"An abundance of provocative ideas . . . Thoughtful readers will whole-heartedly savor this book." —*Publishers Weekly* (starred review)

Praise for
THE HEART AROUSED

"His message is straightforward. . . . By harnessing the powers of attention and conversation, he says, poetry can unite the inner world of the soul with the more structured world." —*The New York Times*

"David Whyte makes the reading of poetry a matter of life and death. His writings have moved me and changed me. If corporations would listen to him they would not only be better places to work, they would make money." —**Pat Conroy, author of** *The Prince of Tides* **and** *Beach Music*

"*The Heart Aroused* is truly extraordinary. It brings a poet's ever-deepening imagination to the world of business and work. It steadies us, gives us grounding, and offers profound images for locating our work deep in the soul. The very style of the book presents a new dimension of language and reflection, with a contemplative tempo that could help us radically and fruitfully reimagine the workplace." —**Thomas Moore, author of** *Care of the Soul* **and** *Soul Mates*

"David Whyte's images resonate to the core. As a poet who has taken his work into the corporate world, he pioneers a vision that is at once practical and illuminating." —**Marion Woodman, Jungian analyst and author of** *Leaving My Father's House*

"With this insightful book, David Whyte offers people in corporate life an opportunity to reach into the forgotten and ignored creative life . . . and literally water their souls with it. The result is a . . . book that can truly heal." —**Clarissa Pinkola Estés, Ph.D., author of** *Women Who Run with the Wolves*

"A corporate analyst who quotes Dante, Yeats, and Blake? Whyte, a maverick business consultant, wends his way through office and board room finding occasions for poetic reflection. . . . Readers willing to lay aside workaday preconceptions will learn ways to look for the hidden patterns of labor and creativity that can give new meaning to corporate employment." —*Booklist*

NONFICTION

Crossing the Unknown Sea: Work as a Pilgrimage of Identity

The Heart Aroused:
Poetry and the Preservation of the Soul in Corporate America

POETRY

River Flow: New & Selected Poems 1984–2007

Everything Is Waiting for You

The House of Belonging

Fire in the Earth

Where Many Rivers Meet

Songs for Coming Home

The Three Marriages

REIMAGINING WORK, SELF AND RELATIONSHIP

DAVID WHYTE

RIVERHEAD BOOKS

New York

RIVERHEAD BOOKS
Published by the Penguin Group
Penguin Group (USA) Inc. 375 Hudson Street, New York, New York 10014, USA
Penguin Group (Canada), 90 Eglinton Avenue East, Suite 700, Toronto, Ontario M4P 2Y3,
Canada (a division of Pearson Penguin Canada Inc.)
Penguin Books Ltd., 80 Strand, London WC2R 0RL, England
Penguin Group Ireland, 25 St. Stephen's Green, Dublin 2, Ireland
(a division of Penguin Books Ltd.)
Penguin Group (Australia), 250 Camberwell Road, Camberwell, Victoria 3124, Australia
(a division of Pearson Australia Group Pty. Ltd.)
Penguin Books India Pvt. Ltd., 11 Community Centre, Panchsheel Park, New Delhi—110 017,
India
Penguin Group (NZ), 67 Apollo Drive, Rosedale, North Shore 0632, New Zealand
(a division of Pearson New Zealand Ltd.)
Penguin Books (South Africa) (Pty.) Ltd., 24 Sturdee Avenue, Rosebank, Johannesburg 2196,
South Africa

Penguin Books Ltd., Registered Offices: 80 Strand, London WC2R 0RL, England

The publisher does not have any control over and does not assume any responsibility for author
or third-party websites or their content.

Copyright © 2009 by David Whyte
Page 369 constitutes an extension of this copyright page.
Cover design by Emily Osborne
Book design by Nicole LaRoche

First Riverhead hardcover edition: January 2009
First Riverhead trade paperback edition: January 2010
Riverhead trade paperback ISBN: 978-1-59448-435-3

The Library of Congress has catalogued the Riverhead hardcover edition as follows:

Whyte, David, date.
    The three marriages : reimagining work, self and relationship / David Whyte.
        p. cm.
    Includes bibliographical references and index.
        ISBN 978-1-59448-860-3
    1. Self-help techniques.   2. Work—Psychological aspects.   3. Self-management
(Psychology).   4. Marriage.   I. Title.
    BF632.W495   2009   2008042129
    128—dc22

PRINTED IN THE UNITED STATES OF AMERICA

10   9   8   7   6   5   4   3   2   1

For my loving wife,
LESLIE

and

In memoriam
JOHN O'DONOHUE
1956–2008

CONTENTS

We should not feel embarrassed by our difficulties, only by our failure to grow anything beautiful from them.

ALAIN DE BOTTON

No one could find me in this strange hiding place. I moved the chair ever so quietly back toward the wall and drew back my feet so that those searching for me would not see those two polished shoes peeping out on the white, immaculate kitchen floor. I tried hard *not* to imagine the concern and wonderment at my recent unexplained disappearance as I sipped at the glass of red wine and looked down again with renewed effort at my notes.

My refuge was a chair placed between two massive gleaming refrigerators in the equally massive kitchen that stood next to the room in which I was about to speak; all this on the very top floor of a sprawling bank building in Johannesburg. Though it was light and warm inside the building, it was dark and very cold outside on the high central plateau of South Africa and the night full of frigid, glittering stars. It was a night to think of origins and the specific place of humanity amongst it all, but the lit interior of the building gave out that international projected sense of abstract corporate power that could have placed it anywhere in the world from Singapore to Seattle.

I was hiding because, humanity or not, I was in a very difficult place at that moment. I needed precious time to myself to come up with a theme very quickly for a talk I was about to give in thirty minutes. I wanted to be a thousand miles away from this audience, many thousands of miles away, to be precise. It was all made worse by the fact that I had given a very good week of seminars, not only within the bank but to the wider artistic community in Johannesburg, and they were all therefore expecting more good stuff and had all told those who had not heard me to come along and hear this poet fellow who could address things in a way they might not have heard before. I would have preferred expectations to be very, very low for this evening. Not only that, but this particular talk was to be to executives and spouses, and had to be relevant to both. The creative center of all this attention, however—the speaker, that is—was completely exhausted and as dry of inspiration as they were full of anticipation. I could hear the buzz of excitement next door, and it made me realize how empty I felt right down to the pit of my stomach, as if someone, somewhere had pulled a plug and the last dregs of energy and enthusiasm had drained away at last. I thought of slipping out like some artistic rock star and really disappearing, leaving only the memory of my past triumphs. I was done, dried out, running on empty and ready for a bottle of wine, never mind a glass, drunk not between two refrigerators in a South African bank building but at home by the fire, with family, with friends, with those especially who did not look to me for inspiration.

In fact, I would have given a lot to be sitting somewhere else drinking that wine; actually, I would have given a great deal to be anywhere else in my life. In fact I suddenly saw myself back in the rose-colored past, as a kid in Yorkshire, in short grey flannel pants, adjusting the big safety pin that seemed to hold them up for a good stretch of my childhood, and which I hid on the inside of the waist. For a moment I found myself looking down at the scuffed knees below the line of those remembered pants: knees that carried me through the local fields and the very local fights of a very rambunctious childhood. That kid could never have imagined sitting here in this humming, oblong metal canyon, about to go on in front of a sophisticated crowd in a faraway, future city; he could never imagine the worries and frets and necessities of the adult mind. I thought about him and what he had wanted to do when he grew up. I thought about my son, my daughter, my wife. I thought about myself suddenly, almost as a stranger, sitting here at this threshold in my life, a stranger at least in the eyes of that rascal kid with his pocket full of holes and pebbles, looking up at me between the refrigerators, in childish puzzlement at my worry.

I waved him off, back into his happy past, and looked at my watch in the all-too-unhappy present. I had been sitting here for ten minutes, and it was now twenty minutes to eight. Twenty minutes until I was on, and I still had not even a glimmer as to what I would say. I heard a stray voice in the kitchen doorway asking another if he had seen me anywhere. I looked down, pulled in the one stray toe that had now wandered beyond the sight line of the refrigerators, exposing me to discovery and stared at my notes.

A big part of the trouble I was now in, had come, as it often does, in the form of a wonderful compliment. The head of the bank, who had invited me and hosted me in South Africa, had been incredibly hospitable to my wife and me, and had also insisted on attending every one of my talks. I had then taken it almost as a point of honor to keep him surprised and interested the whole week and not repeat myself, as speakers are wont to do. The effort had gone very well until this evening, when the cumulative effect of finding something new or at least saying the old in a new way over a dozen long talks during the week had brought me to my knees as far as new material and new insight were concerned.

Part of the way I have always worked is through memorized poems, my own and others', of which I have a few hundred and which I bring to bear on a given subject. It had all happened naturally that way because I had always loved committing poems to memory and I somehow managed to build my work around it. But sometimes you could easily forget what you remembered, and so I had the first lines of all these memorized poems laid down in a multipage list. I would add to this list only as each poem passed the invisible test of being solidly in my memory. It was this that I looked at so earnestly as the minutes ticked away. I was often unnaturally proud of this list, but it was doing me absolutely no good at the moment. It was now a quarter to eight.

In my case, looking at notes is always a sign of desperation. I never prepare for talks this way. I rely on a general day-to-day inquiry that comes to fruition by talking out loud in front of an audience. I always feel the invitation made by attentive, listening ears makes the talk as much as any individual giving the speech. My exhaustion, therefore, had given me a temporary loss of faith in the way I usually hold the conversation. I turned the pages over and realized that I wasn't even seeing anything on the blessed pages, never mind synthesizing anything from the lines. I lifted my wrist again; it was ten minutes to eight, still nothing, and the buzz was getting louder, the questions as to my whereabouts a little more animated through the kitchen door.

There was other trouble waiting for me in that crowd this evening: the face of my wife. That face at the end of a week when I had been working nonstop, hogging all the limelight and barely able to have a real conversation with her, and I was supposed to give a speech, brazen as you like, on bringing work together with all those other human imponderables of family and self. I could just imagine her at the table, giving me that beautiful but wry smile, putting her hands together so politely at the end with her new South African friends, and saying to herself, Well done, very well said. Mr. Gold-Plated B.S.

I looked down at the blue hands of my wristwatch: five minutes to eight. The interesting thing about wristwatches as objects of desire is that when advertised for sale, they are always worn in situations of extreme timelessness—climbing a rock face, flying a plane, sitting with your son—as if by their purchase we will be absolved of time and no longer besieged by its swift, uncaring passage.

Time was moving very swiftly indeed as far as coming up with a decent theme. Work, life, balance. I dismissed the last word from my mind and from the talk. Poets have never used the word *balance*, for good reason. First of all, it is too obvious and therefore untrustworthy; it is also a deadly boring concept and seems to speak as much to being stuck and immovable, as much as to harmony. There is also the sense of unbalancing that must take place in order to push a person into a new and larger set of circumstances. Gazing blankly at my notes, I suddenly remembered, as in a dream, another talk that I had given, at the other end of the earth, as a guest lecturer at the University of Anchorage on a very, very cold snowy day in Alaska. Emerging from a veritable blizzard into a lecture hall with an unknown crowd of students, I realized that my adventure in getting there had completely pushed from my mind the subject of this particular class. I asked them to tell me what their usual subject was for this afternoon. One fellow at the front put up his hand and said, "English composition." The title floored me a little, because no serious writer ever thinks about *English composition*, and if he did it would mean he had temporarily lost his mind or his way as a writer. *English composition* is for those looking from the outside in. *English composition* is to real writing as Sunday school is to Moses before the burning bush. I started hesitantly, knowing I had to find a different ground on which to walk as I spoke, and finally found the way in when I overheard myself say, "English decomposition." Suddenly the students were interested. I found myself talking about all the ways in which you have to break down and discompose your ordinary speech in order to say something real and worthwhile. . . .

"There you are," said the voice of the sound technician, holding up the lapel mike for me with one hand and holding the battery case in the other. He stood in the space framed by the two refrigerators, looked off to the side and said in a loud, excited voice, "I've found him, hiding in the kitchen." Thank you, I thought. I looked at my watch again. Eight o'clock, nothing, absolutely nothing, except that clue about being discomposed and the image of Moses before the burning bush.

My banker friend made the wonderful introduction I didn't want and didn't deserve and didn't want him to give. I thought of how much time human beings spend in circumstances they would never willingly choose for themselves. I thought of why this might be so. I would have been much happier with "He's done great all week, now let's all let him have a really off night and still love him at the end." The room went quiet. I looked out at the assembled executives and their partners and the singles without partners, and I looked at my own wife sitting with her new friends. As much as my spouse loved me, she would be as fierce a judge of what I had to say on work and relationship as anyone in the room. I had to find words that spoke to all the different listening ears, especially to my wife's ears. I had to speak to something in the work we seek, to something in the partner we have sought and won or even sought and lost, and even, I thought, to something that little kid in the short flannel pants is still looking for, looking for in me and still, in a sense, waiting to grow up. I took a deep breath and then said, out of nowhere and to my everlasting surprise, "I would like to speak about . . . the three marriages."

The current understanding of work-life balance is too simplistic. People find it hard to balance work with family, family with self, because it might not be a question of balance. Some other dynamic is in play, something to do with a very human attempt at happiness that does not quantify different parts of life and then set them against one another. We are collectively exhausted because of our inability to hold competing parts of ourselves together in a more integrated way. These hidden human dynamics of integration are more of a conversation, more of a synthesis and more of an almost religious and sometimes almost delirious quest for meaning than a simple attempt at daily ease and contentment.

Human beings are creatures of belonging, though they may come to that sense of belonging only through long periods of exile and loneliness. Interestingly, we belong to life as much through our sense that it is all impossible, as we do through the sense that we will accomplish everything we have set out to do. This sense of belonging and not belonging is lived out by most people through three principal dynamics: first, through relationship to other people and other living things (particularly and very personally, to one other living, breathing person in relationship or marriage); second, through work; and third, through an understanding of what it means to be themselves, discrete individuals alive and seemingly separate from everyone and everything else.

These are the three marriages, of Work, Self and Other.

A word on this word *marriage*: Despite our use of the word only for a committed relationship between two people, in reality this book looks at the way everyone is committed, consciously or unconsciously, to *three* marriages. There is that first marriage, the one we usually mean, to another; that second marriage, which can so often seem like a burden, to a work or vocation; and that third and most likely hidden marriage to a core conversation inside ourselves. We can call these three separate commitments marriages because at their core they are usually lifelong commitments and, as I wish to illustrate, they involve vows made either consciously or unconsciously.

Why put them together? To neglect any one of the three marriages is to impoverish them all, because they are not actually separate commitments but different expressions of the way each individual belongs to the world.

This book looks at the dynamics common to all three marriages: first the recognition of what an individual wants, then a pursuit, then the hope to circumvent the difficult but necessary disappointments, and ultimately, in the face of that disappointment, the full recommitment to the vows we have made in each of the three areas, spoken or unspoken.

The Three Marriages looks at the way each marriage involves a separate form of courtship and commitment, each almost a world unto itself that then must be rejoined together. The end goal: In these pages I am looking for a marriage of marriages.

The main premise of the book becomes also its final conclusion: We should stop thinking in terms of work-life balance. Work-life balance is a concept that has us simply lashing ourselves on the back and working too hard in each of the three commitments. In the ensuing exhaustion we ultimately give up on one or more of them to gain an easier life.

I especially want to look at the way that each of these marriages is, at its heart, nonnegotiable; that we should give up the attempt to *balance* one marriage against another, of, for instance, taking away from work to give more time to a partner, or vice versa, and start thinking of each marriage *conversing* with, questioning or emboldening the other two. As we discover, through the lives and the biographies I follow in this book, how each one of the three marriages is nonnegotiable at its core, we can start to realign our understanding and our efforts away from trading and bartering parts of ourselves as if they were salable commodities and more toward finding a central conversation that can hold all of these three marriages together.

THE TASK

The Three Marriages looks at the triumphs and tragedies of human belonging in three crucial areas that most individuals simply can't avoid: in relationship, in work and in all those strange and inexplicable inner ways we belong to ourselves. It seeks to understand the often accident-prone, the sometimes triumphant, the very often comic and the too often tragic and disastrous, human attempt to belong to something or someone other than our very well-known but very often very, *very* boring, established selves. It looks at what happens along the way when we become more interesting: when we get out of the dynamics of self-entrapment and fall in love—with a person, a future, a work, or with a new sense of self.

At the same time, *The Three Marriages* looks at that other equally strange human need, to be left completely and utterly alone, trawling the deep riches of an inner peace and quiet, where the self can actually seem lithe, movable, limitless and inviolate, invulnerable to those invisible wounds delivered by *partners and spouses*, unharassed by *commitments*, inured to the clamor of *children* and untouched by the endless nature of our *meetings*, all of which come as a result of a deep-seated, not-to-be-suppressed, inherited human need to belong—indeed, that constant, basic need we cannot ignore—to be part of a bigger conversation than the one we are having now.

The Three Marriages, then, attempts to reframe our language and our thinking to move away from a phrase that is deeply misleading, a phrase that often becomes a lash with which we punish ourselves, a short sentence that can lie like a weight on our shoulders and seem irremovable: *Work-life balance.*

The understanding of this book is that in the deeper, unspoken realms of the human psyche, work and life are not separate things and therefore cannot be balanced against each other except to create further trouble. The book most especially tries to dispel the myth that we are predominantly thinking creatures, who can, if we put our feet in all the right places, develop strategies that will make us the paragons of perfection we want to be, and instead, looks to a deeper, almost poetic perspective, a moving, more untouchable identity, a slightly more dangerous but more satisfying sense of self than one defined by ideas of balance.

The Three Marriages looks at the way we actually seem to function—as a kind of movable conversational frontier, an edge between what we think is us and what we think is not us. Following the lives of Robert Louis Stevenson, Jane Austen, Charles Dickens and others, it tries to illustrate the way we can still make a real life even when crowded by other identities, or even when unbalanced and intoxicated with desire, or even when we are disappointed in work or love, and perhaps the way, at the center of all this deep love of belonging and this deep exhaustion of belonging, we may have waiting for us, at the end of the tunnel, a marriage of marriages, a life worth living, and one we can call, despite all the difficulties and imperfections, our very own.

BOOK ONE

The Three Marriages:
Work, Self and Other

CHAPTER I

Some Definitions

THE FIRST MARRIAGE:
THE ONE WE USUALLY MEAN

Marriage is a word loaded with associations; not only the longed-for associations with the mythical horse and carriage that carries us off *in perfect felicity*, as Jane Austen described it, but also the whispers and echoes it finds in our mind, depending on the particular partnership our own parents made. Each of us has a profound inherited notion of marriage or partnership from the success or failure of our own parents in their commitment to each other and their ability or non-ability to bring us up.

To the unconscious mind, the coming together of our parents gave birth to our own growing and was the foundation of our present adulthood. We look at the pictures of our astonishingly youthful mother or father all those years ago, looking intently into the camera and see ourselves waiting for them in their future. Their commitment, however long or however transitory, is the ultimate background to the foreground we now explore as consenting, independent adults. To children, the union of their parents, good or bad, in a still photograph or in a moving memory, is the mythic meeting of the two gods who brought them into life and who provided, by their presence or by their disturbing absence, the surrounding universe of their growing.

Our attempts to make a successful marriage as adults often depend on the image we carry of marriage from our childhood. Inhabited by two wise and benevolent gods, marriage can be a paradise for children, a seedbed, a garden; a safe cradle for the seasons of their coming and going, and subsequently, an unconscious anchor for their going out in the world. But at its worst, inhabited by angry, unhappy or absent gods, it can be a lonely, constant battleground, a weed-strewn plot, an underworld where things seem to come only to die. Most often it is both, with the weather of life blowing through according to outward circumstances and to the trials and difficulties of married life but also the extent to which children may make life difficult for the ones who brought them to birth. It is fascinating to think that each of us as children, by our very appearance in their lives, either brought our parents' romance to a temporary end or kept them from reviving it in the way they had known it before we appeared.

Many a marriage grinds onto the rocks of parenthood with a shock that was never quite anticipated when both parents were happily thinking of names for the newly arriving child. Many free themselves again and rise with the tide of a new arrangement of their love, but many also struggle to find the ability to think of themselves as a couple again, their past romantic desires lost in the labors and logistics of parenthood.

Arriving in the middle of all this, children experience close up and in parallel, often without speaking, all the affections and exiles of their parents' marriage and become not only a close and unconscious student of their relationship, but a sobering mirror of marital happiness and unhappiness from the moment they are toddling around the kitchen, distinguishing right from scolded wrong. The lessons of marriage are read very early into the textbook of a child's mind.

Even in their unhappiness, children who grow up within a bad marriage are alert to other happier marriages in the world; like a moth to the flame the young imagination flutters toward happier families in neighboring houses or to ones that exist only on the television screen, as if, in that constant looking, the search for a happy human partnership were entwined deeply in the human genetic code. A young but unhappy child almost always has an instinctive sense of the kind of family he would like to have been born into. Our myths and fairy stories are full of infants led out into the forest to die, being found and adopted, and as the story unfolds, restored to their rightful parentage.

The internal pictures of marriage we carry into adulthood often represent the need to return to this rightful parentage. The instinctive human approach to the word *marriage* always includes our own biography. I do remember as a young, newly married man in my twenties, feeling an urgent necessity to create a marriage and a form of parenting that would set all wrongs to rights and fill each of the gaps I felt so keenly from my own growing. With maturity and a truer sense of my own sins, I find myself with an almost opposite perspective, trying to live *up* to the example of self-sacrifice that I now see my parents endured in order to provide for their son and daughters and see us right in the world. But the original instincts seem to be a necessary blindness for each generation.

Marriage, that profound commitment to another, officially or nonofficially, that longing for daily physical communion with a particular person, is also at its best an unconscious compact to improve the world and the future toward which the couple faces. "The triumph of hope over experience," said Dr. Johnson, his tongue only partly in his cheek, speaking of the prospects of a second marriage. He could equally have said it about the first—the one we hope for unconsciously, as young children.

That hope, of course, is shared by almost all but the most embittered or disappointed. A single person may run a thousand miles from the possibilities of marriage, glorying in self-determination. Yet there is almost always a corner of the young imagination reserved for the man or woman who will bring all this wonderful self-determination to a shattering conclusion. The young want independence until they glimpse the ideal marriage of their imaginations to which they will give themselves up. There are those strong characters who will never marry because they never find the outer representation of their inner hopes and they refuse anything less. Their marriage is with a future, yet to be encountered, ideal, but one, they are often prepared to admit, that may never happen.

Even if we do run one, two or three thousand miles from it all and set our face against commitment or marriage, we find the expectation of others for us, especially as we get older, astonishingly high, as if our refusal to seek a mate offends some deep human communal necessity or reminds too many of the possibility of their own future loneliness. We may also find that our ideas for marriage fall far outside the understanding of parents or society. We may, in our teens, discover we are gay but want exactly the same outer rituals and normality for a married life as the heterosexual population. We may, alternatively, want to remain officially unmarried yet seek out the same depths of love and commitment as those who have gone through the ceremony.

When it comes to our refusal to commit, especially as we mature, society can seem like a broody expectant parent wondering when the first grandchild is going to come along. A gay individual especially, can find all of this societal pressure reversed in a way that puzzles and shames: discovering as they grow into adulthood that their own need for marriage is actually a fiery trial for the societies that surround them, who offer no understanding to the conundrum they are presented with. For every individual, then, heterosexual or not, marriage in all its forms is an enormous and simultaneously private and public question.

The first marriage is the first of the three big marriages and the three big questions—the three questions others ask us repeatedly through our lives, and the three questions we ask ourselves repeatedly in the mirror: When are you going to get married? When are you going to get a job? And, When, oh when, are you going to grow up?

Most of us grow up only *during* a marriage or a work-life or a sweeping self-examination, not before them. Strangely, despite this fact, in the marriage ceremony we commit to all the ideals beforehand, in public, before parents, before friends, before extended family; as one comedian said, before strange foods we will never eat again, and I might add, before crowds of perfect strangers we may never meet again.

The act of marriage is an act of faith and an act of courageous imagination as much as it is an already established fact. In our ideal imaginations we stand together in a church in the Cotswolds, a cliff edge in Hawaii, a synagogue in Israel or a wide tent on the edge of the Egyptian desert, surrounded by a crowd of loving support. But actually, it doesn't matter; even if our declaration is limited to an elderly, hard-of-hearing Elvis impersonator in a Las Vegas wedding chapel, society and the state vests even in that lowly "king" the omniscient eye of absolute, lawful witness. We have been seen to commit publicly and the solid die for our future is cast. Historically, of course, the "king" has loomed much larger and the perceived witness has been much wider and deeper. In almost all societies we have committed in marriage beyond society, beyond the present moment of history, beyond any earthly king and given ourselves in a new way to God.

Whether we are devout or atheist, or just wish to be told what to say to get through it all, the marriage ceremony is a distilled, magnified, knee-wateringly don't-let-me-think-about-this-too-much, out-loud promise to whoever is listening in this life or the next, that we are on a journey with this woman, or this man, and that we are making wonderful and frightening commitments that are not lightly shed if ever shed at all, future divorce or no.

The first marriage, then, the one we most commonly use the word for—two people entwined for as long as we can imagine the future lasts—is emblematic; is a representation of, is in many ways a magnified dramatized public version of, all those other commitments we make in life, in work, and even in that third, inner marriage, where we forge the silent internal nature of our outer character. It is a code or cipher for the human heart, saying that we will manifest in public an original, very particular, very private and very passionate commitment, and abide by it through any dark loveless nights of difficulty ahead.

First Short Conclusion

The first marriage stands alone in the human imagination as one of the great primary commitments of an individual life. But it is also a metaphor for all the other commitments we must make, and its spoken vows are a representation of all the unspoken promises we make,

especially with those other two, equally untamable marriages, with our work and with our self.

WORK: THE SECOND MARRIAGE

We may be able to evade emotional commitments to others in
marriage or relationship through a steady, stubborn refusal, by
rehearsed, detailed explanations to mother or simply by telling
the whole world to go away, but work in all its forms may be
even harder to ignore, simply because it is tied so much to actual
daily survival. By definition, all of us, living at this time are
descended from a long line of survivors who lived through the
difficulties of history and prehistory; most of whom had to do a
great deal of work to keep the wolf, the cold and the neighboring tribe from the door.

Work was necessity; work meant food, shelter, survival and a
sense of power over circumstances. Work was and still is, endless. Work, even with inordinate riches and imperial power,
never goes away. Money is no defense. Money means obligation,
but also the need for that money to work for itself, which causes
more work for the one who gained all the money in the first
place.

Power and money together mean only that we are then surrounded by supplicants looking for jobs and money, all of whom
have to be addressed, told to go away or organized.

There is no shelter from the calls of work. Find a corner to stretch out in, away from other eyes and lecturing voices and eventually our own conscience, built on millions of years of evolutionary survival, comes looking for us; tells us to get up and do something useful, *for God's sake*. The refusal to contribute, to find a work, a métier, a marriage of self and necessity, is seen as a deeply ingrained taboo by almost all societies; tapping into that same common root of survival we sense in society's need for us to find and commit to a mate.

As in the first marriage, the great questions that touch on personal happiness in work have to do with an ability to hold our own conversation amid the constant background of shouted needs, hectoring advice and received wisdom. In work we have to find high ground safe from the arriving tsunami of expectation concerning what I am going to *do*. Work, like marriage, is a place you can lose yourself more easily perhaps than finding yourself. It is a place full of powerful undercurrents, a place to find our selves, but also, a place to drown, losing all sense of our own voice, our own contribution and conversation.

It has always been accepted as a singular triumph on the part of an individual human being to find real happiness in work *or* in marriage. I remember being told once that in medieval England one particular shrine is said to have granted miracles to any married persons of long standing who had never wished themselves *unwed*. No actual miracles were ever recorded at the site. I have never been able to find a reference to this mythical religious site, but to my mind, it *should* have existed. Equally, in the marriage of work, it would be hard to find even the most zealous executives who in their secret hearts didn't imagine walking away from it all at some dark time in their onward progress.

In many ways, work *must* be a marriage; otherwise, why would we put up with so much over the years? We must have made hidden vows somewhere to follow something larger than the difficulties of the everyday.

But work is not only necessity; good work like a good marriage needs a dedication to something larger than our own detailed, everyday needs; good work asks for promises to something intuited or imagined that is larger than our present understanding of it. We may not have an arranged ceremony at the altar to ritualize our dedication to work, but many of us can remember a specific moment when we realized we were made for a certain work, a certain career or a certain future: a moment when we held our hand in a fist and made unspoken vows to what we had just glimpsed. For some it may come very, very early.

EARLY INTUITIONS OF ADULTHOOD

At the tender age of eleven, I used to sit on a low stone wall out in the fields of my childhood Yorkshire and look toward the high moors that lined the western horizon. This high moorland always stood, in my young mind, for the horizon of my future life. There, looking toward those brooding and often snow-covered hills, I would daydream my way toward an adulthood where, again and again, I would see myself as a grown man, onstage, speaking to large groups of people. I did not know what I was saying in the daydream but everyone *did* seem to show at least a little interest: an intuited dynamic very close to my present mode of public speaking. Where did that image come from? Perhaps from some invisible faculty inside a growing boy already intuiting the essential nature of the conversation for which he was made. More specific to my central vocation as a poet, I would imagine further into the future and see families gathering around a kind of high-tech rock pool in their futuristic homes reading my poetry as it appeared mysteriously, line by line, in the surface of the pool. A close intuition of the computer screen and the Internet, perhaps, for one, who, at that time could not consciously imagine either? A conversation yet to occur, of which I wanted to be a part, some intuitive faculty within me, working hard to discern the future horizon of my work.

Work is a constant conversation. It is the back-and-forth between what I think is me and what I think is not me; it is the edge between what the world needs of me and what I need of the world. Like the person to whom I am committed in a relationship, it is constantly changing and surprising me by its demands and needs but also by where it leads me, how much it teaches me, and especially, by how much tact, patience and maturity it demands of me.

Like marriage and relationship, work is a constant invisible question, sometimes nagging, sometimes cajoling, sometimes emboldening me; at its best beckoning me to follow a particular star to which I belong. If children move into their late teens with no inkling of their future *vocation*, not even a glimpse of the star, it is time for the adult world around them to become rightly and increasingly worried. At this point a seemingly wrongheaded but determined direction is far better than none at all. It may be, in fact, that most of the great work done by individuals through history has often been accomplished through long years of dedicated wrongheadedness. Wrong direction or no, human societies have always intuited the powerful necessity of a gravitational pull youths must follow to find their way. The difficulties and necessities of work, like those of marriage, need some larger perspective, some greater view than the irritations and obstacles of a given day.

An extreme experience of this lodestar; this compass heading, this invitation from the far horizon, occurred about two hundred years ago, in Wordsworth's "Intimations of Immortality." It is a horizon that lives simultaneously in the past from which the young Wordsworth has come and in the future to which he goes.

> *Our birth is but a sleep and a forgetting:*
> *The Soul that rises with us, our life's Star,*
> *Hath had else where its setting,*
> *And cometh from afar:*
> *Not in entire forgetfulness,*
> *And not in utter nakedness,*
> *But trailing clouds of glory do we come*
> *From God, who is our home:*
> *Heaven lies about us in our infancy!*

Shades of the prison house begin to close
Upon the growing Boy,
But He beholds the light and whence it flows,
He sees it in his joy;
The Youth, who daily from the East
Must travel, still is nature's priest,
And by the vision splendid,
Is on his way attended.

There are two very sobering lines that immediately follow this and pull us up very, very short, but perhaps we can return to those later, when we come to talk about how natural it is to lose our way in any of the three marriages. The essential understanding is that although work can so easily *become* a prison, if we follow that essential light, which feels at times as if it was born with us and accompanies us on our way, there can be a way out of those shades of the prison house that begin to close upon the growing boy or girl.

My own son, having gone out into the world and in his second year at college, showed me around his first tiny, independently inhabited rented home as proudly as if we were touring five thousand acres in Montana. At the end of the tour, he suddenly turned to me and with an equally sudden, stricken change of face, said, "But Dad, I never realized how much gas and electricity cost."

Shades of the prison house begin to close
Upon the growing Boy,
But He beholds the light and whence it flows.

Concentrating on paying the bills will only get that young man a job and keep the lights on, but following that other light he knows well and has known well all his life will create a vocation that will embolden him to sacrifices that will pay for everything that is necessary.

One of the most powerful thresholds children cross into adulthood comes through the sexual revolution that occurs in the very fibers of their being, turning them initially upside down, but eventually toward the ultimate necessities of committed relationships. It is interesting to think of an equivalent line in work that children must cross where their comprehension of the world is revolutionized as they slowly come to realize there is labor in the world; that the food on their table and the roof over their head may not have been won lightly and that their work in the world will be as much about providing for others as about providing for themselves. It can be a stone-cold sobering arrival or it can be a careful apprenticeship. For some children this is well understood at seven years old, according to the manner of their upbringing, the income of their family and their early introduction to actually doing something for others. Other more gilded youths I have known, with $60,000 a year in tuition plus living expenses at Stanford paid for without a blush, may take it all for granted until their twenty-seventh year.

Work waits. Reality waits. The conversation cannot be averted without our becoming a shining example of immaturity to those we know. Like our parents' marriage to each other, their sense of dedication to work, in or out of the home, is one we inherit, take on and ultimately test against our own experience. No real long-term satisfaction is possible in work without treating it as something much larger than a series of jobs. I must find, pursue and commit to my vocation as I would to another person in marriage or relationship.

Second Short Conclusion

Happiness in the second marriage of work, like happiness in the first marriage with a person, is possible only through seeing it in a greater context than surviving the everyday. We must have a relationship with our work that is larger than any individual job description we are given. A real work, like a real person, grows and changes and surprises us, asking us constantly for recommitment. In work, we have often made secret vows; sometimes we do not know ourselves what those vows are until we look back with some perspective on the actual nature of the work we have accomplished.

SELF: THE THIRD MARRIAGE

Perhaps the most difficult marriage of all—the third marriage beneath the two visible, all-too-public marriages of work and relationship—is the internal and often secret marriage to that tricky movable frontier called ourselves: the marriage to the one who keeps changing at the center of all the outer relationships while making promises it hopes to God it can keep. What is heartbreaking and difficult about this inner self that flirted, enticed, spent time with and eventually committed to a person or a career is that it is not a stationary entity; an immovable foundation; it moves and changes and surprises us as much as anything in the outer world to which it wants to commit.

Love in the words of Shakespeare may be *an ever fixed mark,* but the person, the self who loves, is not. Nor is the person who works a work, navigates a career. They are both a long, turning wave form moving through experience with a kind of changing, revelatory seasonality, carrying all before them like a tide, surprising everyone with their twists and turns and contradictory flows. We are each a river with a particular abiding character, but we show radically different aspects of our self according to the territory through which we travel. As Seamus Heaney said in one poem, *You are neither here nor there / A hurry through which strange and known things pass.* Now a swift-moving stream, now a slow traverse, at midlife perhaps nothing but a dried-up stretch of seemingly lifeless gravel, becoming a lake again, then by a strange summary on the hospital bed, an estuary, a giving out, a transition into the next existence.

In the midst of a seemingly endless life, however, we can spend so much time attempting to put bread on the table or holding a relationship together that we often neglect the necessary internal skills which help us pursue, come to know, and then sustain a marriage with the person we find on the inside. Neglecting this internal marriage, we can easily make ourselves a hostage to the externals of work and the demands of relationship. We find ourselves unable to move in these outer marriages because we have no inner foundation from which to step out with a firm persuasion. It is as if, absent a loving relationship with this inner representation of our self, we fling ourselves in all directions in our outer lives, looking for love in all the wrong places. The other timeless metaphor for this internal configuration has been a source or a well, a place to drink from, as if somewhere, there is a constant invisible outflow, a flow from which we might be refusing to drink.

Often our inability to draw on that inner well can become more and more painful the farther we get from the water. If we are involved in the outer world in ways that betray our conscience or deeply held beliefs, then even simple internal questions can become very difficult to ask. As if we intuit that drinking from the well will clear our eyesight and help us see what is real in the outer world and that once we have built that outer solid wall, brick by brick over long years through equally long effort, the gift of seeing that reality is the last gift in the world that we want.

Not only can we become afraid of these internal questions, but also we can become terrified of the spaces or silences in which these questions might arise. The act of stopping can be the act of facing something we have kept hidden from ourselves for a very long time. The third marriage, then, especially in today's world, where we have created societies and commercial environments that claw at us from morning until night, can be the most difficult marriage of all. To the outward striver—that is, most of us—it can seem as if this internal marriage is asking for a renunciation of the two outer marriages. Feeling this can come as almost a relief, a way out, for in the name of our many responsibilities and duties, we can use it as the perfect excuse not to look inside at all, feeling as if our outer world will fall apart if we spend any time looking for the person who exists at the intersection of all these outer commitments.

THE NEED FOR SILENCE

All of our great contemplative traditions advocate the necessity for silence in an individual life: first, for gaining a sense of discernment amid the noise and haste, second, as a basic building block of individual happiness, and third, to let this other all-seeing identity come to life and find its voice inside us. In the Buddhist tradition the ability to be happy is often translated into English as "equanimity," roughly meaning to be equal to things, to be large enough for the drama in which we find ourselves.

Almost all of our traditions of instruction in prayer, meditation or silence, be they Catholic, Buddhist or Muslim advocate seclusion or withdrawal as a first step in creating this equanimity. Small wonder we feel it goes against everything we need to do on the outside to keep our outer commitments together. Intimate relationships seem to demand endless talking and passing remarks; work calls for endless meetings, phone calls and exhortations. In the two outer marriages it seems as if everything real comes from initiating something new. In the inner world we intuit something different and more difficult. It can be disconcerting or even distressing to find that this third marriage; this internal marriage, calls for a kind of cessation, a stopping, a fierce form of attention that attempts to look at where all this doing arises from. For the busy mind, for instance, it is almost impossible or even painful, to stop and read the following:

> *In the beginning of heaven and earth*
> *There were no words,*
> *Words came out of the womb of matter*
> *And whether a man dispassionately*
> *Sees to the core of life*
> *Or passionately sees the surface*
> *The core and the surface*
> *Are essentially the same,*
> *Words making them seem different*
> *Only to express appearance.*
> *If name be needed, wonder names them both:*
> *From wonder into wonder*
> *Existence opens.*
>
> *Tao Te Ching* (translation by Witter Bynner)

Existence opens. "Thank you," we say, "but I don't have time. Please give it to me in three bullet points that I can look at later, when I get a moment, when I retire, when I'm on my deathbed or even when I'm actually dead, surely, then, there'll be time enough to spare." Trying to be equal to Lao Tzu's opening remarks in the *Tao Te Ching* when we have no practice with silence and the revelations that arise from that spacious sense of reality can be like a novice violinist trying to play the opening notes of a Bach concerto. We can be so overwhelmed by the grandeur of the piece that we give up on our beginning scales.

The third marriage to the internal self seems to be to someone or something that in many ways seems even less open to coercion or sheer willpower than an actual marriage or a real job. Not only does this internal marriage seem to operate under rules different from those of the other two outer contracts but it also seems to be connected to the big; we might even say unbearable, questions of existence that scare us half to death and for which we have no easy answer. Like a skittish single unable to commit to the consequences of a full relationship, we turn away from questions that flower from solitude and quiet.

> *I wish I knew the beauty*
> *Of leaves falling*
> *To whom are we beautiful*
> *As we go?*

asked poet David Ignatow, not only allowing himself to face the necessity of his own demise but hallowing and making real and beautiful his own present life.

———

Third, Slightly Longer Conclusion:
Marriage with the Self

The marriage with the self is difficult because it is connected to the great questions of life that refuse to go away and which are also connected to our own mortality. In the silences that accompany a strong internal relationship with the self we see not only the truth of our present circumstances and a way forward but we also realize how short our stay is on this earth. Life waits for us in this internal marriage, but death waits for us also. The sudden absence of our partner waits for us. The end of our work or our retirement waits. The hospital bed waits. Right now, in some obscure medical appliance company in a corner of a bleak industrial estate, the very bed on which we will lie, trying to get the great perspective, is perhaps being manufactured as we read. We don't want to know, of course, but all our great contemplative traditions concerned with this marriage, say, this willingness to look at the transitory nature of existence, are not pessimism but absolute realism: life is to be taken at the tilt, you do not have forever, and therefore why wait? Why wait, especially until your faculties have atrophied or your youth has gone, or you have lost confidence in your self? Why wait, to be, as the poet Mary Oliver says, "a bride to wonder"? To become a faithful and intimate companion to that initially formidable stranger you called your self?

BOOK TWO

Love's First Glimpse:
Looking for a Mate,
a Job, a Life

Happiness is somebody to love,
Something to do,
And something to hope for.

CHINESE PROVERB

CHAPTER 2

The Classic Case:
Love's First Glimpse
of Love Itself

*A glance can both submit and subvert; it can be sharp or shy,
scornful or adoring; it can be a near cousin to scrutiny—
but it almost always assumes a degree of mutually
encoded knowledge. A spark is struck and apprehended;
the head turns on its spinal axis; the shoulders freeze; the
eyes are the only busy part of the body, simultaneously
receiving and sending out information, so that a glance
becomes more than a glance. It is a weapon, a command,
or a sigh of acquiescence.*

CAROL SHIELDS

As living beings we can't help paying attention to things other
than ourselves. Though we might be weak or wounded in one or
more of them, we have all the five senses through which to create a constant subliminal conversation with the world outside.

We may not set out to look for a relationship: for a job or a better understanding of ourselves, but if we are sincerely paying attention, we most often end up with all three of them, whether we want them or not. We find ourselves in these relationships because we were made to be both aware of and entangled with the world through our senses. Our ability to survive depends on the acuteness of our senses, but the same faculties that help us to pay attention to what is around us, to ward off threats and seize proffered opportunities, are also the same senses by which we are beguiled and intoxicated and made to fall in love.

This falling in love can occur in a multiplicity of ways. We have the remarkable ability as human beings to fall in love with a person, a work, or even an idea of ourselves. That is, we create a relationship that has a perfected image of what we first encounter, a sense of longing for the perfect person, the ideal work, the full potential of our own character. We fall in love through seeing, hearing, touching, tasting, intuiting and longing. These senses are constantly mediating the frontier between what we think is a self and what we think is other than our selves.

First, we have eyes, taken mostly for granted, with which to see a new moon or a tiny memo. We have ears, not fully appreciated, with which to entertain a grand opera or a humble opinion, and we have those tireless hands used every day to pull others toward us or push them away; most especially we have a tongue with which to taste, to give voice to desires or to lash others with our pent-up disapproval. We also have the intellect to contrast and compare, to measure carefully and weigh things in the balance. Then, beneath them all, untiring but seldom listened to, we have that sixth sense acknowledged in almost all traditions: a swirling internal formation called the intuition, the imagination, the heart, the almost prophetic part of a person that at its best somehow seems to know what is good and what is bad for us, but also what pattern is just about to precipitate, what out of a hundred possibilities is just about to happen, in a sense, an unspoken faculty for knowing what season we are in. What is about to die and what is about to come into being.

We follow this constant internal seasonal round of living and dying throughout our lives, trying to understand what it is we need, what is coming to fruition and what we have to let go of. In the first half of life we especially look for clues as to what lies ahead of us. Looking out of the windows of our parents' house, we want to know both how to belong to that world through a work and what specifically we should belong to in the sense of a community, an organization or an idea. At first, that waiting world appears to hold a level of complexity that seems beyond us.

We start paying attention to this world before we are born. Our ears, medical research tells us, have us fall in love with our mother's heartbeat and then, as we grow as unborn children, to the sound of both our parents' voices resonating, far outside that protected tidal beat of the womb. We shush a baby to sleep because the sound mimics that internal swirl of amniotic fluid in which the child was first formed and felt safe.

When we leave the enclosed safety of the womb at birth, our new eyes look immediately for a face, for a breast, and our fingers reach out, curling and uncurling as if trying to compass the physicality of the world, as if testing and retesting both the presence and the possible absence of something, as if testing the very ability for touch itself.

At birth we fall in love again with our mother through our visual and physical senses. In a sense we come already equipped with the knowledge of what to look for. Far inside each of us is a foundational ground that recognizes *mother*. Our survival depends on it. We look for nourishment and protection in those first moments but also, ultimately, underneath it all, though we do not know it, for something that is actually preparing us one day for leaving that same loving protection, for an enabling force helping us to stand on our own two feet.

It is intriguing to think that the first falling in love that happens to a person has at its base something that must also, at the end, take the person beyond that cradling hand. Our first love is something that has the seeds of its own demise right at the center of its very necessity. It may be that within the seed of any relationship, any work, any established sense of identity, is an internal intuition of how it will eventually disappear. Something inside the protective walls of our happy relationship, our settled career, our established sense of our self may be preparing us, willingly or unwillingly, for an emancipation, a life beyond it which if intuited too early might be frightening to us, beyond our ability to reach.

SEEING THE OTHER:
LOVE'S FIRST GLIMPSE OF LOVE ITSELF

We fall in love, then, because of the senses, but we fall most deeply; most abidingly, in love because of some internal foundation of recognition and belonging to which all of these external senses lead.

At the age of only nine, in the medieval Florence of 1274, the young Dante Alighieri first saw Beatrice when she had just reached the age of eight. The sight of her overwhelmed him. She wore soft crimson with a girdle around her waist; she seemed both restrained and pure.

> *In that moment I say truly that the spirit of life, that spirit which lives in the most secret chamber of the heart began to tremble fiercely so that I felt its agony in the least pulsation, and, then, trembling, it said this to me:* "Ecce deus fortior me, qui veniens dominabitur michi:" *Behold a god more powerful than I, who, coming, will rule over me. At that moment, my natural spirit, that which lives in the high chamber to which all the spirits of the senses carry their perceptions, began to marvel deeply, and, speaking especially to the spirit of sight, spoke these words:* "Apparuit iam beatitudo vestra:" *Now your blessedness appears. At that moment the natural spirit, which dwells in the place where all our nourishment is brought, began to weep, and weeping said these words:* "Heu miser, quia frequenter impeditus ero deinceps!" *Oh misery, how often will I be troubled from this time on!*
>
> Dante, *La Vita Nuova*, lines II, 13–27 (translation by D.W.)

Dante put those lines into Latin for special emphasis. *Heu miser*: Oh misery! His emphasis speaks to one of the abiding themes of this book—that many of the hopes we hold for a particular marriage are never consummated in the way we originally imagined. That a marriage with a person, a work or a religious sense of self is its own mistress; goes its own way and has its own future, which we must follow and accommodate ourselves to. The great dramatic tension in Dante's work lies in the fact that both he and his reader know he will have his heart broken, yet Dante will keep making the context larger and larger for us to tell us why this difficult, human path is necessary.

The background to Dante's foreground narration is the wonderful vista that opens up behind his continued disappointment. If the ways of God are being justified to a man, it is a difficult justification for all of us, as if his heart will be made whole only by having it broken many, many times. Already Dante is telling us that this particular falling in love will lead to a marriage larger than any one man or woman can encompass.

Dante also tells us that this falling, this descent into a form of madness, is not just surface lust, though there is a beautiful and very lusty, physical aspect to it all. It is trustable, first, because he was in a nine-year-old's body that most likely could feel the sexual physicality of the world but just as likely could not understand the true dimensions of its eventual consummation. Second, it is a brilliant description of an outer infatuation that finds a firm inner correspondence, a true ground, far inside his own sense of self. The revolutionary aspect of Dante's love, to the startled medieval mind reading his work for the first time, was his breathtaking religious interpretation of earthly love. He was using language that previously had been found only in the Latin of ecstatic monastic contemplatives and putting it into everyday Italian. He was illuminating a bodily sensation that people had intuited in their daily lives, a love found in the words of folk song or story, but his was a falling in love that had not been articulated with the depth, the sophistication or the accuracy he now brought to bear.

Dante was in a sense beginning an intense study of himself through this encounter with Beatrice. He was also looking in detail at the stages of the journey he had begun as a result of his encounter with all she represented. By studying himself, he was trying to find an internal foundation to the momentous encounters that seemed to be occurring on the outside. It was a form of medieval apprenticeship, but this time to the phenomenology of love, in other words, what happens along the way to an individual when he goes through this common but extraordinary process of falling for another: Dante wanted to proceed through this love, as he said later, *from bad to good, good to better, and better to best* (Convivio I, ii, 14).

Whatever his progression, we have in Dante's first meeting with Beatrice the classic case of love's first glimpse by a young man suddenly intoxicated by possibilities that a moment before did not exist. Equally familiar is the destruction of his old identity and the blossoming sense of risk that from then on will highlight a classic masculine bid for the far horizon.

In 1876, about six hundred years after Dante, Robert Louis Stevenson took an evening walk in Gretz, France, and stopped, transfixed, outside a lighted dining room window. Almost the moment he looked through that window he fell instantly in love with a woman he saw sitting at dinner with a circle of friends. Stevenson says he gazed at her for what seemed like hours, and then drew wide the very tall window, which was already slightly open, jumped inside the astonished room and introduced himself. We might be happy to hear that she was impressed enough to want to know more; we will join them in later chapters and follow the further consequences of jumping through open windows in small French towns in front of attractive strangers.

Thirteen years later, in 1889; in the best Dantean tradition, another strategically placed window was playing its part in another momentous meeting. Maud Gonne was at an afternoon gathering, standing under its light near a vase of apple blossom when the twenty-four-year-old poet William Butler Yeats entered the room. Seeing her, he forgot everything he was about to say to impress those present. Over the years she would force him to say far more intelligent and more lyrical things in many poems that would make his name. But she did it mostly through refusing him again and again. Yeats, like Dante, had found his Beatrice, and Maud had found her greatest admirer; the meeting altered both their futures forever.

All these men suddenly seeing women; all these women seeing men seeing them and testing them to see if what they see is real. What of love's first glimpse for a woman? It brings to mind the old saying that a man falls in love with what he sees and a woman falls in love with what she hears. Most recent scientific research seems to reinforce the woman's attentive emphasis on verbal, relational, rather than visual clues: clues as to sincerity, clues, perhaps, as to whether the man is *really* capable of *seeing* her. Not that a woman doesn't rage lustily for the George Clooneys of this world, but over time she seems to continually check that the image is not too small for her, not idealized in a way that actually excludes the particular details of her life. She also seems, according to the studies, to be looking for clues as to intelligence, as to vision for the future, as to fitness to be a father. Though no individual woman or man wants to be held to any generalization, this mutual but gender-based, checking and rechecking does seem to occur again and again through human history.

We could say that this dynamic is just as true for what we might call the masculine part of a woman when she catches sight of something or someone she realizes she desperately wants and needs. But the classic feminine, bound intimately to the biology of procreation, though she may be equally pierced by the dart of love, must follow a much more careful path. She risks childbearing, she risks being vulnerable as a possible mother, to the later discovered insincerity of the pursuer, and in a way a young male cannot fully imagine. If she has the least bit of sense about her she must test again and again to see if her first intuitions were true. But first she must allow herself to be literally smitten, that is, struck a blow that subverts her normal sense of propriety. Listen to that soon-to-be expert on manners, the young Jane Austen, describing herself with her first love, Tom Lefroy, at a ball. "I am almost afraid to tell how my Irish friend and I behaved. Imagine to yourself everything most profligate and shocking in the way of dancing and sitting down together." Take it another step and read Paul Alexander's description of Sylvia Plath walking into very dangerous territory on her first meeting with the poet Ted Hughes. "As soon as Hughes made a move to kiss her on the neck, Sylvia, ready to show that she could hold her own in such matters, reached up and bit his cheek so hard her teeth broke skin, causing him to flinch. Somehow it did not seem possible to continue, so they stepped apart. Certainly Sylvia had found her match, though Hughes had found his too. Moments later, as Hughes left the room, Sylvia could see blood trickling down his cheek."

Sylvia Plath's bite was both an invitation to address her as a sexual equal and a warning to let Hughes know she could hurt as well as be hurt. It is a fiery, youthful communication conveying a very different kind of testing chatter than the one Jane Austen was used to. At either end of the spectrum, mannered or not, a woman must test and try the pursuer to see if the fiery path to a deeper consummation is possible.

Nonetheless, it can be deeply disappointing to the feminine psyche when it is not even given the opportunity to test, rebuff and tell the masculine to go away. As Jane Austen said in a letter to her sister, Cassandra, about one disappointing ball: "There was one gentleman of the Cheshire, a very good looking young man, who I was told wanted so much to be introduced to me. But as he did not want it quite enough to take much trouble in effecting it, we could never bring it about."

Whether we be male or female—a woman with a highly developed masculine side who knows what she wants, or a man who can discern and discriminate in the midst of hot pursuit—the two dynamics seem to call for a necessary form of marriage between desire and discrimination, whatever kind of man or woman we are.

In the early stage of relationship, without the creatively destructive dynamics of desire and longing, our protected sense of self cannot be destabilized or subverted from our old way of being; we cannot be chaotically reorganized to accommodate ourselves to anything fresh. A certain state of blinding ecstasy seems necessary for navigating the first crucial thresholds of a loved one's recognition.

I remember a close friend of mine worrying that in marrying for love he felt his powers of logic were clouded. Should he wait until, in effect, he wasn't so much in love anymore? "There is a tide in the affairs of men," I almost found myself shouting out loud. Letting that dramatic Shakespearean inclination sweep by, I found an equally dramatic part of me, from far within my own married state, wanting to cry out, "Why would anyone in his right mind *logically* choose to marry?" In effect, both partners must suffer a kind of logical self-impairment to make the commitment. A marriage is creatively destructive of both partners' cherished notions of themselves. Despite the initial hopes of perfection, what one partner wants will not occur; what the other partner wants will not occur. Both are left with the actual marriage: a radically new conversation that is built on the razed foundations of their former identities.

An old time-tested perspective, is that a true marriage is never just an arrangement, though with luck it may grow from one. It is almost like a mutual invitation to which both partners must respond wholeheartedly. It includes as much of the future in its gravitational pull as it does any present particularities. It is something that lives over the horizon as much as it exists in the here and now. It is full of keen daily pleasures and shattering disappointments. From all of these early, optimistic appearances and depressing disappearances we realize we have had a first glimpse of secret imagined possibilities, until now unspoken.

Short Conclusion:
On Falling in Love for the Long Term

For any long-term happiness in a marriage, almost everyone would agree that falling in love is an absolute necessity, whether it is before, or as in many cultures, after the ceremony. Falling in love comes through an illogical but real glimpse of a future possible perfection. The passion and ecstasy of that experience of perfection act as a kind of indelible foundation in the memory that gives the couple a ground on which to build and shelter through all the future troubles that lie ahead of them. If falling in love is the basis of marriage, and if good work is a form of marriage, why, therefore, would our happiness in a work have any different kind of foundation? For happiness in a vocation over time we must fall in love with our work, before or after the commitment to a particular career, no matter the seeming impossibilities of that first perfect imagining; no matter the difficulties that lie between us and a future consummation of our hopes. In the foundations of love for another person, we have the basis for understanding the second, parallel marriage, and also the basis for a next chapter, falling in love with a work.

CHAPTER 3

Vows Made for Me:
Falling in Love
with a Work

We can fall in love with a work as easily or as accidentally as we can with a person. Looking at the biographies of many of those who have achieved something beyond the ordinary, we often find in each of those lives, some threshold of realization, some concentrated foundational insight they experienced, often quite young, that acted like a prior announcement of the drama to come. These events are rare and momentous, and can be difficult because they have to be lived up to long after the experience has receded into memory, so much so that we often have a part of us actively working hard to forget and dismiss that rare experience and consign it to the past or to myth. As an antidote to this aptitude for forgetfulness and returning to the ordinary, I am tempted to start this chapter with the rarest of the rare, to start at the very top and only then work down, from the seemingly unreachable, to a place that seems possible in our own workaday lives.

Once upon a time and long ago, in a much simpler time, a young and very uneducated girl walked out into the woods surrounding her home and received instruction from the three saints she happened to meet on her way: Saint Catherine, Saint Michael and Saint Margaret. Their dictates were clear. She must drive out the foreign forces occupying her forlorn land, they said sternly, and she must reinstate the true prince and have him crowned again in the greatest cathedral in the land. A cathedral that still lay in enemy territory. The young girl grew up with a firm persuasion of her task in life from this and other startled meetings. Taking small steps, one after the other, she slowly convinced powerful men further and further up the hierarchy of society to believe in her visions, until she was introduced to the court of the prince himself. On the appointed day, though the prince disguised himself among his followers to test her, the young girl chose him out immediately though she did not know him by sight. Then by whispering a secret into the prince's ear that only he could know, she astonished the prince into acquiescence and made him listen to her advice. She then led the armies of the almost defeated nation to an astonishing series of victories and saw her prince crowned king in the reclaimed holy cathedral.

We might ask ourselves what this pleasant fairy story has to do with an attempt to look at the practical world of work—a work, we might add, that takes place amid the grit of an everyday reality, except this is no fairy story, and there was a great deal more grit about in her day than any of us are likely to meet in our protected postmodern glass-and-steel workplace.

This girl actually existed in history, and her life and its events are precisely chronicled and verified by the scribes who lived in her time and the historians who have followed the path she trod. She lived from 1412 to only 1431, and her name itself seems to belong to fairy tale or myth: Joan of Arc. We have mythologized that name to the point of nonexistence, which is to say we find her courage and her purity pointless because it is so far beyond us, and being so far from it ourselves, we would rather not think about it, or her, for that matter. Yet she did exist. She was poor. She was uneducated to the point of illiteracy; she knew no one; she had no military training; she had no understanding of politics; she was completely successful in what she set out to do.

The story of Joan of Arc lies at the very far limits of our ability to understand real dedication, in this case the ability to create something far reaching out of a seeming nothing. It goes beyond even that far, far-off limit when we learn that she was betrayed by the very prince she served, and executed by the English she had driven from his lands. Her dedication was based on the exhilarating but frightening conversations she experienced during her religious visions, and during her final trial by the English, we learn, she could have recanted her visions and saved herself. Reading this, we are most likely to say, No, thank you. We want to be happy in our work, not a beautiful and exemplary sacrifice. But her story is the pure template from which many other, much humbler stories of success are built.

She heard something, she saw something, she followed what she saw and heard. It was as simple as that. She listened and had faith in what she had heard even though others could not conceive of what she had experienced. She grew afraid, like all of us, of what she had understood and what she had to do because of this knowledge. Then she was cajoled, strengthened and even threatened by what she secretly knew, and then as the pressure grew, scolded by what she had seen and heard, she drove on through seemingly insurmountable difficulties to see those visions come to life in the literal splendor of a coronation.

Again and again, it seems, it is the memory of the initial encounter that is the currency for all the future transactions involving a work. We might not encounter saints, but all of us encounter something when we are young that is almost like an invitation, a beckoning uncertainty that emboldens us not only into the world but also into a surer sense of ourselves. These visions, like Joan's, can also have something of the slave driver about them, driving us on through wind and rain to our imagined goal. I remember vividly, at thirteen years old, seeing Jacques Cousteau sailing across the little television set in a corner of our living room in the North of England, and my mouth and my mind dropped open at the sight.

I stood in the middle of the room, looking and looking and looking at that beautiful ship sailing those vast oceanic horizons, and out of that nonstop looking, immediately conceived a notion to follow that vision aboard the good ship *Calypso*. I spent long hours soaking in the bath each day dreaming myself over blue horizons. I walked over the back fields behind our home and saw myself in diving gear, steering zodiacs along coral reefs; more practically, I gave up all my beloved arts subjects at school and put myself into the salt mines of biology, chemistry and physics. "I could always pick up a book of John Donne," I said to myself. I needed help, and as it turned out, a great deal of help, with ecological genetics. Ten difficult, hard-slogging, exam-clogged, rain-filled years later, relieved only by music, mountaineering and a good measure of alcohol now and again, I found myself, just as I had imagined, a hundred feet underwater at the base of a volcanic reef in the Galápagos Islands, running out of air while being threatened by a tiger shark. I was ecstatic; happy as ever I could imagine. Driven on by those original visions, I had come home. I experienced everything I had seen in the compass of that tiny screen in the infinitely broader vista I saw in those islands.

How we respond to an invitation can mark or maim us for the rest of our days. A life can often be measured against how sure we were in responding to the initial beckoning image. Like Joan, on a smaller, less miraculous scale, our ability to follow our star is also a measure of our belief in the original invitation. I have sober memories of friends who passed entrance exams, as I did, for the elite local school that was a sure track to a brilliant education and an invitation to a much wider horizon than any that our modest Yorkshire working-class parents had inherited. Most of my friends made a great deal of the opportunities offered to them. But there were a few who seemed afraid of what was on offer, and to my young mind, afraid of something it called for in their selves. As if they did not feel worthy of the invitation or felt at some essential level they were not equal to that world into which they were being invited. They had no belief in what they had encountered. What they glimpsed seemed too large for them and some part of them eventually became afraid of it. It might have been they were afraid of an ambitious form of falling in love and the commitment to which it might lead.

It is sobering to think especially of two young men I knew. One did well in class but refused all advancement and responsibility, confining his powers to the circle from which he had come, and passed away, to my grief, extraordinarily young, like a poignant character from Dickens. The other turned down the possibility of university but had no other compelling vocation to replace it; he lives out his former intellectual powers in the small world of crossword puzzles and word games, from which, in a corner of a local pub, he barely raises his head. The great question is: Were they happy? I think not, or I would not mention them in this context. There seems to be a constant visiting dynamic in all stages of life where it appears that we get only the girl, the guy, the work, the job, the sense of self, or a participation in wider creation that we actually feel we are worthy of. If we don't feel we deserve it, then, like a spendthrift heiress, throwing her patrimony to the winds, we do our best to sabotage and give away what we feel we did not deserve in the first place.

Making ourselves equal to the invitation offered by life often begins early on by walking out in the world, the head literally or metaphorically, held high, looking and listening, cultivating a beautiful kind of youthful self-belief in our own senses. Joan was later put on trial by her English enemies and asked about the original experience that had propelled her into such extraordinary conduct:

> *She answered yes, she had received great comfort from him. "I do not speak of Saint Michael's voice, but of his great comfort." Asked which was the first voice to come to her, about the age of thirteen, she answered that it was Saint Michael whom she saw before her eyes; and he was not alone, but accompanied by many angels from heaven. She said also that she came into France only by the instruction of God. Asked if she saw Saint Michael and the angels corporeally and in reality, she answered that she saw them with her bodily eyes as well as she saw the assessors of the trial. And when Saint Michael and the angels left her, she wept, and fain would have been taken with them. Asked, on the same day, if there was a light with the voices, she answered there was a great deal of light, on all sides, as was most fitting.*
>
> Proceedings of the trial of Joan of Arc (translation from
> the original Latin and French by W. P. Barrett)

It is moving to hear, in Joan's testimony, the emphasis she places on the comfort provided by Michael's voice. It is an intuition of all the times she will have to turn to its memory during the unbearable trials that lay in her future. It is equally moving to read: *Asked, on the same day, if there was a light with the voices, she answered there was a great deal of light, on all sides, as was most fitting.* It is this fitting, youthful ability to see and follow the light that enables us to live with a sense of anticipation that we are involved with some great undertaking that has not yet quite come about, but which will soon reveal itself. The belief in the light also enables us to conjure it again and again in the dungeons of our later life when our youthful courage will be put to the test. But making ourselves available in first encounters of youth, we have a chance of an encounter with something beyond ourselves. Youth seems to say, "Let humility come later; we will have no choice in any event but to be humbled by what we are called by." Out in the world looking for good trouble with a solid inner self-belief in what we encounter, we find a robust edge between ourselves and the world, an ability to look for help and an increasing ability to hold a conversation with what comes to find us.

What is remarkable about Joan's rise from obscure peasant girl to national icon in just a few, very short years, is the way she was able to ask for help again and again. Her ability to ask was magnified by absolute belief that she should be helped, that her cause was just and even inevitable. She was somehow persistent enough with the hard-bitten, dissolute commander of a nearby garrison of French soldiers to cause him to waver in his initial derision. When her self-belief shaded into outright prophecy on the exact outcome of a faraway battle, he was overawed into providing her with an escort for a journey to meet the king of France.

We can only imagine Joan's sense of anticipation before the meeting. The sense that a moment is ours all ready for the taking is a powerful arbiter of success, whether it is an audience with the king of France or an interview in high office in downtown Seattle. Confidence and self-belief are contagious; they are not a matter of pure arrogance or overweening egotism, they are the sense of being part of a greater story others have not yet discovered and giving off an almost physical sense of invitation to join that story, that disarms and then changes potential enemies into allies.

In order to have a chance of being smitten, of falling in love, we must hazard ourselves on the path that our experiences and revelations open up for us.

Often, we have to fall off a metaphorical cliff. Joan fell in love directly with her God, which is beyond most of us. But Dante fell for his Beatrice, a type of falling in love that most of us have experienced at least once in our lives. Dante also fell in love with his poetry and with the Italian language, and through that falling in love, found a new vocation. Harder to understand is the as yet unknown Deirdre Blomfield-Brown, who ran into a very old, very fierce religious tradition and fell in love with a pure form of void, a vast emptiness that would lead her into her own unusual vocation, and into carrying a very different name, though she could not have known it at the time. Deirdre Blomfield-Brown is perhaps the least-known personality whom I follow in this book. Her name and her ordinary background represent us all in our wish to emerge from the bland, background noise of life into something more unique, more our-selves, more generous and more courageous.

But whether we fall for Beatrice, for a work or for the great void, it does not seem to matter what we fall for to begin with so long as it puts us to dreaming and imagining, so long as it puts us in a real conversation with something other than ourselves and so long as it does us no actual harm. A nephew of mine fell in love, very early in his life and very seriously, with washing machines: their buttons and their dials, their interior belts and drums, the secret ways of their repair and maintenance, how they were made, how they functioned, how they felt to the touch—in short, everything they represented. We may start anywhere and in any way, but the encounter asks the same of us. Those first glimpses lead us into worlds that eventually test, as with Dante following his Beatrice, Joan and her saints, and Deirdre with her desperate void, our sense of worthiness for a task much larger than the initial invitation.

Sometimes the first glimpse is just that: a mere fleeting glance, a touch on the shoulder, a crooked and beckoning finger; the kindly but tough aunt who takes us under her wing and directs us toward something more bracing and risky than our parents are prepared for. It may be in the form of an advertise-ment in a journal for a really scintillating job for which, at pres-ent, we have no preparation or qualifications. It might be found in a certain air of happiness and satisfaction we see in a man we meet in a bar, who is happy to talk about his endeavors and breathes both excitement and contentment as he talks.

Sooner strangle an infant in its cradle, said William Blake, exaggerating like all good storytellers, in an attempt to get near the truth, *than nurse unacted desires.* Refusing to fall in love with a vocation and thereby refusing the necessary insanities for the path ahead is hardly ever a passive process where everything goes into neutral; it is actually corrosive on the personality and character of the one who repeatedly says no to something that keeps on whispering yes. *No more things will happen,* says the poet Rilke, *No more days will open / and even the things that do happen will cheat him.* The child who is done to death in Blake's poem might be the part inside us that loses its life when we turn away from our own innocent but necessary expectations of the world. We may not meet Saint Catherine, Saint Michael and Saint Margaret in our youth, but the tiniest thing can speak to the alert mind and change its future forever.

PRIMARY IMAGES OF WORK:
A DIFFERENT "PLANE" OF EXISTENCE

A friend of mine, one whom I came to know well in my early twenties, when I lived in the mountains of North Wales, fell in love long ago, not with a woman or a saint, but with a tiny, brass plane used for shaving wood. As a child he had found himself sitting beneath a neighbor's workbench amongst the drifting wood shavings of a beautifully organized workshop. He looked up at seven years old and saw the older man lift that exquisite little brass object with its perfectly slotted blade above a piece of flat, glowing cherry so that the tiny instrument caught the light.

In my friend's imagination that plane still hangs there now, forever framed in that light flowing through his neighbor's workshop window, and to this day, that image still informs everything he does in his work. The sight of that beautifully made plane in that perfectly organized workshop was everything for him. Everything from that moment would be bent to living his future life around that unassuming tool and all its other brother and sister implements. He admired the furniture the man used to make, but most of all he fell in love with all the necessary tools and the care with which they were made and maintained. He also fell in love with all the names: bow and band saw, rasps and routers, oak and ash. I remember, too, that he had a very soft spot for the perfect little bubble in the level. Just as important, he also became entranced with the way his neighbor worked. The man spent one-third of his time preparing, sharpening and oiling the tools, arranging the wood, clearing the way ahead; only one-third actually working; and the last third of his time busily clearing, sweeping, tidying and hanging all the beautiful things back in their proper places.

By the time I came to know him, my friend had grown into a very fine carpenter, and I particularly enjoyed, cup of tea in hand, observing him at work in his own well-organized palace of a workshop. As I drank my tea and watched him bustle happily about the place (one of the more pleasurable occupations of being idle), I would often think to myself that the level of craftsmanship he put into the cabinets he constructed was really just a surface over the real virtuosity he revealed in actually doing the work itself.

When he lifted a chisel up to the light, with its glowing, well-oiled wooden handle and its bright edge, you knew he was holding something that meant a great deal to him. You had a suspicion that preparing the materials and the tools was far more important to him than the mere necessity of actually having to use them. Cleaning, arranging and sweeping were final and daily satisfactions for him. Though he struggled in his marriage and his personal life, in his work he was well matched. He had found a very loving partner. As a young man not yet sure of my future, I always emerged from his workshop with some of that happiness just as happily rubbed off on me and would walk on beneath the purple hills of Snowdonia, thoughtfully outlining a perfect writing studio for myself, a studio I knew waited for me in my future life, with all the books arranged just so, and perhaps, but not necessarily, a view over water or mountain.

PRIMARY IMAGES OF DIFFICULTY

Sometimes our work begins not with a bright plane caught in gold light, but with something darker and more difficult. Something not wanted. Sometimes we begin with images that are the opposite of nourishing and inspiring; sometimes the first image is one of imprisonment and the wish for escape. Yet these first images can form the foundation for a work that is both liberating and inspiring.

Charles Dickens grew a great, long, weighty bookshelf of a life directly out of his childhood struggles. You could say it grew directly and literally out of imprisonment.

Charles' father had struggled constantly to keep his family above a rising tide of debt. When Charles turned twelve years old, despite his love of learning and books, his father looked to him for help with money. Despite his age, Charles was told to forget about an education, he must do his part and take a job—at Warren's Blacking Company. Charles was horrified. Warren's was a manufacturer of boot blacking operated by a family friend in a series of filthy, run-down houses deep in the slums of London. Surely his parents couldn't mean it?

His father and his mother ignored their son's distress. They were pleased and excited about Charles' possibilities for working his way up through the company under the eye of their friend. To the young boy who loved more than anything, time with his books, his prospects suddenly seemed as dark as the jars of polish onto which he had to paste labels ten hours a day. The premises were dismal, the floors rotting, the place full of rats and soon after Charles started work, his father sank under his commitments and found himself imprisoned for debt. From then on, young Dickens' life seemed to become a kind of metaphor for incarceration. We might be surprised to know that Dickens' entire family, as was usual at that time, came to live at the Marshalsea debtors' prison.

Before Charles began his day's work, he would breakfast with his family in his father's prison room. Then, after working all day, he found his despairing way back to the same place for dinner. He was deeply impressionable and deeply wounded by the absolute way his talents and his way in life seemed to have been neglected and forgotten.

> *But for the mercy of God, I might easily have been, for all the care that was taken of me, a little robber or a little vagabond.*

He had become invisible, he realized numbly. He had become one of that mass: the poorest of the poor, and like the invisibles with whom he now worked, a member of a teeming working-class community of the unnamed and the unnoticed that until then he himself had barely seen. In the midst of this, doing who knows what, perhaps staring at a label for the thousandth time, perhaps walking out through the gate of the prison into the smoky London air, perhaps lying in bed in the dark of his father's prison room, Charles Dickens swore to himself he would work his way out of this invisibility. He would fight his way out with words. He would fight with those words for those who had been forgotten, like himself.

> *In the little world in which children have their existence, whosoever brings them up, there is nothing so finely perceived and so finely felt, as injustice.*

This quotation from *Great Expectations* stands almost like a vow, a representation of a fierce internal marriage to the seed of his future work, not only as the brilliant storyteller who could turn a pretty penny or two, but one who stood for all those in society we so easily see as expendable. He became not only an articulate representative of the Oliver Twists and Little Dorrits of this world but also, by the time of his death, an arbiter of Victorian social change that would improve the lives of the destitute immeasurably.

Charles Dickens' singular imagination changed the imagination of a whole society around him. In a sense he enabled the privileged, reading classes to take notice of people they had not been able to see before. He taught them to see something that had already been right before their eyes. This societal revolution depended on Dickens' having made an initial, unwanted visitation to the underworld of dirt, impoverishment and invisibility. In later years, he would bless his early lack of fortune. He saw it as the seam of ore from which he excavated his characters, his stories and his passion for social change. Dickens reminds us how easy it is to swap the rich struggling particularity of our given life for an abstract, too easy inheritance that would lead to our not seeing, to our not participating and to our refusal to care.

VOWS MADE FOR ME

Good work can begin in the interior of a well-ordered workshop, in the underworld of darkness, imprisonment and poverty or looking at the upper world of mountain and sky, as it did to William Wordsworth, who lived two hundred fifty miles to the north of Dickens' London. Two hundred fifty miles, and far from all that London smoke and dirt, but not very far from impoverishment, lay the mountains, lakes and wooded valleys of Cumbria. The English Lake District had become home to a coterie of poets, chief among them William Wordsworth, who had grown in those mountains and who, like Dickens, tried to make ordinary things visible to those who walked right by them with barely a glance. Wordsworth's ordinary things were, in a parallel to Dickens, the men and women who toiled in the fields or walked the roads begging from place to place, but also the cliffs and mountains that stood above them and that used to horrify the educated society of his youth. Wordsworth taught the eye and the intellect to appreciate wildness in a landscape and in a person. He looked at that part of creation that could not be contained by ordinary social conversation. He saw the redemptive in a leech gatherer, and heaven in a mountainside.

Coleridge wrote a masterly sentence describing the effect of his friend Wordsworth's work on the mind of the reader, saying his work gave "the charm of novelty to things of every day, and so excites a feeling analogous to the supernatural, by awakening the mind's attention from the lethargy of custom, and directing it to the loveliness and wonders of the world before us, an inexhaustible treasure, but for which in consequence of the film of familiarity . . . we have eyes, yet see not, ears that hear not, and hearts that neither feel nor understand."

Wordsworth was attempting to see, hear and feel for a society that he felt had forgotten certain basic, foundational truths.

To every natural form, rock, fruit, or flower,
Even the loose stones that cover the highway,
I gave a moral life: I saw them feel
Or linked them to some feeling: the great mass
Lay bedded in a quickening soul, and all
That I beheld respired with inward meaning.

The Prelude, Book III, "Residence at Cambridge"

No matter the multitude of inward meanings, Wordsworth had a long, hard toil of making his name and his poetry tell. He began his adult life under tremendous pressure from exasperated guardians who had looked after him tetchily, from his orphaning at thirteen to his being admitted to university and who, above all, and like any self-respecting guardians, wanted him to get that most necessary thing—a decent job.

Wordsworth's guardians had paid for him to go to St. John's College, Cambridge, where he found both the teaching and the landscape depressingly flat, especially compared to the richness of his school years among the mountains of Cumbria. Returning home for a summer vacation now seemed to him like returning to paradise. He had that experience many of us have in young adulthood when we return for the first time to the childhood home that nurtured us and grew us and are suddenly able to see it as if for the first time. We get a glimpse of what we took for granted and can see it now as a unique inheritance.

Racing down to the small ferryboat that would take him across Lake Windermere, Wordsworth realized how much the place lived in his imagination like an invisible structure. Back amongst those very visible mountains, he had such a powerful experience of home ground that it seemed to set up an echo that allowed him to understand the right, true ground of his own work and vocation. In this homecoming was his first glimpse as an adult of the love that would stand behind his work.

He describes this moment in *The Prelude*, the biographical poem he wrote to try and chart the growth of his awareness. It is a moment famous in English literature, and a compelling example of someone falling in love with his future and finding, in that falling in love, a sense of dedication to which, through the rockier moments of his future career, he would return again and again. I can never read this short piece without feeling the sheer physicality of the experience. First, because I walked the same mountains year after year in my own growing, and second, because I used to read him back in my tent in the late summer light as someone who spoke to the intensity of my youth in a way other, tamer authors could not approach. I felt both companionable and conspiratorial with him but also confirmed in my own intense searching. He made me feel as if I had been walking with him every step of the way without knowing it and as if I could follow him to whatever destination he decided on. He was an invisible companion in laying down the foundations of my own future work.

We can join Wordsworth ourselves on this particular walk and witness how the world seemed to ripen around him until it formed into something momentous; something ready to be harvested, something worth his dedication. Wordsworth was on his way from a midsummer night's dance, walking in the first light of dawn, making his way back to his home village of Hawkshead.

Two hundred ten years later, two terms need a little explanation: *grain tinctured*, meaning "dyed scarlet," and *empyrean*, meaning "heavenly."

> *Two miles I had to walk along the fields*
> *Before I reached my home. Magnificent*
> *The morning was, a memorable pomp,*
> *More glorious than I ever had beheld,*
> *The sea was laughing at a distance; all*
> *The solid mountains were as bright as clouds,*
> *Grain tinctured, drenched in empyrean light;*
> *And in the meadows and the lower grounds*
> *Was all the sweetness of a common dawn,*
> *Dews, vapours, and the melody of birds,*
> *And Labourers going forth into the fields.*
> *Ah! need I say, dear Friend, but to the brim*
> *My heart was full; I made no vows, but vows*
> *Were then made for me; bond unknown to me*
> *Was given, that I should be, else sinning greatly,*
> *A dedicated Spirit. On I walk'd*
> *In blessedness, which even yet remains.*

I made no vows, but vows / Were then made for me is a beautifully wrought phrase that says, in effect, that life comes to find us as much as we go out to find it. Which could be a line from a Hallmark card except for the radical imaginative step he asks us to take next: life can find you only if you are paying real attention to something other than your own concerns, if you can hear and see the essence of otherness in the world, if you can treat the world as if it is not just a backdrop to your own journey, if you can have a relationship with the world that isn't based on triumphing *over* it or complaining *about* it.

Wordsworth tells us that we put ourselves at the center of the world strangely, by eliminating our concern for the smaller self. When something beautiful and overwhelming like a waterfall or the morning light on a mountainside takes us outside our worries, we are put in a privileged position that is far more than the ability to appreciate a good view.

Hearing and seeing without the filter of interpretation is seen by Wordsworth as the act of reaching the real conversation at last and it is this conversation that does all the work of helping us find our way into the future. Wordsworth is pointing out a marker for us, a milestone. Saying, in effect, that when we have this experience, this is where we are on the map. You have glimpsed your homeland, and the rest of your life now has to do with making that first glimpse into paradise, a living, daily reality.

> *On I walk'd*
> *In blessedness, which even yet remains*

He says to tell us that he has reached *here* from *there*.

Wordsworth's *vows made for me* is a moment in time, an experience rarely put into everyday language but one that appears again and again in the mouths of those who have navigated these absolute threshold experiences of dedication.

It is a help to us when someone is able to pass this experience on as a recognized marker for understanding what is happening in the intensity of the moment. It has been said before, by other now glamorous teachers and amongst other, more exotic mountains. Dogen Zenji, a formidable Japanese Zen master, said, " If you go out and confirm the ten thousand things, this is delusion; if you let the ten thousand things come and confirm you, this is enlightenment." Dogen Zenji's statement is a way of describing a dynamic that occurs in very fierce states of attention built up over years of contemplative practice, but closer to everyday life, it has also been experienced in the midst of a depression, getting into the passenger seat of a friend's pickup truck, and reading the first line of an open magazine that says, "There is nothing wrong with negativity," as Deirdre Blomfield-Brown did in 1974. Perhaps, in that moment of difficulty, 175 years after Wordsworth, Deirdre saw her depression as a thing in itself, like a mountain or a cloud, with its own life, its own necessities, and therefore worthy of respect, more like a doorway than an obstacle. It was a path to follow, not an error she had made that she should eliminate.

Being smitten by a path, a direction, an intuited possibility, no matter the territory it crosses, we can feel in youth or at any threshold, as if life has found us at last. Beginning a courtship with a work, like beginning a courtship with a love, demands a fierce attention to understand what it is we belong to in the world. But to start the difficult path to what we want, we also have to be serious about what we want.

Following this path through increasing levels of seriousness, we reach a certain threshold where our freedom to choose seems to disappear and is replaced by an understanding that we were made for the world in a very particular way and that this way of being is at bottom nonnegotiable. Like the mountain or the sky, it just *is*. It is as if we choose and choose until there is actually no choice at all. When the level of attention reaches a certain intensity, as it did for Wordsworth that midsummer's morning, then the person who has been looking suddenly feels as if he or she has been sought out by the world, sought out, acknowledged, named and recognized. The only question is whether you will respond, whether you will not turn away, whether you will turn toward it—whether, in effect, you will become *a dedicated spirit.*

This acknowledgment seems to arrive in a multitude of ways: in glamorous, earth-shattering ways, accompanied by a view over the mountains, through the private inner intensity of depression, or it can come about more easily, more subtly, by others noticing something of the way we are made before we have got there ourselves.

THE RECOGNITION OF OTHERS

When I first made my home in the United States and settled in at an educational center near Seattle, I was surprised to find that of all the many titles that people had given me, "poet" was one that somehow seemed to catch the imagination of my new colleagues. It was a surprise to me that they had caught sight of a very private and, in many ways, secret core, but I had said very little about those aspirations; I had not written for years, and there was little corroborating evidence to earn the title. Still, I was introduced as the poet so many times and started to feel so embarrassed about it, that after a while I decided I had better get on with it, so as not to let down those who had seen something I dared not as yet fully acknowledge myself: it was a slow, subtle and secret start line that led to other, more shattering declarations.

The mountains were calling Wordsworth. The impoverished and unnamed were calling Dickens. Three saints ganged up on Joan of Arc for what we would call a good telling-off. Dogen Zenji said the ten thousand things came to find him every day and by extension could, with a little work on our part, find all of us. Everything, our great contemplative and artistic traditions tell us, is waiting for you to take your place in the conversation. Why not follow the path that is beckoning you? Why not acknowledge that you are already on your way home?

I wrote the following piece as if looking in the mirror, as if giving myself a good telling-off, one of those times when we have to remind ourselves about something we may know already but are in danger of forgetting.

EVERYTHING IS WAITING FOR YOU

Your great mistake is to act the drama
as if you were alone. As if life
were a progressive and cunning crime
with no witness to the tiny hidden

transgressions. To feel abandoned is to deny
the intimacy of your surroundings. Surely,
even you, at times, have felt the grand array;
the swelling presence, and the chorus, crowding
out your solo voice. You must note
the way the soap dish enables you,
or the window latch grants you freedom.
Alertness is the hidden discipline of familiarity.
The stairs are your mentor of things
to come, the doors have always been there
to frighten you and invite you,
and the tiny speaker in the phone
is your dream ladder to divinity.

Put down the weight of your aloneness and ease into
the conversation. The kettle is singing
even as it pours you a drink, the cooking pots
have left their arrogant aloofness and
seen the good in you at last. All the birds
and creatures of the world are unutterably
themselves. Everything is waiting for you.

from D.W., *River Flow: New & Selected Poems 1984–2007*

Conclusions: Falling in Love with a Work

Our great, historical, mythological and contemplative traditions continually reiterate one thing: A good or even great work is never just of our own choosing, though it may not be achieved without our particular gifts.

To glimpse our vocation, we must learn how to be sought out and found by a work as much as we strive to identify it ourselves. We must make ourselves findable by being seen; to do that we must hazard ourselves and make ourselves available to the world we want to enter. Finding and being found is like a mutual falling in love. To have a possibility of happiness we must at the beginning fall in love at least a little with our work. We can choose a work on a mere strategic, financial basis, but then we should not expect profound future happiness as a result.

Further Conclusions

This is not a lonely road; untold numbers of people have gone before us in history. Untold numbers have had the same experience of having things seem to move on their behalf, in what seems, inexplicably, like a compact or an arrangement that has been waiting for them all along. Many of these stories are exemplary and helpful to us in the present particulars of our life, whether we look out from a palatial London office on Canary Wharf or from a depressing bedsit in Pimlico. We can read into the details of those stories and biographies to help us remember the greater dimensions of our involvement.

Final Conclusion

The dynamics that have driven many admired and courageous figures to great works through human history are
the same ones we encounter on a lesser scale in our everyday lives. Our first glimpse of what we see may not seem
as great, or the eventual sacrifice demanded of us as profound, but then again, they might just become so, because
none of us knows the conclusion of the story upon which
we are embarked.

Final Final Conclusion

A real work, like a real love, takes not only passion but a
certain daily, obsessive, tenacious, illogical form of insanity to keep it alive. Once you have experienced the real
essence at the beginning of the affair with a work, the
task, as in a marriage, is to keep the work, the company,
the initial image with which we fell in love, alive. We
want to be surprised again and again by where our work
takes us and what kind of person we are becoming as we
follow it. Like a love, or a sense of our selves, we can nib-
ble and negotiate at the edges but the central core of the
relationship is actually nonnegotiable. A real work cannot
be balanced with a marriage in a strategic way, a little bit
on that side, a little bit on the other; it can only be put in

conversation with that marriage, as an equal partner. All the strategies for making them work together will come from understanding that central conversation. And what is that conversation? What is the thing called the self that drives home from a work and walks through the door into a relationship? Who is it who goes out the door in the morning and leaves a loved one, a husband, a wife, a daughter, a home behind and looks to a new future in the day?

CHAPTER 4

The Doorless Door:
Youth's First Glimpse
of the Self

Who lives at the center of all this commitment? What is that thing at the center of our identity that every religious tradition in the world insists we have? What is the soul? Is there a soul, a central faculty of belonging? All people intuit an interior self at the center of their everyday being. But this being seems even more stubbornly difficult to come to know as a hoped-for partner or vocation.

This intimate internal self seems to love and labor in a completely inconsistent way. Like a completely distinct person, it does not seem to be ultimately knowable. Like a real person, it seems to want to go its own way. Our reluctance to investigate its character can be reinforced by its seeming behavior. One moment we find it relishing life, the next resenting everyone; one day finding freedom, the next feeling suffocated and surrounded. We discover it wanting one thing and then having us say out loud the complete opposite, and quite often, it seems, to its own continual surprise.

The mystery deepens when we realize that this self seems to have two conflicting core competencies: one, the ability to find its way home by sheer instinct, to know what is good and nourishing for it; and the other, just as well developed, to sabotage both itself and what it loves the most, to destroy not only the home, but everyone who lives in it and for good measure, the carefully constructed path it followed to get there.

This interior self can seem impossible to track down. If we want to meet a possible partner, we can look to our immediate circle of friends, we can survey our colleagues with a discriminating eye, or desiring a great deal of undiscriminating and disastrous fun, sign up with an Internet dating company. If we are looking for good work, we can search through advertisements, talk with career counselors or follow doggedly in the wake of a Jacques Cousteau or a Warren Buffett. Where, we ask ourselves, do we meet the self?

We know from accounts we have read that an encounter with the self sometimes involves a visitation, a form of intense experience: perhaps a high Himalayan valley, a devastating loss, a battlefield? It also seems to demand silence and something, the Dalai Lama insists, is called self-compassion. All of which are very difficult to put on a to-do list. Picking up a book on the mystic traditions can be very intriguing but keep us at a wondering distance.

I remember my first encounter with Dogen Zenji years ago in the quiet upstairs library of a house where I stayed. I read:

> *To study Buddhism we study the self*
> *To study the self is to forget the self*
> *To forget the self is to become*
> *Enlightened by all things*

And wondered if I would ever come to really understand it. From someone of Dogen's stature, we know we might be hearing something true, but we also might be a little puzzled that our hard-to-arrange date with the self might come to an end as soon as we have introduced ourselves. It sounds like another possibility for disappointment and rejection, of which we already have plenty in the other two marriages. It is interesting to note that the dynamics of a true love, a true work and what, in Buddhism, has been called the true self, are essentially the same. None of them is amenable to command and control. We establish a relationship by in effect establishing a conversation with that tricky customer we happen to be involved with in that particular marriage. Tricky customer number one might be our spouse; tricky customer number two, our job; and trickiest customer of all, our self—and the last one, by the way, we seem to have the least choice over. Normally in relationship, a slowly evolving conversation begins to inform us as to whom we are involved with and helps us to uncover, in each step of getting to know that prospective partner, whether we want to make a further commitment. In the relationship with the self, we know from the beginning that we have no choice. Yet strangely, despite this inevitability, at the beginning of the getting-to-know-each-other stage, there seems to be little or no cooperation.

Philosophers over the centuries have constantly puzzled over this self, which seems to go its own way, and fretted daily over inconsistencies in following their own carefully constructed theories. Arthur Schopenhauer despaired daily about his constant search for a wife, though his philosophy said again and again it was only a means to misery. Simone de Beauvoir called for a dignity and an identity for women that were not defined by males, and was all the while enslaved in her affections and the pattern of her days by her love for Jean-Paul Sartre. There seems to be a current deep inside all human beings that flows in exactly the opposite direction from many of the heartfelt declarations they make on the surface. Who is it? Who lives beneath all the philosophies?

FIRST STEPS TO THE SELF

The first steps have long been acknowledged to be very painful. We often want self-understanding, but not until we feel we are strong enough to take the insight. Like an awkward teenager on a first date we can find ourselves attempting all kinds of surface manipulations in order to make an introduction to the stranger inside. The interesting dynamic is that although we might really want to find out who we are underneath it all, in the end, we also want to find out how marvelous we are. We want to learn how to be humble, but we want that humble self to have prophetic powers or know exactly the right thing to do, or be able to create the ideal life. We want it to hold sway over all circumstances. We want, in effect, to find images of perfection.

It is interesting to note that the spiritual longings of a young man or woman are almost always intimately connected to a form of idealism. Through this self-enlightenment they will change the world and become that incarnation of perfection they have always wanted. Perhaps the intuition is correct. There is a necessary way in which we fall in love with a template, an idealized form of what we want ourselves and our world to be, just as we seek on first meeting, the perfection in another person or perfect job satisfaction when we look for a career.

Realizing we are looking for an ideal, we might think we should be more mature; we might think we should turn toward a more sober reality and get back to the real world. But innocence might be entirely appropriate for our first glimpse of the self, just as it is appropriate in a young man or woman first exploring the world. And just as we hide things from ourselves at the beginning of a relationship or a job, so in the search for self-knowledge it might not be useful to know every obstacle that lies in our path. If we were really aware of the particular brick walls and unending difficulties that lay ahead of us in finding just a little of that true self, we might lock ourselves up in a padded room with a towering pile of *Hello!* magazines and never have a profound thought again. But youth seems to be made generation after generation to make the world in its own

image, and must have the world as it wants it. It must also imagine itself into the person it wants itself to be; it must find corroborating evidence that this life will be different from all lives
that have gone before it.

I find something quite remarkable, speaking from experience, in the freedom of the young male. In its late teens and
early twenties it seems to love bringing itself into sharp contact
with immovable objects; it loves to suffer minor wounds and
walk on unperturbed. Its abilities to travel to exotic, far-flung
places on almost nothing per day, to sleep in any position and on
any surface, its constant search for friendship and like minds
among other travelers and its deep sense of happiness and timelessness when it finds that companionship are admirable and
necessary. The young psyche, man or woman, at its best, also
has a natural bent toward traveling light, to austerity in the
name of adventure; to a shared sense of participation in doing
without. The band of brothers or sisters is a phenomenon deep
in the evolutionary makeup of the young. It is representative of
the young psyche's wish to make friends with the world and
with its peoples. The young also must feel that it will be just as
easy to remain sure friends with their deeper selves as it will be
to keep that happy band together through the decades to come.

The young face looks into other eyes of other selves and sees
itself in them, and it looks for far horizons, not for imprisoning
walls. It is an electric, sociable ability that we take for granted
in youth, not knowing how that propensity for friendship and
adventure might fade. As one elderly woman, distressed that
the teenagers in her area were taking to drugs instead of far

horizons, told a journalist, "They have the greatest, most potent drug of all, *youth*—and they won't even realize it until it is gone."

A BULL'S EYE AT YOUR BELT

Perhaps a strong concentration of that potent drug in his veins enabled Robert Louis Stevenson to climb through a window from a village street in France, in front of perfect strangers, and declare himself to a surprised woman sitting at the end of the table, whom he would then follow to the ends of the earth. Stevenson was a man who knew how to keep his youthful enthusiasm alive long after its usual sell-by date was past. One of the playful rituals of his childhood days stayed with Stevenson into his adulthood, and acted like a metaphor for his ability to discover and rediscover the self and find out what it wanted from the big world that awaited it. Stevenson's world was one in which you could be kidnapped, find buried treasure or jump through open windows rather than go round by the door to introduce yourself. Despite having had a sickly, constrained childhood, he believed there was something alive and glowing at the center of a human being that could animate and embolden all outward activity.

In an essay written as an adult, Stevenson remembered an annual ritual from his boyhood in Scotland. Every September, when the nights began to draw in, all the boys of his area would buy small tin lanterns called bull's eyes, light them, attach them to their belts and then button them beneath a thick winter top-coat. This done, they walked through the streets and out into the neighboring fields alone without showing a glimmer of light from the lantern, until they were challenged by another wandering, tightly buttoned boy; then the coat would be opened like a secret compact and the hot, smoking, hidden source displayed. The memory struck Stevenson as a way of describing the constant light he felt lived inside him. "The essence of this bliss was to walk by yourself in the black night, the slide shut, the topcoat buttoned, not a ray escaping . . . a mere pillar of darkness in the dark; and all the while, deep down in the privacy of your fool's heart, to know you had a bull's eye at your belt, and to exult and to sing over the knowledge."

Stevenson felt one of the great tasks of youth was to keep that core light alive through the difficult transition into adulthood. It was not only necessary for a sense of happiness and joy but also a source of the courage necessary for all the challenges of courtship and pursuit in the three areas of human life: relationship, work and self-knowledge. He saw that light as a central arbiter of courage. In other words, without the interior light, faint heart could never win fair lady; without that fierce sense of interiority, you didn't jump through the window as Stevenson did, you went round by the door or did not trouble to risk your self at all. You stood stuttering out in the dark, wishing some unforeseen circumstance outside yourself would introduce you to this woman. Stevenson's delighted appearance through the window, he knew, would enable those he surprised to recognize his sincerity if he revealed his light in the right way. The witness to this event does in fact say that Stevenson's unconventional appearance caused immediate celebration and spontaneous delight.

Stevenson's work as an author was a kind of continual invitation to readers to make their own parallel, unconventional appearances in the world. Stevenson felt that everyone had a kind of poetry inside, but most conventional people were like poets who had died young and were still living on in ghostly fashion through an ordinary life wondering why nothing seemed touchable or real anymore. But he did feel that this half-dead soul inside could be revived, and that, dead or alive, almost everyone had something inside that "lived, buttoned under their topcoat . . . the spice of life to its possessor. Justice is not done to the versatility and the unplumbed childishness of man's imagination. His life from without may seem a rude round of mud: but there will be some golden chamber at the heart of it, in which he dwells delighted: and as dark as his pathway seems to the observer, he will have some kind of bull's eye at his belt."

OTHER PEOPLE'S QUESTIONS

Stevenson reminds me of a similar sense I had of that glowing youthful interiority. As a young man, I was particularly horrified to discover how seriously the doctrine of original sin had affected our history in the West. The smoke-blackened stone of the local church seemed to represent the ugliness of that inherited approach as I passed it, year on year, on many a dark, thoughtful night. I could understand that there could be something deeply selfish and flawed at the center of the human psyche, but that flaw lived in companionship with many good qualities and to isolate it and make it a lash on the backs of believers was repellent to me.

The belief that, born to darkness, we needed to be saved by a future intercessory light, seemed to go against the everyday evidence and delight of my childhood: that sense of a hidden bull's eye burning away in the center of my chest. It *certainly* seemed to go against the evidence of the community that surrounded me. My Irish and Yorkshire family and friends were no paragons of virtue, but they were people who, in the midst of their many flaws and multitudinous setbacks, in the midst of scraping by penniless from week to week, always seemed to want to do the right thing. The notion of being born with a built-in bias to sin also seemed simplistic and unnuanced, and seemed to say more about Saint Augustine, the deeply unlikable, guilty puritanical cohorts who came after him, and the anxieties of the dying Roman age he was born into than anything that was true about the world I inhabited.

Now, of course, sixteen hundred years after him and half my life later, coming to know myself a little better, I know what he means. There is a dark core to be found in all human behavior when love, care, shelter or a sense of self are withdrawn unwillingly from us and we then try to recover them through fair means or foul. But this is different from saying that human beings are necessarily born to be ruled by that shadow. Sensing that burning center of vitality so strongly myself as a young man, I was also at a loss to understand why we should need an intercessory force from the outside to reveal something that already seemed so present. Walking the fields near my home, looking at the broad moorland skies to the west, I seemed to have a daily experience of grace from things that were already in force rather than from something that would come to me only if I behaved well and kept my nose clean.

The instinctive rejection of the doctrine of inherited sin by a young man or woman is sane, necessary and self-protective. Just as the young Augustine himself said, "Give me chastity, O Lord, but not just yet," so the young must find their own way through the brick wall of their own skin by believing in something as yet hidden, worth bringing to light.

It seems to me that a good appreciation of sin will come later, in any case. Perhaps no mention of original sin should be made to us until we are forty-three: thirty-nine, perhaps, if we are quick learners, so that we can understand its spirit without taking it too literally.

Youthful innocence is, in effect, a way of paying a deep kind of attention to the world; a van Gogh–like courage, looking out at a potential canvas others have lost the ability to see. To lose your innocence is to rob yourself of a particular pair of eyes and a profoundly attentive set of ears. Coming to our original sin later allows us to find out how subtle that notion of sin actually is and how much the notion of original sin has been a very original way to control others rather than a way to understand our own awkward ways. To fall in love with a deeper sense of self, we must start with the ground we stand on in youth: our own half-grown hopes for the world. For the first glimpse of the self, everything must be possible; Tir na nÓg, the land of the young, as the Irish would say, is, after all, just a step away. We do not need to know with this first glimpse that it might demand your whole life to take that one short step.

Being young and trying to catch a glimpse of the depths, of the true self, of the soul, or whatever human beings have called it over the centuries, we often find ourselves surrounded by bossy, hectoring voices trying to short-circuit our personal experience by superimposing their own disappointments. Much of this bossiness masquerades as an education. It is especially magnified in Britain at this time, where children are worried, threatened, stressed, depressed and overexamined at frighteningly regular intervals from a mere five years old until college. The whole dynamic looks like an unconscious living death wish, wished particularly on the next generation by those who have suffered from a long and uninterrupted tradition of bossiness in those islands.

Even if the intuitions of original sin are sometimes accurate, and there is a need at times for control of the darker emotions, to the young, that is not the point. To find the first mirror of our soul we must fall in love with that reflection, and what, may I ask, has ever been the point of giving anyone in love, warnings or detailed advice?

COMING TO OUR OWN QUESTIONS

Just as the doctrine of original sin was one I had inherited, but which made no sense to me, all of us live amid a thicket of questions forced upon us that are not our own, or at least not our own way of asking them. One of the first great steps we take in looking for a glimpse of the self depends on our ability to learn how to ask our own questions; the ones that make sense to us, no matter how simple they might seem. The first step toward the self is the step of discerning what questions are our own, and what questions we have been bullied into by others seemingly taller, more adult or more educated than we are.

A good few years ago, I spent a long day in Amsterdam look- ing at a series of van Gogh's self-portraits. Van Gogh to my mind would be one of the great and original questioners in the history of painting. Someone who asked very simple, almost primitive questions of the world he looked upon. I was about thirty-five on that day I walked around the modernist museum that holds his work, ready, perhaps, for another step down, down toward the self that seemed to be waiting for me underneath my endless surface travels. After a long afternoon in front of the paintings, what struck me was the lack of self-indulgence in these portraits: no self-pity, no look-at-poor-me. Each time van Gogh painted himself, you felt he was actually capturing a way he was paying attention to the world in that particu- lar epoch of his life. He was, in effect, painting the threshold he was looking out from. He seemed to look out bravely, too, even from under a bandaged ear, at a world that looked back just as fiercely.

Afterward, excited by some fleeting intuition, I hurried back across the park to my hotel room, sat at the small writing desk, which faced a wall mirror, and wrote the title "Self Portrait" across the top of a blank page. When I looked up at the mirror, the first line following the title surprised me; it had nothing to do with the line of my chin or the bridge of my nose. I was in fact looking underneath that reflection and seeing a question staring out at me that seemed to have lodged in me like an arrow years before. What was strange about it was that I realized it wasn't my own question and it didn't belong there; it was someone else's question that I had taken on, thinking it was important to me because it had been important to others. The question was "Is there one God, or are there many gods?" "People have been killing one another for centuries over this one," I said to myself. It was a supposedly important question that I was just discovering in the poem, but was not in the least bit important to me, at least in the way it was asked.

SELF PORTRAIT

It doesn't interest me if there is one God
or many gods.
I want to know if you belong or feel
abandoned.
If you can know despair or can see it in others.
I want to know

if you are prepared to live in the world
with its harsh need
to change you. If you can look back
with firm eyes
saying this is where I stand. I want to know
if you know
how to melt into that fierce heat of living
falling toward
the center of your longing. I want to know
if you are willing
to live, day by day, with the consequence of love
and the bitter
unwanted passion of your sure defeat.

I have been told, in that fierce embrace, even
the gods speak of God.

from D.W., *River Flow: New & Selected Poems 1984–2007*

Asking in my own way, sitting in front of that mirror and that blank page, I got to the one God beneath the many, but I had got there under my own steam. It is always a little bit of a shock to realize how singular each of us is in the way we hold a conversation with life. We each have a particular way of shaping ourselves in the world. To take on someone else's conversational style and to keep repeating other people's questions as if they were our own is to exhaust ourselves. It doesn't matter if it is the thoughts of Socrates or Susan Sontag. Read and admire, but then go back to first principles and ask the question yourself, in your own way. Dare to disagree.

Looking up at the mirror in my Dutch hotel room after finishing the poem, I had to wonder how many other questions I had living inside me, exhausting my powers, that were not my own.

As I look at the poem now, it's a young man's poem. But it's a young man standing at the threshold of a new maturity. There is also a sense that it is a young man just beginning to face up to all the inevitable defeats that come out of that first necessary faith in victory.

But first and always we need, perhaps, like Stevenson, a sense of possible victory: a falling in love with our future possibilities. Without it, youth might not be worth the name, and there could be no possibility of leaving that static, staring hopefulness in the street as Stevenson did, to climb bravely through a window and find your happiness.

Conclusion: On Spontaneously Vaulting Through Windows

We have something inside us that we sense wants to get out into the world. We share this intuition with almost all people who have ever lived. Again and again this interiority is seen as a kind of light, a source of illumination for both ourselves and others. All of our storytelling traditions, whether they be the Bible or Stevenson's *The Amateur Emigrant*, ask us to step toward that light, to step bravely toward what we think is a deeper, profounder and bigger self, no matter that it might disintegrate on first contact and no matter that we do not start with a good definition of what we are stepping toward. There is no first step toward self-knowledge without hazard or risk to the surface self you already know. To begin with, the interior self is above all unknowable and untouchable.

Conclusions About the Illusions of Youth

Youth *is* the metaphor for all original enterprises. The illusions of youth are only temporary but they are natural, and most important, they will be seen to hold their own logic and their own truth in the end. These marvelous youthful illusions are as follows: The self was made for the world. The world was made for the self. Everything in the world is constantly coming to our door with clues as to how we belong. We only have to follow those clues and we will find our way home. Leave all obstacles and disappointments for the future; in our search for the self, life will provide all the opportunities in good time to temper and make wise our original youthful fire.

Hectoring Advice
on All the Unwanted Hectoring Advice

Youth is rightfully resistant to the hectoring abstract advice of others rather than their encouraging, compassionate particularity. The innocence of youth is necessary again and again through the thresholds of a life no matter our chronological age. Therefore, at any time of life, follow your own questions; don't mistake other people's questions for your own. Fall in love with your own questions so that you can commensurately be disappointed by them at a later date. See innocence not as something to be replaced by experience but as a necessary way, no matter your actual age, of paying attention, without which you cannot begin a new cycle of investigation. Fall in love with the possibilities ahead. At least to begin with, be infatuated with an imagined perfection. Let your hoped-for intuitions be true until they are proved wrong. What else will carry this difficult marriage, this pursuit of the self, through all the other difficulties to come?

BOOK THREE

The Joy of Pursuit: What We Think We Are Worthy of in This World

CHAPTER 5

The Pursuit of the First Marriage:
The Classic Case Again:
Early Stage

In my memory I see myself standing by an empty road at five o'clock one late-summer dawn of my very early twenties; hitchhiking to London from the mountains of North Wales. I was emboldened by my sudden move and looked back at the line of those mountains with some confidence as I faced the quiet road. It was one of those mint-fresh mornings when you can feel the heat to come, even through the first cool air of the day. A Volvo emerged from the mist-wreathed distance, saw me alone at the roadside and pulled in to pick me up.

I had woken that morning with a desperate desire to see a woman with whom I had spent the early part of the summer. Though she had grown up in England, she had a Greek father, and we had met in a small whitewashed seaside town on the island of Crete. She had opened the door of the hostel she managed, and we had fallen for each other the moment we locked eyes, right there, on the doorstep. I had a letter to deliver to her in my right hand from a friend, but she had to ask me for it twice, as I had dreamily forgotten all about it. We had six weeks together. Six weeks that every man and woman should enjoy at least once in their lives; then, just as suddenly, it was over. A fleeting postcard from a friend had brought me home.

The postcard reminded me of another possible marriage: the one with my vocation. I had failed a biochemistry exam, and if I knew what was good for me, I should hotfoot it back to Bangor, North Wales, and sit the mandatory retake exam in August.

I returned. The examination was over; I had passed. I closed my books, and the Greek light flooded back into my mind, and with it the vision of my loved one's face and with it her very long, dark hair.

"Where are you off to, young man?" asked the man in the Volvo. "To London," I said. "To see someone I just met in Crete. She's finished her work running a hostel there and she's come home for the winter." He was very pleased for me, smiling at the thought, until, that is, he found out that this woman had absolutely no idea I was on my way. His face fell. He gripped the steering wheel and shifted his position in the seat. He started gently, and then with increasing emphasis to tell me that this was probably not a good idea. Not a good idea at all. I remembered the Greek light; I remembered her movements in front of the wine-dark sea. It seemed like a very good idea.

I was dropped off at a wonderful place for hitching, just at the top of a hill in the broad fields of Shropshire. Trucks would strain up the hill and be traveling at no more than twenty miles per hour as they reached the top of the rise when they would see me, thumb extended, wearing a handsome Faeroe Island sweater. Ten minutes later I climbed into the cab of a big farm truck carrying bales of hay. "Where are you heading, young fella?"

Again, initial enthusiasm at my attractive destination followed by head shaking, unnecessary gear changes and again, much shifting in his seat when he found out the minor detail of my unannounced arrival. He turned to me still shaking his head and uttered a rural phrase straight out of Thomas Hardy. "My grandfather allus said, 'Women'll throw you further'n gunpowder'll blow you.'" I laughed, but the swirls of gunpowder cleared immediately in my mind so that through the battlefield of life and relationship, I could see her again, in my mind's eye, in the Mediterranean light, sitting by the arched window of her bedroom, quietly sewing.

Five or six rides and an equal number of wagged fingers, sucked teeth and much unnecessary gear-shifting later, I arrived, slightly shaken, at the door of my sweetheart's house. By then I knew already that disaster and disappointment accompanied my visit, not just because of the oft-repeated advice from my transporters, but because I had taken a red London bus for the last few miles to her house and she had actually been out on the street when she saw me through the bus window. No detailed note telling me our relationship had come to a natural end could have been as eloquent as the distress her upturned face registered in that brief, unguarded moment.

A WONDERFUL LOSS OF CONTEXT

We don't have to know the future course of Stevenson's life to guess that leaping through that evening window led to trouble. We don't need to know Jane Austen's biography to predict that an episode of outrageous ballroom flirting might lead to severe disappointment. We know that Joan of Arc's bravery led to her death. We can almost hazard a prediction that Dante and Yeats were unrequited in their passions exactly because of their perfect adoration of Beatrice and Maud Gonne, respectively. We have no idea how the well-educated but otherwise unremarkable midwestern woman from Indianapolis, looking over at the magazine, will find any version of herself in its pages. The understanding is that the path ahead is at first unrecognizable and will wend through territory we could not have associated with our journey.

We are always given plenty of warnings about the path ahead. "The course of true love never did run smooth" has been repeated down the centuries to those who will not listen, exactly because it is so stubbornly true; it is a phrase that has never really helped any of the afflicted it was meant for. Its very annoying cousin "There are plenty more fish in the sea" is even less help to each generation new to the stomach-rending nature of true love's even truer disappointment. Despite all outside, best hopes, the one in pursuit of a passion has always been armored against all advice, good or bad. Strangely, this self-determined wish to create one's own world, real or not, seems to be absolutely necessary.

Passionate love seems by its very nature to be a loss of context; it also seems to involve a necessary and helpless inability to save the one who is driven by it from what clearly lies ahead. It is in effect a form of unilateral disarmament. Part of its very nature seems to be an unconscious drive toward vulnerability. It may be that we must put aside the powers of self-preservation and negotiation that are necessary to preserve life on the surface in order to follow the hidden nonnegotiable conversation, which will reorder, and reimagine us, preparing us for the possible marriage to which our falling in love leads.

Logic, by necessity, has nothing to do with energy needed for the initial pursuit. Many years later, a witness to Stevenson's entrance through the window that crucial evening of 1876, described it in this way.

> Then in the dusk of a summer's day, as we all sat at dinner about the long table ... there was a startling sound at one of the open windows giving on the street, and in vaulted a young man with a dusty knapsack on his back ... He was tall, straight, and well formed, with a fine ruddy complexion, clustering light brown hair, a small tawny mustache, and extraordinarily brilliant brown eyes.... I gazed at him in spell-bound admiration.

Stevenson's eyes were brilliant because in seeing Fanny Osbourne for the first time he was most probably looking through a pair of eyes similar to those of Dante, almost six hundred years previously, when he saw Beatrice for only the second time, a full nine years after he had first met her.

> *It happened that on the last one of those days the marvel-ous lady appeared, robed in the very purest white, between two gentle ladies both older than she was, and passing me on the street, she turned her eyes to that part of the road where I was standing almost fearfully, and with that inef-fable graciousness for which she must now be rewarded in eternity, she greeted me with such perfection of manner that I seemed at that moment to plumb the entire depth of possible bliss.*
>
> Dante, *La Vita Nuova*, III, 3–10 (translation by D.W.)

Fanny's perfection would have been in the eye of Stevenson, the beholder, whose eye was also plumbing the depths of all pos-sible bliss in her presence.

But Stevenson had come across his Beatrice in a very com-plex form. Fanny Osbourne was American, ten years older than the twenty-five-year-old Stevenson, subject to bouts of pro-longed illness and already married. Indeed, sitting with her at the table were her eight-year-old son and her eighteen-year-old daughter, both of whom she had taken from the very difficult but charismatic husband she had left behind, six thousand miles away, in far, faraway California.

Fanny was also, to begin with, far more impressed with the traveling companion who had accompanied Stevenson to

France, his handsome cousin Bob, to whom she was soon introduced.

Stevenson's ardor soon overcame the immediate problem of her attraction to his cousin; his constant attentions and wit also drove away any thought of the many problems that loomed over their future together. As an Edinburgh Scot, he had never met an American woman before, and he was deeply attracted not only by her glowing eyes and her boyish good looks but also by her fine, outspoken, almost naive way of expressing herself. For his part, his seriously witty and unremitting approach convinced her not only of his sincerity, but eventually of her own affections for the young traveler.

The details of how they actually came together in France do not seem to have been recorded by their friends, but Stevenson and Fanny Osbourne settled happily into living the expatriate artistic life for two years, until the summer of 1878, when Sam Osbourne in distant Oakland, California, suddenly recalled he had a wife and family and insisted they return to join him. Fanny departed with her children for the Atlantic crossing but left Stevenson with the understanding that it would be an opportunity to immediately petition for a divorce.

A NOT-SO-WONDERFUL LOSS OF CONTEXT

To Stevenson's distress, nothing happened with the divorce, and he found himself in a great deal of unremitting heartache. To help him forget his troubles, perhaps to raise a little money to pursue Fanny to America and definitely, to delight posterity with his writing, he took off to the South of France on a long walking holiday and then wrote *Travels with a Donkey in the Cévennes.*

This timely heartache produced one of the pioneer classics of outdoor literature, for which Stevenson designed one of the world's first sleeping bags and in which he presented to readers for the first time the idea of camping as an enjoyable activity for its own sake. The book is dominated by the unforgettable character of Modestine, a stubborn, Machiavellian and manipulative donkey, who constantly gets the better of her supposed master.

The constant battle of wills with Modestine is a clear allegory of his attempt to control the very relationship that he had once possessed and which had now deserted him. The book is beautifully self-deprecating, and Stevenson finds himself constantly put in his place by the iron will of the recalcitrant Modestine. His ability to admit defeat in the face of the donkey's insistence on going its own way must have prepared Stevenson for the stubborn emotional struggle ahead.

Stevenson left Modestine with some relief at the end of his Cévennes journey. He returned to Edinburgh only to find a cable from Fanny to say she was ill and needed him. Without hesitation he bought a ticket on the *Devonia,* a classic transatlantic liner, which was about to leave from the Clyde River in his native Scotland. The ship duly left Greenock on the seventh of August 1879, with Stevenson on board, pensive and almost penniless, setting out for an unknown future and a very unknown America.

As he looked back over the rail of the *Devonia* to see the coast of Scotland disappearing behind him, the radical simplicity, the almost foolish simplicity of what he was doing must have struck him forcibly. "A sinful, mad business," his engineer father had said, letting him go but refusing to put a penny in his pocket to help him along.

But Stevenson's pursuit of love was all of a piece with his pursuit of travel. Although he paid eight guineas to secure a room with a writing table, it still put him with the huddled masses in the ship's steerage, eating bowls of Irish stew and drinking a concoction that seemed to lie midway between tea and coffee.

Stevenson realized that though he was involved in the pursuit of a woman, the emigrant masses around him were actually involved in the pursuit of a life and probably would never return to their difficult, original homes. He saw the parallels and the stark differences of these very different forms of necessity.

He called his memoir of the voyage *The Amateur Emigrant,* and acknowledged the discrepancy between his goal and those that surrounded him. He kept far from the first-class passengers drinking proper tea from proper china, whose background he shared but whose snobbery distressed him deeply, and instead, wrote away in his thin-walled cabin amongst the poor, listening to "the rattle of tin dishes as they sit at meals, the varied accents in which they converse, the crying of their children terrified by this new experience, or the clean flat smack of the parental hand in chastisement."

STOWING AWAY: HIDING FROM OUR OWN FUTURE

In his walks about the ship, the future author of *Treasure Island* and *Kidnapped* was intrigued to meet a knowing cast of characters who had stowed away in odd corners of the ship. He found, as I did in stopping cars when hitchhiking long distances, that there was a whole art to the task of getting aboard: gangways, artful explanations (steep inclines, handsome Faeroe Island sweaters) and then (unlike me) remaining mute and hidden.

Stevenson included a whole section of his memoir on the art and science of stowing away: how to go about it, which liners to choose and how to remain incognito on board. (His editors and his father took fright at the encouragement to lawbreaking and together struck it from the final manuscript.) It was as if he realized that any great enterprise demands some form of illicit voluntary abduction, some way of literally hitching your self and your enterprise to a star, aboard whatever Volvo is leaving the mountains or whatever vessel is leaving shore. Falling in love is subversive to societal order, and its pursuit can never follow abstract rules arranged by others with no knowledge of the particularity of the person pursued. Love is individual, as Dante rediscovered, and must be given a larger world than the one that society is prepared to allow it. Dante sanctified it with a religious, almost beatific context. Stevenson saw it as being stolen away. The abduction was a kind of relief from the imprisoning forces of society and the duties that surrounded and besieged an individual.

All of Stevenson's future fiction would look at this dynamic of abduction: the sense that we are continually being stolen away by circumstances, that in a way we do not, to begin with, give our full consent to the journey. To Stevenson, and to close observers of this dynamic, there is a part of us that does not want to pay the full fare. We do not want to be paid-up official participants of whatever is taking us along. Finally, all of us want to hide from the consequences that await us if we become fully visible in the migration.

It could be that this need to hide has to do with a refusal to come up into the light of day until our new identity is formed and the new world fully on the horizon. It could be an intuited sense that something is in a delicate embryonic form and must remain enclosed and sealed off; left to breathe a different kind of air. A sense also that even whispering it to ourselves, never mind declaring ourselves out loud, might kill it off, stop us from catching the boat. Partly because we may still not be ready for it, we might be afraid of what we are giving birth to and, as in the old fairy stories, plan on leaving it out to die on the bare mountain, keeping us safe, like an old wicked stepmother, from what may usurp us in the future.

THE MASCULINE VERSUS THE FEMININE PURSUIT

Whatever new identity we form in our wish to secure a future marriage, we come up against something ancient and immovable in the difference between feminine and masculine understandings of a pursuit. I know of no examples in my own life where a woman has pursued a man in this chasing-after, geographical one-continent-to-another sense, and not been an object of pity, often to the man she is pursuing.

A woman pursuing a man in full light of day is tempting very ancient fates. I would not accuse the feminine of passivity, however: to my mind, a woman pursues a man beneath the current of everyday events, not by jumping on a ship, though that may come as a culmination, but by testing the reality of a relationship by continually conversing with herself and with other women, in effect pursuing a slowly building consensus within and without her as to whether this might be the one.

Her pursuit is more collaborative, with others and with the evidence; his, more often undertaken alone, the goal not discussed with others but more often willfully hidden from them.

In a woman's pursuit, such as Fanny Osbourne's active-receptive waiting for Stevenson in faraway Oakland, she is looking in anticipation toward Stevenson in her own way, but her pursuit takes the form of positioning herself to be found. She sent the cable, and whatever it said (we do not know), it was an effective invitation to follow. To pursue a man overtly and geographically would be to travel alone with her decision instead of in the company of her corroborations. Her pursuit is ultimately a pursuit of the sincerity in the man's pursuit, to see if it is real. A woman can be convinced by the persistence of a pursuit if it does not constitute harassment. A man tends to find any pursuing woman whom he didn't like from the first a form of harassment itself.

INCOGNITO

Whatever the gender details, history is full of both men and women who have felt passions that have been too hot to touch, so much so that these passions are fearful even to the one who is experiencing them. No wonder there is often a necessary dynamic of hiding, even from oneself. Stevenson knew, like most men on a passionate enterprise, he was traveling incognito, leaning against the rail of the *Devonia*, barely letting the strangers around him know what he was after or what he was about. In an amusing section of *La Vita Nuova*, Dante hides his central, all-consuming passion for Beatrice, pretending he is actually interested in someone else.

> *One day, this most gracious lady [Beatrice] was sitting in a place where words about Mary the Queen of Glory were being spoken, and I was standing where I could see my bliss. Halfway between her and me, in a direct line of sight, sat a gentlewoman of a very pleasing appearance, who looked at me again and again as if fully surprised by my gaze, which seemed to be directed at her.*
>
> *Many began to notice her glances in my direction, and watched them, and I heard someone saying, as I left this place, "See what a devastating effect that lady has had upon that man." And, when she was named, I realized that the lady they referred to was the one whose seat*

*had been halfway along the direct line which extended
from the most gracious Beatrice and ended in my eyes.*

*Then was I greatly relieved, sure that my secret had
not been revealed to any other through my glances. And I
thought at once that this lovely lady could be a screen to
hide the truth, and so well did I play my part that in a
brief spell of time those who talked about me were sure
they knew my secret.*

*With this woman I concealed myself for some years
and months, and to make others believe me, I wrote certain little things for her in rhyme which I do not include
here unless they could be as a way to speak about the most
gracious Beatrice; therefore, I will leave them all out except for the ones that are clearly in praise of her.*

Dante, *La Vita Nuova*, V, 1–23 (translation by D.W.)

Con questa donna mi celai alquanti anni e mesi. With this woman
I concealed myself for some years and months . . . as if Dante
was arranging a necessary disappearing act, a kind of self-im-
molation. Stevenson knew how close this need for invisibility in
the pursuit could come to a literal disappearance.

On reaching New York, Stevenson wrote to a friend: "I am
not very well; bad food, bad air and hard work have brought
me down. . . . I have been steadily drenched for twenty four
hours . . . immortal spirit fitfully blinking up in spite." Then,
on the crowded, stifling-hot, fourteen-day rail journey across
a barely inhabited continent, he wrote again: "I had no idea
how easy it was to commit suicide. There seems to be nothing

left of me; I died a while ago; I do not know who it is that is traveling."

Stevenson is speaking to a loss of foundation that accompanies all of us in the midst of real trial and tribulation, to an urge to move off the radar screen, to create a kind of stealth profile and disappear, sometimes literally.

He also reminds us, as we accompany him on his sea and land crossing, how much human beings looking from the outside of this passion want to keep themselves intact and aloof. As I follow him from the distance of a hundred thirty years, I find myself wanting to be on the same voyage, but in first class, going down to see him in his colorful, characterful milieu, every now and again. It is probably because I have a choice. I am following someone else's passion pleasurably at my own writing desk; Stevenson did not have a choice because of the way his love hovered like a Beatrice in his imagination, but also because of the integrity of his three marriages, the way, traveling each of those journeys, toward a love, a book to be written, a sense of self, they were inextricably knit together.

In a very clear way, the privations that Stevenson endured in his passionate pursuit of Fanny Osbourne were exact parallels to the privations that brought him close to the subject of his writing, and eventually to a less deceptive understanding of himself. It is particularly surprising to find him looking underneath all his natural daily joy and finding the part of him that could easily end it all. It is a mark of his courage that he runs straight at it as soon as he sees it, as if it is as worthy of investigation as anything outwardly more optimistic, and even at that door he is ready to go through and learn from what he finds there.

All of Stevenson's disciplines were to do with the close encounter. The understanding that deep in the conversation; deep in the attempted meeting itself, is the only place you can find the answer to the great ancient human questions he was coming to himself, such as: Is the one I am pursuing, my true love? Is my work real, and is it any help to others? Is that strange thing I call myself, semi-imprisoned in a small cabin, among the tight crowd of other, traveling strangers, equal to all the things it loves and longs to encounter?

The Short Conclusion

In the pursuit of a marriage, dignity is a dispensable luxury.

The Longer Conclusion

The pursuit of another with hopes of a marriage of hearts and minds involves a dismantling of our usual daily self-protections. There is a sense of a current larger than one we have generated ourselves, carrying us off to as yet unknown places. There are roads to be taken, tides to be caught and places to go, a sense of drama, urgency and necessity.

The pressing dramatic qualities that accompany the pursuit are all diagnostic features that the passion is a real one and worth following. For those who can garner at least a little wisdom amid the madness, there is also a sense that the journey itself will provide the test of whether what we are pursuing is good for us, real or lasting.

There is also a sense of abduction, of the pursuit not being a fully voluntary affair. With the sense of being stolen away comes another form of self-protection through sleight of hand and secrecy. The enterprise is barely believable to ourselves, so how can we explain what is really happening to others? Under these circumstances, no advice should ever be given to those in love. Blood should issue from our lips before we say a word of warning to friends, relatives or even our children. They will go their own way and cross any oceans in their way. Who, in that state, has ever listened to anything but what they wish to hear?

CHAPTER 6

Opening a Tidal Gate: The Pursuit of a Work Through Difficulty, Doubt and Distraction

It is a great help to follow the likes of Stevenson and Fanny Osbourne, Jane Austen and Dante. It sets one to dream, to think about being called out to greater things like a Joan of Arc or a Wordsworth or a Dickens, but at the end of it all, when we put any book down, no matter how inspiring, we are left facing ourselves in the mirror and the need to get up each morning, walk out the door and live our own lives.

As I write my way through these characters, I look naturally for the moments in my own life that parallel theirs. Wordsworth makes me think not only of taking a mountain walk, but taking it alone. Jane Austen somehow wants me to bring a keener eye to other people's marriages. Joan of Arc asks me how courageous I could really be if tested, and under what circumstances. Dante asks me if the woman I married is really my Beatrice.

(She is certainly going to read this, it must be so; I wouldn't dare ask it in public otherwise.) Yet Dante says I must pursue her on a daily basis no matter how familiar she may have become or how well I think I know her. Yet my work at this moment actually comes down to making all those literary parallels real for a reader, a stranger I have not met, and to do it by filling the next blank page with something surprising, something pleasing, something this stranger might want to read.

My work is not a walk in the mountains, it is not surveying the undercurrents of a ballroom, it is not leading troops on the field of battle. It is writing the next word. This task elicits no sympathy from the gnarled steelworkers of this world, but put a brawny, no-nonsense, iron-fisted steelworker in a closed room with a blank page for an hour and you will soon have him donning his mask and very happily getting back to perspiring in front of hot buckets of molten steel again. All of us remember the blank page from childhood, no matter if we never lifted a pen again after graduation.

I once read an amusing little book whose title I cannot recall or find, written by an editor, about her long experience trying to obtain manuscripts from her authors. Finally tiring of the string of imaginative excuses for not finishing books over the years, she yearned for a brief, truthful explanatory note from at least one author that said simply: "The book is not finished because I have not written any words."

It would have been more accurate to say that there were none of the right words. They could have sent many, many words, but they would have been prosaic, unsurprising or disappointing, or jumbled; they would not have lived up to the ideal that the author first desired.

Writers or not, all of us face the same dynamic in our work. There are lots of actions we could take to pursue a work or a career, but we often don't begin, because we don't feel the grip, the connection, the current that can carry us across such a wide tract of water. In effect we leave the beckoning blank page of our life completely empty because we don't have confidence in the particular first sentence that confronts us. It is a consistent dynamic across time and history that what we most feel as human beings, faced with all the possibilities, is how far those possibilities are away from us. Almost always, we come across the part of us that can't do it or doesn't want to do it, or that wants to take a long holiday and then do it.

The interesting thing about a work life is that it is very much like a workday. Most of the hard work is done by simply turning up, facing the task at hand and moving forward, inch by inch, foot by foot, until we look around, admittedly after a much greater time than we expected, but surprised to see it has all been done.

Like a good workday, a good work life must be accomplished in the midst of all other competing demands. *Nel mezzo,* "In the middle," as Dante said, putting those first two words on the very first, very blank page of a very, very great work, the *Commedia.*

The other interesting thing about a work life is how different it is from a workday. The tasks we face on a given day are often around specific actions, or specific conversations we need to undertake. The tasks we face in pursuing a work life more often have to do with intangibles, with what cannot yet be touched or spoken, and very often with the great intangibles of our unhappiness. In a good workday you are more often than not trying to make other people happy; in a good work life you are trying to make your self happy. In a work life we must treat the intangibles as seriously and as practically as we treat the touchable, doable tasks of a given day. To do this we must use a different language and a different imagination from what we might use at a desk or a workbench; we must locate a form of current different from the one that powers our laptops or our power tools, an internal current inside the imagination, inside the body that is determined to flow out around all external obstacles and find its way home.

THE TIDAL GATE

It was just an ordinary lunch, but it had profound consequences in the months that followed. To begin with, it had been difficult to make any room in my busy day to meet with him for the meal. Busyness was an integral part of my identity that year. I *was* extremely busy, after all, besieged by what seemed like unremitting and unending deadlines. Not only that, but his request for the lunch seemed to arise from a much more leisurely approach to life that had me very much annoyed on the phone. In my busyness I was put off by an irresponsible sense of repose on his part, a sense that he had plenty of the time that I did not have, which in some little place at the back of my mind irked me. Luckily, I was able to rise self-righteously above my self-righteousness and be impressed enough by his persistence to make room for the meeting.

My work had become important to me in a subtly corrupting way. I ran the educational program of an organization dedicated to environmental teaching, and my scheduled busyness was a wonderful measure of my self-importance. I felt that I was affecting hundreds of people directly and thousands of people indirectly. I therefore felt it was worth killing myself a little for it. Here at last I was educating at least some of the masses about the big ecological picture to which my degree in marine sciences had led me.

My time out in the Galápagos Islands had been a time for falling in love with the natural world that surrounded me; it had also given me a real sense that I was contributing something good to the world. My job had been to educate people and protect the wildlife at one and the same time as I escorted groups around the national park areas. It had also given me a frontline sense of living with nature. That daily sense of intimacy with the wellsprings of life gave me a constant sense of clear energy and vitality. Now, however, I felt I was in a more settled phase of my vocational marriage with the natural world, meeting my responsibilities in wider human society. I had the equivalent of children in the relationship. Now I was giving back, working on my metaphorical children's behalf, being responsible. But the reflection in the mirror every morning was not good. In the

midst of such constant, unthinking busyness, such a close application to the work, and the paper on which it arrived, I barely
glanced out of the window at the surrounding waters that I was
so earnestly trying to save. I had entered treacherous waters,
waters and currents that acted like a form of forgetting, an
ancient form of amnesia that has so often lured the traveler
onto the rocks and away from his intended course, since the day
Odysseus left Troy to find Ithaca and home.

But I did not have the wisdom of an Odysseus. He was sen-
sible enough to have his crew tie him to the mast so that any
beseeching sirens would not tempt him ashore, I had not secured
myself to anything and was easily lured by wailing, seductive
calls, especially by the seductions of my own self-importance. I
seemed to gravitate to them gladly, as if I was ready for a bit of
amnesia after all the intensity and idealism of following a
glamorous vocation in the Galápagos; as if, strangely, I needed a
rest from underlying truths and wanted to bask on the wonderful shallow surface of things for a while. Once I had this particular job and position, the seductive Harpies had lured me out
of the packed passionate and communal steerage that Stevenson loved so much into a very isolated, snobbish first class and
then, with just a song or two more, off and away from my good
ship *Devonia* altogether.

By the time I sat down for this lunch, my ship was nowhere
to be seen and well over the horizon without me. I had been
drawn onto a magic island of constant busyness where all my
colleagues seemed to be under the same happy island spell,
moving hypnotically from fax to printer to filing cabinet to

meeting, like an elaborate court dance, with everyone seeming to have the same lovely comforting foundation of constant work as an identity, and gladly so.

From the forgetful shores of my busy, enchanted island home I heard a voice across the lunch table speaking to me as if from far away. "I need your advice. You have a degree in marine sciences and I have a problem. The problem is where the Maxwelton stream meets the waters of the Puget Sound. Do you know where I mean?"

I nodded. I knew exactly the place he meant: a lazy curve of water gathered out of marshland that came to an abrupt end at a large opening under the coast road at Maxwelton Beach.

"Have you ever looked down into that culvert?"

I thought of the last time I had used the word *culvert*; it had been a very long time. *Culvert, culvert, culvert*, I said to myself, a good strong word. Then I imagined myself on the road, head down over the side, looking into the culvert. No, I told him. I had never looked in.

"Thousands of chum and coho salmon used to migrate up that little stream until 1910, when a tidal gate was built across the stream to help drain the marsh behind it. When they built that gate, it stopped a salmon run that had been occurring, season after season, ever since the last glaciations, about ten thousand years ago."

I was shocked by the power of his roll-on sentence and the sudden image of the forlorn salmon unable to enter the stream. I thought of the gate closing for the first time, letting the water drain from the marsh to the ocean but then refusing to let the tide back in; I thought of the returning chum and coho crowding in the shallows of the beach, scenting their home stream slipping out through the gate but with no way of following that flow home, the end of a ten-thousand-year tradition of return. They would have died there with the olfactory cries of home calling to them in vain. I thought of the original farmers on the island and how virtuous they would have felt in their work of draining the marsh. How much satisfaction they would have had that long-ago day they fitted the tidal gate. How they would have gone to bed without a thought for what they had brought to an end, just as I would have done if I had grown in that time. Just as I was now, I thought to myself, sensing some gate I had built, halting an inner migration, a tidal gate firmly closing off the creative flood, put together in a short year, by my unthinking busy hands.

Lunch came to an end. All I had to offer him was encouragement. I don't know whether to him, I seemed engaged in his problem or not; I was a bit lost in the surface conversation. His words had the strange effect of touching me at a level far beyond his immediate practical need, as if I had opened a gate inside and felt a long-neglected current stir and with it the very faint possibility of some kind of return. I knew I was far away from his problem and engaged in some kind of internal selfishness, which had not given much time to anything other than itself for a long time. I am sure he felt I was in some kind of reverie, not entirely present. My degree in marine zoology culminating, after all those years of study, in a simple nod and an agreement that indeed, changing the tidal gate was a great thing to do.

I said goodbye to him, shook hands and walked home, promising what help I could: I left my desk to run itself that afternoon and instead sat down at the kitchen table looking over the waters of the sound below and took out a blank piece of paper. Something very particular now seemed to be calling me back out of my self-concern; I wanted to find out exactly what that particular thing was.

THE CHALLENGE

I looked down at the blank white paper, which lay on the table like a challenge in itself, asking me to lay out the dynamic exactly, as if putting questions into my mouth. At this stage it is so easy to want to turn away from our own faculties of attention and turn something else on: the radio, the television, the lawn mower, to want someone else's voice, someone else's work, anything but your own voice or the very necessary task that awaits you beneath the household chores. This invitation to the depths, this challenge to get below the surface, is a dynamic that faces not just the writer but all people who really want to know what is eating at them, what is asking to be addressed, what lies beneath the surface busyness.

"When was the last time you thought about the salmon?" I said to myself, banishing the mower to the back of my mind. "I mean, really thought about them, the way you used to think about them?" Here was the signature animal for the whole stretch of coast from northern California to Siberia, the creature whose migratory patterns through the vastness of the North Pacific were difficult to fully credit or believe.

I wrote out a few names. King salmon, silver salmon, Copper River salmon, chum, coho, pink salmon. Noble, delicious fish whose health represented everything else that should be healthy about the whole oceanic system and the people who lived on its shorelines. I remembered the astonishing way these fish find their way back to an often tiny home stream, using a detailed chemical memory of the water they have passed through with even, perhaps, a sense of star formations and the earth's magnetic field to find their way home.

I thought of the papers on my desk, some of them about salmon, but all just papers, just information, just work to be done, information to be conveyed. It was then, with the image of the salmon gliding between kelp, I started to get close to something at the very heart of what had brought me into the field in the first place, something that had been of overwhelming importance to me as a young boy: a visceral sense of empathy with creatures and worlds that were not my own.

I remembered a series of quotations I had memorized in my teens as if needing to tell myself of the need to remember what I knew then into my future.

The secret of genius is to carry the spirit of childhood into adulthood.

THOMAS HUXLEY

Genius is nothing more than childhood recovered by will, a childhood now equipped for self-expression with the capacities of an adult.

BAUDELAIRE

If a child grew into adulthood according to early indications we should have nothing but geniuses.

GOETHE

I do not know what I may appear to the world, but to myself I seem to have been only like a boy playing on the sea-shore, and diverting myself now and then finding a smoother pebble or a prettier shell than ordinary, whilst the great ocean of truth lay all undiscovered before me.

NEWTON

The Child is Father of the Man.

WORDSWORTH

In my early teens, I had looked around at the strange world of adults and saw with a kind of horror that almost all of them seemed to be preoccupied with the details of life in such a way that they had lost sight of the greater picture. Adults seemed to have forgotten basic elemental and joyful relationships with clouds or horizons or grass that seemed necessary to be a full participant in the creation I saw around me. This form of false maturity, this slow forgetting, was late in coming to me but I had fallen for it at last and it was now beginning to smother me.

I realized that the salmon had just become a currency of exchange in my educational barter system, a commodity instead of a noble form of individuality. In fact my whole approach to work had become commoditized. No longer a pursuit but a kind of defensive stasis, things bargained back and forth at the outer edge with very little transacting at the center.

In my reverie over the page, I remembered the years of hard slog in sciences that got me to the Galápagos, and in particular I remembered a marine zoology professor at Bangor University in Wales who had looked at me in horror when I told him I had taken up diving. He thought it quite touching but almost unsporting to actually go down there and see the living versions of things he saw mostly under a microscope. I had walked away shaking my head; laughing to myself; but in my recent approach to work I was fast becoming a newly minted version of him.

DRAWN BY DISTANCE

I exchanged the paper with the list of salmon for another blank sheet. I didn't like the next question that was beckoning to me now. What could I do to help open that gate in the Maxwelton stream, and what could I do in parallel to open up that current of childhood engagement which I had felt so strongly until recently? The key question had to do with my own contribution to the present circumstances: When had I erected a barrier inside me that let things out but did not allow them back in? (As good a definition, perhaps, of stress and burnout as could be made.) By what steps had I forgotten the promise I had made as a child not to fall into a false form of maturity, which is actually a form of nonparticipation, of not seeing, not hearing and not imagining?

I could feel the ease with which I would become like so many people who had originally astounded my child's mind, people just trying to make ends meet, people trying to keep the lawn cut and the mortgage paid who had made me shudder as an adolescent. I knew the necessities of the mortgage now and the lawn was there to be cut, not mocked; I had got beyond basic adolescent superiorities but this newly discovered inclination to mediocrity frightened me. I knew, looking at that blank piece of paper, that I had to get back into some current that would take me away from this limbo. The siren calls of lawns and mortgages beckoned, but I had to stop my ears and look elsewhere. Lawns and mortgages are not monstrous in themselves, yet perhaps that's why they are so dangerous and can take the fight and the future from so many individual lives. Some other swift, moving current, surely, would save me.

The tidal gate I had to open inside me was a kind of mirror image of the one presented to me over lunch. While my friend worked on the outside to clear the way for a salmon run, and while I gave him whatever help I could to accomplish that, I had to clear the way for some internal migration to start again. Something had to move. I had to get back to a home stream.

A BLANK PAGE—AN OPEN SEA

Lifting the pen above a blank sheet of paper is an iconic moment. That is, it stands not just for the writer, for a Stevenson, a Dante or a Jane Austen, but also for the building contractor about to lay out a foundation or a baker counting out her ingredients. It stands for the importance of first steps, where each of those first steps taken has to be judged finely to prevent all future steps from coming to a very sticky end. In bread making the preparation is paramount. The measures are important, the ratios of flour to yeast, of flour and yeast to water. Kneading and the exact strength of that kneading have to be finely gauged. The recipe is tried and tested and must be begun as it is finished, according to how you want the crust to emerge and the bread to taste. In building a house, the building contractor must lay out the lines of the foundation exactly. He must consult the plans, measure and remeasure, check and recheck. The consequences of getting it wrong multiply and become more and more embarrassing as the work proceeds.

But what if we have no recipe to consult? What if we have no grand architectural plans? What if we do not know what we are building or baking? And what if that lack of knowledge of what to do and where to go is debilitating, and therefore, as it is to most human beings, slightly, or for some, deeply depressing? What if we really do have a blank page?

Contractors may have a level and a chalk line to lay out the line of a wall, but they have no fixed mark for building again if their business fails or if they lose half their company through divorce or worse, injure themselves so that they cannot do the physical work anymore. The tangibles of work are built every day out of the intangibles of intent and commitment. How do we proceed when there is actually not meant to be a plan, because we are actually working with a way of being, a slowly building conversation between what we want for ourselves and what we are most afraid of?

CONFRONTING DEPRESSION

Looking at the page, I felt like the Maxwelton salmon must have felt. I could scent the stream home but couldn't get there from here. I felt that caged feeling that seems to rob the world of possibility. One of the hallmarks of depression is that its semi-darkness steals over us without notice; our slowly diminishing circle of reference becomes a self-fulfilling, self-reinforcing dark star, where nothing can escape to transform our view of the horizon, a horizon that now seems to be right against our face. Still looking at the page, I thought of the German-speaking poet Rainer Maria Rilke. His work carries some of the best descriptions we have in literature of the trapped feeling of depression and distraction. The state we enter when we have lost our tide. Rilke is especially good in this territory of the blank page; for long years he was unable to get to his work as a writer, and when he did he had great difficulty putting anything down. He knew the territory well and in these lines, he is beginning to show himself the way out. He is a very good companion to those who feel trapped.

> *It is possible I am pushing through solid rock*
> *in flintlike layers, as the ore lies, alone;*
> *I am such a long way in I can see no way through,*
> *and no space: everything is close to my face,*
> *and everything close to my face is stone.*
>
> *I don't have much knowledge yet in grief—*
> *so this darkness makes me feel small.*
> *You be the master: make yourself fierce, break in:*
> *then your great transforming will happen to me,*
> *and my great grief cry will happen to you.*
>
> (translation by Robert Bly)

Rilke asks us not to try and get around the feeling of stuckness itself but to see it as having as much right to a place in our life as our other free-flowing accomplishments. He sees anything that is real that presents itself to us not as a barrier but as a necessary next step. The inability to write is just as real as the ability to go full steam ahead to the bottom of the page. He asks us to go right into the exile and sense of burial itself, as if our malady is not the visitation of loss itself but the inability to feel it fully. He suggests, in effect, that our ability to know what we want is first of all, often marked by an early and profound experience of its very absence. In a sense, he is saying that one way to come to love is to do without it for a long, long time.

One way to come to the first line is to stare out the window for a very long time. Tapping the pencil against my forehead, I thought of another poem that Rilke wrote in the midst of his struggles with the blank page—what could be called his first truly fine poem, one I had memorized as soon as I read it because I was so impressed by it. Not only was it the first poem of Rilke's that we can recognize as being very, very good, but it was in fact a doorway to a kind of freedom. The first poem where a brilliant Rilkean use of sound appeared, where the sound of the words themselves carried the experience he was describing without any further explanation.

Still staring at the paper, I thought of how comforting Rilke's life can be to those who struggle with the specifics of their work or how to put those specifics into action—for those, especially, who stare at blank pieces of paper or stare at their partners when they ask for a divorce. He is a good counselor for any individuals whose organizations don't want them anymore and an even better advisor for those who have suffered the cruelest rejection of all, the ultimate dismissal that comes with self-hatred: the dynamic where we start to reject our selves before anyone else can get there first.

Rilke did know, looking at the empty sheet of his life, that he truly, truly wanted to be a poet, but he also came to the understanding that his first poems were truly, truly mediocre.

Despite his difficulties and the depression that accompanied them, the young Rilke tried everything he could to get into the poetic stream, to open a tidal gate, to get home—including marching around Prague with yellow gloves on, carrying bouquets of lilies. He was the perfect poetic poseur without any of the seeming talent to achieve it *except* a mighty living *wish* inside him that led him from one creaking gate to another. That willingness to follow what was after all just a powerful beckoning uncertainty led him to two radically transforming influences: a powerful woman in the shape of the intellectual Lou Andreas-Salomé and the equally powerful and charismatic sculptor Auguste Rodin.

Lou Andreas-Salomé took the young poet off to Russia under her intellectual, imaginative and sexual wing for six months, and under her tutelage and lively personality he began to engage with his writing as a serious apprenticeship. But Rodin's influence, though less entertaining, led to Rilke filling a very specific, very blank page with a now famous poem, "The Panther." Rodin taught Rilke how to see and to be transformed by what he saw.

Rilke stayed with Rodin in Paris in order to write an essay on the sculptor and his work, something Rilke soon found almost impossible to do, faced with the gargantuan energy, drive and productive capacities of his subject. The young poet had come close to the sun, the source of all creativity, but he couldn't work out where all the energy came from, and all he could feel was the scorching heat of comparison between Rodin's unstoppable energies and his own hesitant attempts at writing. Rodin naturally became impatient with all this very uncharismatic and very irritating scratching on bits of note paper, and the sculptor's massive hand soon pointed Rilke to the Paris zoo, where Rodin told him impatiently to choose an animal, any animal, and to watch it, for days if necessary. The instructions were to look and look and not to even think about writing until he couldn't do anything but write. You can almost hear Rodin: "Now go and stop pestering me."

If we think of Rodin living out his days trying to bring out foundational patterns from lumps of stubborn living rock, he must have been well prepared to see something difficult but possible in the immobile Rilke. Rodin knew how the imagination worked with inner and outer correspondences, how it seeks echoes between what it feels inside and what it can apprehend outside itself. He must have known that Rilke's imagination would naturally be drawn to an animal that represented the very pattern of his own imprisonment, his own stuckness. We could see Rodin's instructions to Rilke as being like the blows of another more metaphorical chisel, another form of sculpture, helping to hew the young poet out of his self-entrapment.

As the title of the poem that resulted tells us, and as Rodin might have guessed, Rilke chose a big animal, a panther, enclosed in a small space. Rilke describes the powerful creature trapped by the iron bars of a heartbreakingly small cage at the Paris zoo, constantly moving, pacing this way and that.

THE PANTHER

In the Jardin des Plantes, Paris

From seeing the bars, his seeing is so exhausted
that it no longer holds anything anymore.

To him the world is bars, a hundred thousand
bars, and behind the bars, nothing.
The lithe swinging of that rhythmical easy stride
which circles down to the tiniest hub
is like a dance of energy around a point
in which a great will stands stunned and numb.

Only at times the curtains of the pupil rise
without a sound ... then a shape enters,
slips through the tightened silence of the shoulders,
reaches the heart, and dies.

(translation by Robert Bly)

Rilke re-created the iron bars in the poem with a series of continuous flat vowel sounds that have readers reciting the original German feeling as if they had the taste of metal in their mouth.

Sein Blick ist vom Vorübergehen der Stäbe
so müd geworden, daß er nichts mehr hält.
Ihm ist, als ob es tausend Stäbe gäbe
und hinter tausend Stäben keine Welt.

The reader looks out from behind the bars as the panther would look. In the natural world, the panther would leap on any creature in such close proximity, closing the circle of instinct and action, killing the observer. Here the metal bars stop that closure; the image reaches the panther's heart, but there it dies, because the panther cannot leap.

Rilke has written the dynamic exactly for all those who see the possibilities of life but cannot seem to do anything about them. Where invisible bars seem to lie between them and what needs to be done. What were the bars for Rilke?

First: His mother's disappointment that he was a boy and not a girl. Her repeated need to dress him as a girl, and her constant, controlling presence that kept him away from other boys and from the outside world.

Second: His father's patience snapping at his wife and her constant mollycoddling, and his unceremoniously packing his son off, at ten years old, to a brutal Prussian military school.

We can imagine the confusion. All efforts first dedicated to becoming something he was certainly not, a girl; followed by all other efforts dedicated to his becoming something he was also certainly not, a soldier. No wonder Rilke cultivated the persona of the outsider: someone looking in on life from the other side of an impenetrable barrier, someone who didn't quite feel himself.

Rilke's magnification of this dynamic of distance is very useful for every other human being who will come to read him in the future, because, as many of our religious traditions constantly remind us, not feeling quite ourselves is actually the normal human condition. Most of us have this sense of just missing in a more refined form and can easily shade it over with robust actions dressed up as what look like the right actions. Rilke just happened to have such a distilled essence of the experience of not belonging that it could not be covered up. He could only confront it or be destroyed by it.

Rilke's memo to us: *We are all strangers to the world, to our work and to our selves.*

In "The Panther" Rilke identifies the dynamic exactly. He has also taken the first step to freedom by identifying it in written speech and thus freeing it from the page. A burden shared is a burden halved. An ancient abiding dynamic of human existence is the ability of something, once fully admitted, to begin to change, and to change quite often into its opposite. The Greeks called this *enantiadromia*. The word names an underlying dynamic of time and space, that once a season has been recognized and announced, it is already beginning to leave and turn into the next.

When he sees the bars clearly, they start to disappear. How do we know they disappear? What is the difference between what Rilke is doing and someone just indulging in his own sense of imprisonment?

First, he opened a door he had wanted to open for a long time, and in doing so he did good work—he wrote a brilliant poem. To Rilke, being happy or, in the California sense, *aware* because of it would have been irrelevant. He was doing his work. He had visited home ground once, and now he knew, even through many other imprisoning bars to come, that he could find his way back again. The experience had been fully lived in the poem and became part of the insight he could offer to others.

Second, he asks us to treat barriers not as things to be overcome but as representations of a bigger pattern whose shape we cannot as yet see. "Sweep the corner any size," Dogen Zenji would have said. Bars are not a problem; bars are telling me I have not yet seen but could be just about to see a dynamic I have never been able to name before.

Rilke's ability to locate the enclosing bars inside him is not just the experience of a poet but the experience of any people who suddenly realize how much they have been standing in their own way. How much they have been refusing to see the dynamic that constantly immobilizes them.

It can be extremely sobering to stand on the outside of people who are completely frozen, unable to take another step despite the excellent advice everyone else may be giving them. Despite the fact that we know that if they just persevered in an area where they have talent, things would start to happen. But they have decided that progress is impossible that way, and they are sticking by it even if it means their complete immobility.

INTO THIN AIR

As both boy and man, I spent many years rock climbing and mountaineering, and some of those years teaching the art to others. Hanging off a cliff face beside a person who is stuck, terrified because of it and who refuses to move is an educational experience. An interesting phenomenon with beginner climbers is that they absolutely want to put their foot on a hold in such a way and at such an angle that it is bound to slide off. It is as if it is so self-evident that they are in a dangerous position that they are going to prove it to the world. They lean into the cliff so that their fearful, perspiring face is scraping up against the rock. They try to get as close to the rock face as possible with the whole length of their body. This naturally puts their feet at a downward angle; this naturally makes their feet slide off. They will cling even more desperately, and repeatedly slide their foot off the hold, looking at you with some satisfaction to show that once again they have demonstrated that it is impossible for it to stay there.

Patient and compassionate requests; spoken in a very low, very calm voice: to lean out, to bring their feet more at ninety degrees to the rock, to not cling so, are met with incomprehension and a look that says they know exactly what their body wants to do and they are doing it. In many ways their clinging creates a false kind of intimacy with the cliff that leads to immobility. By clinging they lose a real sense of contact and real purchase with the rock. You could call their clinging a kind of self-indulgence; it is not like Rilke's sense of real purchase with the prison bars, where the bars become a usable hold, but more a time-honored and fearful "Look at poor me," which is wonderful to experience as long as we are not looking to get out of the situation on the cliff face.

Good poets, like good rock climbers, look not for clinging but for real purchase. People who are serious about pursuing their vocation look for purchase, not for a map of the future or a guided way up the cliff. They try not to cling too closely to what seems to bar their way, but look for where the present point of contact actually resides. No matter what it looks like.

The point of contact is what allows us to take the next step.

Sometimes the point of contact is through the next necessary small task completed; sometimes it is through understanding the depth of our exile, the disenchantment experienced in the here and now, the impossibility of it all. Eventually we realize that not knowing what to do is just as real and just as useful as knowing what to do. Not knowing stops us from taking false directions.

Not knowing what to do, we start to pay real attention. Just as people lost in the wilderness, on a cliff face or in a blizzard pay attention with a kind of acuity that they would not have if they thought they knew where they were. Why? Because for those who are really lost, their life depends on paying real attention. If you think you know where you are, you stop looking.

As a rock-climbing instructor, roping down to rescue a panicked beginner, I experienced what all those imagined guardian angels must have experienced in all their painted guises trying to help human beings through the millennia. "Thanks," we say to the descending angel, "but you obviously don't understand my position. Look," we say to the angel, not overawed in the least by shimmering robes and shining halo, "I will show you, that next step cannot be the one I have to take, because it won't hold me. Please elevate me straight to the top, wherever that may be, and let's get this over with." Our guardian angel might say, "Then you wouldn't be rock climbing," or perhaps in a more literal way, "Then you wouldn't be living." That is the next step, their extended robed hand seems to say, there is no other step and no other way. But you need a different attitude (literally) and a different inclination (again, literally) to accomplish it.

A brilliant little poem by a not-too-well-known Canadian

poet, Alden Nowlan, is also a literary guessing game, in which he looks at the way many authors who are considered authorities in their areas actually had no direct experience of the subject. They looked all the more closely at their subject exactly because they were unfamiliar with it. Any familiarity was made through what seemed like an unbridgeable distance. What they had was an unquenchable desire to know and describe. You must guess the author's name for each description; answers below.

THE SEASICK SAILOR AND OTHERS

The awkward young sailor who is always seasick
Is the one who will write about ships.
The young man whose soldiery consists in the delivery
Of candy and cigarettes to the front
Is the one who will write about war.
The man who will never learn to drive a car
And keeps going home to his mother
Is the one who will write about the road.

Stranger still, hardly anyone else will write so well
About the sea or war or the road. And then there is the
    woman
who has scarcely spoken to man except her brother
and who works in a room no larger than a closet,
she will write as well as anyone who has ever lived
about vast open spaces and the desires of the flesh:
and that other woman who will live with her sister and
    rarely leave her village, she will excel

in portraying men and women in society:
and that woman, in some ways the most wonderful of
  them all,
who is afraid to go outdoors, who hides when someone
  knocks,
she will write great poems about the universe inside her.

Far from undermining the credibility of the authors, Alden Nowlan's poem is an encouragement to all of us who look at what seems like an unbridgeable distance between our present lives and the work we want to accomplish. We are comforted to know that Herman Melville jumped ship because he could not stand life aboard a whaler. We are intrigued that Ernest Hemingway spent most of his days away from the fighting, supplying the lines with candy and cigarettes, convalescing or living it up. Jack Kerouac tells us it might not be an impediment to adventure to have a close relationship with our mother. Jane Austen, that chronicler of courtship, asks us to ponder the necessity of marriage itself. We see a kind of integrity in Emily Brontë's intense sense of privacy, while Emily Dickinson's refusal to leave home is an encouragement to all of us to make a universal life out of the particular, sometimes tiny house we have chosen to call our own.

Nowlan probably started his literary list to reassure himself once again that feeling far away is a normal human experience and that feeling far away from our own life and our own work can be an essential part of its very discovery. Feeling far away is to be examined and understood rather than disliked and dismissed. In fact, Nowlan asks us to look at the particular way we feel distant and to see it as a very particular way of looking at the world that no one else possesses and that bestows very precise insights. He is asking us, in effect, to have confidence and even faith in the particular forms that our own exile takes.

WRITING THE POEM

Sitting at the kitchen table, thinking about distance and looking from very far away at shadows of my own work life, I was ready to be honest about the dynamic and then gain a little purchase from that honesty. I was ready to have a little faith. First, then, all the ways I hadn't thought about what I was supposedly working *for* . . .

I wanted to hear exactly how far from home I was, without trying to argue against it. I was ready to examine the manner of my own exile.

SONG FOR THE SALMON

For too many days now I have not written of the sea,
nor the rivers, nor the shifting currents
we find between the islands.

For too many nights now I have not imagined the
    salmon,
threading the dark streams of reflected stars,
nor have I dreamt of his longing,
nor the lithe swing of his tail toward dawn.

I have not given myself to the depth to which he goes,
To the cargoes of crystal water, cold with salt,
Nor the enormous plains of ocean swaying
beneath the moon.

I have not felt the lifted arms of the ocean
Opening its white hands on the seashore,
Nor the salted wind, whole and healthy,
Filling the chest with living air.

I have not heard those waves,
Falling out of heaven on to earth,
Nor the tumult of sound and the satisfaction
Of a thousand miles of ocean giving up its strength on
    the sand.

But now I have spoken of that great sea,
The ocean of longing shifts through me
The blessed inner star of navigation
Moves in the dark sky above
And I am ready like the young salmon
To leave his river, blessed with hunger,
For a great journey on the drawing tide.

Getting a clear sense of the distance between my present situation and the life I wanted closed the gap immediately. The last lines gave me an absolute sense of physical current. As if, like the salmon themselves, I was on a gradient of sensitivity that would take me out of my exile into the oceans and bring me back again. The moment I said exactly how I hadn't felt the tug, the current opened and I was following it home.

I had a powerful physical sense of the salmon but also a very real sense of feeling at home simply because I was on my way there. It was a home I would reach, through writing my way there. That was the particular migration on which I had to embark. If I taught in the future, it would be as a result of my writing and not instead of it. My job was not to abstract the life of the oceans and parcel it up into educational sound bites but to make it real for myself and for others in language against which our normal defenses have no power. Writing, in other words. Poetry, in Wordsworth's words, would be my life's star, my light of navigation. How it would play out, I didn't know. But I was hungry again for the right thing and already feeling the drawing tide that would help carry me out of that place.

Optimistic Conclusion

The tidal gate was replaced with very little help from me, but every year since it was changed, the salmon have returned to the Maxwelton stream in increasing numbers. The whole focus of the stream has changed from being a mere outlet to a home, not just for the salmon, but for a whole community of creatures who live with them. Farming practices have changed along the stream; the local schoolchildren are involved, and the seasons are now marked by the first returning salmon being spotted in the stream—all this from one man's idea to change a single tidal gate.

Harder Conclusion

The motivational speakers and self-help books are all wrong: there is no way of creating a life where we are full participants one hundred percent of the time. There is no way of being fully human without at times being fully stuck or even completely absent; we are simply not made that way. There is no possibility of pursuing a work without coming to terms with all the ways it is impossible to do it. Feeling far away from what we want tells us one of two things about our work: that we are at the beginning or that we have forgotten where we were going.

Remembering what we have forgotten is a first practical step home; the opening of a tidal gate that brings us into contact with the larger, stronger currents of existence. Exile and forgetting are natural states for most human beings, but so are remembering and recalling. All tasks are completed through cycles of visitation and absence. We should get used to this cycle and integrate it fully into the way a work or a vocation is achieved and not hold ourselves to impossible standards that are often quite tedious, giftless states, in any case.

It may in fact be, that the very essence of what individuals have to offer the world is through a close understanding of their weaknesses and blind spots—blind spots in themselves or in others. The very dynamic we confront when we feel it is impossible is the very dynamic we will put into the work, a dynamic that will make it distinctive and entirely our own.

Anticipated question at this point in the conclusion

What about a Mozart or a Shakespeare, who both seemed to work full-pelt without interruption?

Answer to anticipated question

A Mozart or a Shakespeare may have written nonstop, but each was also constantly interrupted, and many times, I am sure, by their own untimely needs. The very big difference seems to be that they remembered what they were about and got back on track sooner than most of us.

Mozart was confronted with constant traveling, kings who insisted he used too many notes: an archrival who tried to sabotage him, and a father who haunted him for the span of his days. Shakespeare's theaters were regularly closed by the authorities, his Globe Theatre burned to the ground, and one of his plays was used as a signal for insurrection against the Queen, which led to very necessary but time-consuming conversations with large men carrying halberds. (*Halberds*: tall spears that also have an ax head attached, granting dignity to the one who holds it and a sense of power over those who do not.) He was also a formidable entrepreneur and businessman, a kind of busy, successful Spielberg of his day. For both Mozart and Shakespeare, despite the breadth and volume of their work, more time was probably spent not writing than writing itself. A work is achieved not by creating a hermetic space sealed off from the world, but *nel mezzo,* in the middle of everything.

The imagination and its ability to discern bigger underlying patterns is just as important if not more important than a firm grasp of the details of what we want. The mighty interior wish is more important than mere outward details that seem to tell others that you haven't a clue what you are doing.

Over-the-top but nevertheless true conclusion

In building a work life, people who follow rules, written or unwritten, too closely and in an unimaginative way are often suffocated by those same rules and die by them, quite often unnoticed and very often unmourned.

CHAPTER 7

Searching for a Self:
The Pursuit That Is
Not a Pursuit

As I remember now, I was walking alone in the pine forest, high in the Himalayas and separated from my other two companions by a long valley of white trees and the steadily falling snow. I was breathing deliberately in the thin air, trying to find a path through the forest that was quickly disappearing under a thick white layer, hiding the way and separating me from my two friends, who were now far, far ahead of me in the high alpine valley.

There came a moment, however, when I was forced to stop worrying about that absolute sense of silent isolation. Looking up to catch my breath, I saw that the landscape I had been walking through in such a dogged, concentrated manner was overwhelmingly and breathtakingly beautiful. Though the snow was thick, somehow sunlight permeated the falling flakes from the far end of the valley and each flocked tree was lit with an unearthly background luminescence. The quiet amid the falling flakes was total and profound.

I stopped at the edge of a clearing to put on a down parka, then lifted my sunglasses and propped them in my hair to get a true measure of the surreal colors. I was shouldering my pack again a few minutes later, when across the snowy circle of the clearing, I was shocked to see a figure sitting there on a white horse, absolutely stock-still. I looked back, stock-still myself, because this figure was like nothing I had ever seen before, outside my childhood stories of Marco Polo. The horse was dressed in elaborate silks and the decorated saddle was studded with silver that winked and glinted in the glowing light. The man holding the reins looked out from a fur-lined robe above which his calm, sun-wrinkled and bearded face was crowned with a conical brass helmet. He had seen me before I had seen him. He did nothing but look at me intently. His eyes, though lined, were steady and unafraid and seemed to give off a youthful, ageless benevolence. He sat with an erect ease that also communicated a powerful sense of control and purpose.

I looked back at him across the clearing and in doing so thought I could understand the unspoken conversation occurring between us. I was probably the first Westerner he had ever seen come up into his high valley; no doubt his life would be changed forever by what I represented, but he looked, seeing me, as if he would face it with the equanimity with which he probably faced all other changes. For me, he was the first person I had met out of what seemed like a forgotten past. We looked across the centuries at each other as if an unspoken annunciation of a new world was appearing out of our meeting, one that would be crucial to our separate futures.

We continued to look at each other through the gently falling snow as if we had an agreed understanding that neither of us would attempt to speak. How long we looked at each other I am not sure, but after what seemed like an age, he raised his hand and pointed, appearing to guide me in the direction I was looking for through the forest. Then he lifted his reins and walked his horse off slant-wise, in the direction opposite where he had pointed and left me alone in the silence.

With a quick look at his disappearing back, I stumbled off through the thick snow in the direction in which he had sent me. After the strange meeting I was half panicked and wanted to find my companions and be reassured that I was still in my own time and not stumbling through some kind of illogical portal into the past. The Himalayas seemed to be constantly creating a different context from the one I had left behind me in the West, as if little dramas like the one I had just witnessed should, could and actually did occur on a daily basis.

The snow had a steadily increasing wind behind it now and was fast becoming a blizzard. I had no idea how far it was to the next house or settlement, distracted as I had been all that morning by a circling Himalayan griffon vulture. I was still weak and convalescing from a serious bout of dysentery that had laid me very low the week before. Intent on the sky, I had not joined the day's route-planning conversation, preferring to rest and listen to them at a distance, gazing up through my binoculars at the twelve-foot wingspan and then letting them go ahead on the path. I had not seen them since.

It was not long after leaving the mounted stranger that I realized I had no perception in the now windblown, freezing forest of any way ahead, or if I was even facing in the right direction. It was becoming very, very cold. It was also, I realized, time to stop, to make whatever kind of shelter I could and get into it before I walked into deeper trouble and lost my friends, and the trail, completely.

I had cut my first branch with the big serrated knife I carried in my pack when I heard a muffled shout coming from the very direction in which I had been headed. I ran toward the voice immediately, knife in hand and, breaking through a line of snowy branches, ran straight into my friends. After their initial shock at the appearance of this snow-covered, knife-wielding apparition in their midst, we banged one another on the back and knocked the brows of our snow goggles together in celebration at finding one another. The celebration was short-lived; we had no idea where we were or where the path was. I put the knife away, took out the compass and started walking, leading the others more or less north. I led the three of us with my head down, watching the snow-covered ground and the compass needle at the same time. The other two followed me for about an hour, after which, as we came to the foot of a cliff, we froze at the sound of a nearby screech. It was a very human screech, and it was coming from right ahead of us out of the swirling flakes. As we looked up we could tell it was issuing from the mouth of a very old, bent woman standing beneath a wooded slope at the side of the cliff, who, shielding her eyes, was looking toward us and gesturing for us to follow her.

We walked quickly after her up the slope in silence, following her imprints in the new snow, as if following strange old women in Himalayan blizzards was the most natural thing to do in the world. I walked on silently, watching her dark figure disappearing above, nursing what little convalescent strength I had left with no extra breath to tell my friends that this was the second fairy-tale figure I had met that day.

As the wooded slope turned into bare mountainside, the old woman kept up a very quick pace and I was fast becoming exhausted. Despite her years she was well used to life above ten thousand feet. I, on the other hand, had barely eaten for a week, and if I had been at home I probably would have sat in a chair and read for the next week to get my strength back. There was no sitting and reading here; the woman almost seemed to be loping up the slope ahead of me, taking a path that now wound between short grey cliffs, and glancing behind, I saw that even my fit friends were having trouble with the altitude.

My friends' struggle was not much comfort; by the time we reached the foot of a log ladder that stood against a man-made wall, I was at the end of my physical tether. I stopped, my hands resting on my knees, gasping beside the wall while the woman gave her first smile, shaking her head at the weakness of the young and pointed above her into the mist, up the ladder. Looking up, I could see we were standing beneath a *gompa,* one of those small fortified temples that you often see clinging to the ridges above the high valley floors. They were places of retreat for lamas—Tibetan priests. Many of the *gompa*s we had passed looked semi-ruined, but this one seemed well kept; through the swirling flakes I could see the wall was swept with a new coat of what looked like adobe and the pinewood in the ladder was cut only recently.

We followed the billowing skirts of the woman up the ladder into the falling snow and emerged onto a small, flat area before a large double door. Once we had gathered ourselves on this peculiar windswept balcony, she opened the doors and led us into a room that was half shrine, half living quarters. There was an altar: priceless old tattered religious hangings, statuettes of dancing figures and a strong scent of yak butter from the many snuffed-out candles. In the corner was a low trestle bed above which a small window let the grey light in from the mountain heights. As soon as we were given the signal to sit, I laid myself flat out on the floor and closed my eyes, feeling the room suddenly spin and my strength ebb.

From my horizontal position, I could hear the old woman making Tibetan tea. The tea came in a dusty, bricklike solid-brown ingot, like a bar of Irish turf, that she had to grate and reduce to powder; then put in the bottom of a special wooden plunger and mix with salt, yak butter and hot water. The yak butter was almost always semi-rancid, but after the first shock of drinking it some weeks before, the tea had become a life-giving staple to the high-altitude traveler. It had everything needed in those unforgiving heights to revive the weary: salt, calorie-rich fat, caffeine and hot water.

Undeterred by her hike up the mountainside, the woman went to the plunger with a will, mixing the ingredients together. Soon I sat up against the wall, nursing the tea in my hands and listening to a translation from one of my friends. She was the housekeeper for a very holy man, a lama, who had just left on horseback for the south that morning. Had we seen him? My friends said no. I lifted my finger and said yes. I had met him and he had saved me from getting lost in the blizzard by pointing me in the right direction.

She nodded in satisfaction when this was put to her, as if pointing out the path was the very essence of a lama's job in life; then, in a very matter-of-fact way, she said, yes, yes, yes, the lama had told her early that morning that she might have company, she should be on the lookout for travelers and she should offer us shelter, and point us on the way across the mountains. He was very particular that we take the shortcut over the ridge above to cut out a large bend in the valley and reach the village that afternoon.

"How on earth would he know that?" I said to myself. Perhaps, from this height, you could see miles down the valley among the trees? Perhaps he had a telescope? The Dalai Lama himself was known to be fond of scientific instruments. I sank down again, refusing to think it through. I blanched at the thought of ascending the ridge above, and my experience in wild places told me to run a thousand miles from the word *shortcut*, but I was in no position to argue. We drank the tea, looking at one another as if we were members of a party suddenly being guided by a stern but invisible hand, and shrugged, thanked the life-saving woman profusely and went on our way, down the ladder into the now misty snow and up the ridge.

The ascent was easy enough, but when we reached the path along the ridge, the rocks that made up its knife-edge crown were coated with wet, caving snow that pushed us onto all fours, sliding and grasping for a firm hold as we moved together along the edge. If the snow had nothing beneath it, our feet would push it off and into the thin gusty air, where it would fall off into the nothingness that seemed to lie on either side. It took total concentration and a mighty effort of will, which I could barely muster, to inch along that airy way. At one point I lay panting, spread-eagled across the ridge, my face buried in the wet snow, resting to get my strength back. The others looked back and thought I had slid off the ridge, into the void. They panicked and shouted, screaming my name into the emptiness, stopping only when I raised a fluttering hand out of the white depths. They were finally relieved to see me raise myself and shunt myself along, almost burrowing through the snowy crown toward them.

After the panic, nothing was said; we turned to look down and were relieved to see the flat roofs of the village below us through the clouds and then a gully leading down where the path would have been had we been able to see it.

By the time we had descended the gully and reached the village, my exhaustion had reached the point of delirium. I was not only wet through and very cold, I was in a very, very strange mental and physical state. The village seemed empty, with only the sounds of dozens of prayer flags snapping on their upright poles on the rooftops. The wind moaned through the cliffs surrounding the village. I was the first to reach the narrow stone lane, which was bounded by houses on both sides. When I looked down the lane I could see that each of the houses had a half door, like the old cottages in Ireland, and out of each door, as if each house were a stable, there was a horse looking out into the lightly falling snow. In my fevered mind, I felt as if I had blundered into a scene from *Gulliver's Travels,* and into a village inhabited only by members of the equine race.

My delusion was short-lived. Suddenly, in the small square at the bottom of the lane, a man appeared, his pale saffron tunic standing out among the grey stone houses and the drifting flakes. He lifted his arm above his head, brandishing a large brass key, and started shouting and pointing toward us. Immediately the street filled with a crowd of people streaming out of the houses where only horses' heads had been a moment before, as if the whole village had been waiting for this moment. We were surrounded by what looked like the entire population of the mountain village, smiling and laughing and encouraging us to follow the man with the key, who was now beckoning us off on a path to the left that led straight into the side of a tremendous cliff that overhung the village.

I tried to get my friend to translate a request. Could I lie down somewhere, dark and very quiet, and sleep? But the enthusiasm was too overwhelming for them to see my weakened state. They jostled us along the cliff path, keeping me thankfully upright through their sheer crowding proximity and then stopped where the path narrowed to single file and became a part of the cliff face. Here the path followed a series of hewn ledges out into the middle of the face. I could see that when the path reached the middle of the cliff, it stopped below large carved wooden doors cut into the rock above.

The crowd hung back, murmuring with excitement. Three men, all wearing the same saffron tunics, led us out slowly into the middle of the face. I stopped beneath the door, standing right in front of it between my two friends. I could sense something momentous about to happen. Two of the men stepped up, taking hold of each of the doors as I stood trembling, barely able to stand. In the silence they opened the doors. There was a long silence after the creak of the hinges: then, looking out into the void through the falling snow, through the darkness of the carved arch behind the doors, was a tall, elegant, completely calm, absolutely serene, gold-painted Buddha with curved purple eyes. Those eyes seemed to look out at me with a complete understanding, a form of rested presence that was both calm and at the same time absolutely alive. The sight was so breathtakingly beautiful, my state so profoundly fragile, I dropped to my knees sobbing and then slid to the ground on the ledge, blubbering: all sense of the cold or the exhaustion banished, my face pressed into the grit and poor earth of the ledge, and I cried happily into that ground, as if the rock could take every tear I had, as if I had found a ground on which to rest, that could hold not only my incredible weakness, but my strengths, my will to live and even, at the end of some other long mountain path, my eventual and inevitable disappearance.

THE PATHLESS PATH

It is not surprising to any of us who know what it is like being left behind, whether it is in a high mountain valley or in the isolation of relationship, that when Deirdre Blomfield-Brown found herself in despair over the end of her second marriage, her foundational experience was actually a complete lack of foundation: a loss of ground. She saw herself, in her aloneness, staring into a great depression, a slow internal whirlwind from which there seemed no escape, and which the advice of her spiritual friends—to turn toward the light, to think positively, to get beyond it—seemed powerless to prevent her from entering. To her, she was inching along a ridge with the void on every side.

Looking into the self is often like looking into that void, especially if we come to our search through trauma and loss. There may be a tidal gate inside us to open, but it has often been described, especially in the East, as a gateless gate, or like my adventure that day in the Himalaya, a pathless path. In other words, to begin with, we cannot even see it is there, and we do not recognize it. Something has been lost on the surface, and we cannot as yet see anything that could replace it. If this lack of orientation continues without any outside help, we start to lose faith that there is anything other than our overwhelming experience of being lost. What we then feel is often described as depression. Part of the burden of depression can be the constant sense of not knowing. It can be a release then, to think, that when we first come across the idea of a pathless path, by definition, we are not meant to understand what it means. We are meant to pay a different kind of attention—the kind of attention we might pay if we thought our life was at stake at high altitude—one that starts to change us from the inside out.

We could see depression as a complete loss of attention to anything outside our own sense of disorientation. To be depressed is to feel a vague but constant sense of imprisonment. One of the other diagnostic features of depression is a loss of articulation. Suffering in silence, we often find we cannot even properly tell ourselves how we feel. To do that we have to find a bigger language for ourselves, for which as yet we have no confidence and no energy.

Anyone who has suffered real loss, the loss of a child, a marriage, a well-loved home, has always had difficulty conveying the absolute sense of devastation to those who are at present more fortunate. *As if standing on fishes,* Rilke described it, as if the ground had a life of its own and were swimming away underneath him. Many of us who take the solidity of the world for granted have had glimpses of what it would be like to have that ground taken away. It is hard to convey that sheer sense of faraway physical isolation, surrounded by swirling snow, and separated from the friends who give your journey context and sanity. It's hard to convey the sense of emotional isolation, being left behind by someone you thought loved you and would continue to love you to the end.

It is hard, also, to underestimate the way human beings need a sense of foundation in their lives; good foundations can be consciously felt or taken for granted. I remember being caught in a powerful earthquake in another mountain range, on the other side of the world, in faraway Peru, which for days after, created a literal stomach-churning anxiety in me about the supposedly solid earth on which I stood. It felt very strange to look at the ground as being an untrustworthy entity. I also remember being attacked in the days after that tremor, by a band of locals drunk on corn beer. Though I escaped unhurt, I had a pain in my stomach for two days from the first, direct physical revelation that my fellow human beings could try to kill me for no good reason. This was not the ground upon which I thought my relationship with other men stood. I was not only shocked, I felt bereft. All I could do at the time was take to my bed for forty-eight hours; pull the blankets over my head, and in that claustrophobic darkness, come to very reluctant terms with it.

Sometimes we walk around with the blankets invisibly over our head, talking, conversing, sometimes even laughing, but looking all the time, as if through a glass, darkly. We are traveling, but we are anxious travelers, wondering whether the direction we are following in our darkness will actually lead us off a cliff edge. It was in this empty, anxious, claustrophobic state that Deirdre Blomfield-Brown, knowing little about Tibet, or the Himalaya, or lamas or any of her future, came out of the New Mexico school where she had taught that day and got into a friend's pickup truck to find an open magazine beside her on the front seat.

Facing her, at the top of the page, was the title, "Working with Negativity." The article was written by a man with an intriguing name. Chögyam Trungpa, a lama, a Tibetan Buddhist teacher, but Deirdre did not know she was reading a Buddhist view of the world; she did not know that Trungpa was Tibetan or a teacher. As she read on, she simply said to herself, "This is true." The article asked her to see difficult circumstances and negativity not as a problem but as a doorway to understanding. The real problem, Trungpa said, was negative negativity, when we react against our perceptions and try to escape. Deirdre continued to nod as she read: ". . . There is nothing wrong with negativity . . . it's actually creative and very direct and very . . ." Deirdre did not realize it yet, but she was looking into a well from which others had drunk since the beginning of recorded history.

THE ESSENTIAL HUMAN INGREDIENT

In the pursuit of all three marriages there is one essential human experience that an individual brings to each of them. Anxiety. It does not matter whether we have to climb a snow-clogged ridge in the Himalaya or find a hard-to-get parking spot in the hour before a meeting: it seems to be part of our evolutionary makeup to wake up at night and worry and then take those accumulated worries with us into the day. It also seems to be a real virtue and a core competence. Nature seems to have favored those of our ancestors who did stay up late, sometimes marveling at the clear bright, uninterrupted stretch of stars, but more often fretting under those heavens, not only about the snow that was about to fall, but also about the berries that had been gathered but not preserved, the animal run down but still not skinned, the mate who seemed to be spending a great deal of time around another very attractive member of the tribe, smiling foolishly, while pretending to be doing useful things. Jealousy in all its different forms can often be our preferred mode of anxiety. Many of us are specialists in very particular kinds of worry, being unaffected by physical difficulties while fretting over every word said the previous day. Whatever our choice of concern, worry pursues us as we pursue our goals: whether we look for a mountain path in the woods, for a mate, or far beyond it all, for a God.

WORRY: OUR FRIEND

Worry is the daily faint echo of our transience and mortality. Whatever we hold in our hands will eventually slip away. We will live to say goodbye to all those we know, or they will say goodbye to us. We may pursue or waylay a mate, but then, as human beings, having created a longed-for relationship, we carry worries about parentage to a high art and build elaborate constructs around fidelity: constructs that can be gone over at great length while we are alone, constructs that are further reasons to stay up at night, to ignore the stars, the mountains and the heavens, to plot revenge or to run away, hurt and saddened, into the night.

Worry can even be our friend. In our waking hours we see work and worry as inseparable companions. For many of us, the real midwife of work is worry. We are sure from experience that there is no real work without worrying about what needs to be done to prepare for it, with what needs to be done to carry it out and with what needs to be done to preserve its gains. We work, therefore we worry.

Millennia of worrying under night skies have brought human beings to where the complexities of our contemporary societies have almost reached breaking point. In many ways, our to-do lists have become the postmodern equivalent of the priest's rosary, the lama's sutra or the old prayer book—keeping a larger, avalanching reality at bay. Above all, the to-do list keeps the evil of not-doing at bay, a list that many of us like to chant and cycle through religiously as we make our way to work through the commute.

Postmodern life has multiplied our concerns. Not only do we have to track the particular tribe we belong to and their many doings, we now have the plumber to worry about, the educational expenses, the many, many taxes and through it all, the many, many, many little gadgets to plug in and power up. Little wonder, then, that, made as we are and trained as we are to organize complexity, we are constantly trying to assign each and everything a name so that we can organize it and control it, so much so that it can be tempting to try to name and organize something that cannot be pressured or regulated, this elusive thing called the self.

THE SELF OF NOT DOING

It is natural to try to bring our organizational competences to bear on a domain that seems, like that day in the Himalaya, and like Deirdre's inconsolable depression, immune to our normal everyday skills. But anyone who has spent any time in silence trying to let this deeper hidden self emerge, soon finds it does not seem to respond to the language of coercion or strategy. It cannot be worried into existence. Anxiety actually seems to keep an experience of the deeper self at bay. This hidden self seems reluctant to be listed, categorized, threatened or coerced. It lives beneath our surface tiredness, waiting, it seems, for us to stop.

Stopping can be very, very difficult. It can take exhaustion, extreme circumstances on a wet, snowy mountain ridge or an intimate sense of loss for it to happen. Even then we can soon neutralize and isolate the experience, dismissing it as illogical, pretending it didn't count, then turning back to our surface strengths and chattering away in a false language we have built around our successes.

Success can be the greatest barrier to stopping, to quiet, to opening up the radically different form of conversation that is necessary for understanding this larger sense of the self. Our very success can be the cause of a greater anxiety for further preservation of our success.

The fact is, human beings have worried, no matter when or where in history they have lived—whether they have a job or not, whether they inhabit the top of the building or the bottom, whether they are married or single or even whether they have a great deal of money or none at all. The ability to grow an ulcer and worry is so human that it is strange to think that hardly any other portion of creation indulges in the activity with the depth and sophistication with which we do. If we do see the marks of anxiety in another creature, as I did recently in a dog waiting for its owner to return home, we remark on it and begin to say the animal in question is *almost* human.

But no animal has taken anxiety to the grand heights that we have. Our highly evolved ability to worry and become anxious may have conferred us with survival advantages but it also gave us the ability to sit beneath a magnificent sky and not see a single star, to sit by ourselves and not have an inkling of who that self is, to spend most of a life providing for a family while neglecting to spend the time with them that is an expression of the love that all the providing is supposed to represent. Anxiety about our world, about ourselves; our constant need to compare and contrast ourselves with others, our constant attempt to identify exactly where on the map we find ourselves, divides us from creation as surely as any serpent proffering an apple.

Perhaps our development of a sustained ability for mental and emotional worry was the very apple into which we gladly bit, defending ourselves consciously against creation while at the same time expelling ourselves from the garden where we felt unconsciously at home.

A LAND BEYOND ANXIETY

One of the underlying reasons for traveling to sublime land-scapes such as the Himalaya is to pay witness to a world far beyond our narrow concerns, to enter a cultural world that does not trigger our habitual responses, and at best, to find ourselves then borne along by some other invisible current; an invisible current, that until then we were too habituated to or preoccupied to find. We go there to be free, to inhabit a place where our normal cares are hopefully left far behind.

In the West, almost all of the pivotal spiritual experiences that occurred to men and women in the Bible occurred to those who were cradled by equally powerful biblical landscapes. Many of the men and women in those mountains and deserts were also at the end of their physical and emotional tether—Moses at the Red Sea or by the burning bush; Job in the desert, confronted by a voice out of the whirlwind, telling him to ignore his tremendous material and family losses and turn his eyes to creation, to another form of cradling than the material one he strove to construct to protect himself with every day.

Job is one of the biblical figures we can perhaps most identify with, a man who, of anyone who ever lived, deserved a good, anxious moan about everything, having lost his son, his house, five hundred yoke of oxen, three thousand camels, seven thousand sheep and, as Alain de Botton has noted, looking at this same passage, five hundred badly needed she-asses. Finally and entirely naturally, having questioned God's mercy, he received this reply from the whirlwind carrying Jehovah's voice:

Who is this that darkeneth counsel by words without knowledge?

Whereupon are the foundations thereof fastened? or who laid the corner stone thereof; when the morning stars sang together, and all the sons of God shouted for joy?

Where wast thou when I laid the foundations of the earth? declare, if thou hast understanding.

Hast thou entered into the treasures of the snow?

Canst thou bind the sweet influences of Pleiades or loose the bands of Orion . . . or canst thou guide Arcturus with his sons?

Canst thou lift up thy voice to the clouds, that an abundance of waters may cover thee?

Who hath put wisdom in the inward parts? or who hath given understanding to the heart?

Hast thou an arm like God, or canst thou thunder with a voice like him?

*Doth the hawk fly by thy wisdom, and stretch her wings
toward the south?*

Canst thou draw out leviathan with a hook?

Job 38–40 (King James Version)

Fishing for an answer, Job landed a powerful life form from the deep. A voice that pointed to a deeper context than the one his outer successes gave him, a life beyond his daily life, a sense of riches beyond the ones he could store in his herds or even find in his family. The cruelty of the words from the maelstrom cannot hide some other kindness opening up, a difficult truth of human existence: anxiety, worry and fretting may have helped us to survive, but they cannot help us see the great horizon, the deeper context. Our worries and our need to control those we love because of those worries will not help us to marvel at the natural world, to appreciate a daughter's loving presence, to enjoy a son still alive, or a spouse who is healthy, breathing and with us, not ill, not passed away, not now untouchable.

Hast thou entered into the treasures of the snow . . . ?

gives another context to my struggles on the Himalayan ridge. The voice speaks to a radical and radiant eternal present hidden under the struggles of the moment. Our need to find a way through the snow covers over our appreciation of that brilliant light-filled substance. Perhaps, earlier in the forest clearing, my lama was not pointing at the way, perhaps he was just pointing at the snow. Perhaps we look and look, following the pointing finger, but do not see.

The voice in the whirlwind asks us to see the world without having an ounce of control over it and to cultivate our faith through paying attention to this creation. Job may have been unlucky, but he was lucky in one completely transforming respect: he heard a powerful voice representing a much larger reality than the one he had put together himself.

THE UNBROKEN VOICE

Sometimes the whirlwind is a natural cataclysm speaking to us—powerful elements brought together to remind us of some other, larger context than the preservation of human identities. It is a Hurricane Katrina, an Asian tsunami, or in Deirdre Blomfield-Brown's case, a slow inner-falling part from which she heard a voice, one she slowly had to learn to call her own.

The voice she read on the page of the open magazine was one that had been carried down through the centuries. It had begun in northern India and quickly found a home in the mountains to the north, where it took on the natural inclinations and character of the Botya or Tibetan peoples who lived there. But the extraordinary thing was that in those mountain fastnesses, over all this time, through individuals such as the lama I met in the snowy forest, the voice *had* been maintained unbroken.

Chögyam Trungpa's approach was the product of an insight into basic human anxieties that had begun in northern India, in the sixth century B.C. with the unyielding intention of a young man to get to the bottom of human unhappiness. He was called Shakyamuni, or Siddhartha, but he later became known as the Buddha because of his particular insight into suffering and anxiety and the way to live in and beyond its presence. It was a title particular to his insight and not to his person. The Buddha was not to be worshipped—Buddhism is not in fact, a form of worship; anyone who gained the same insight in the future would also be known as a Buddha. Everyone has Buddha nature; it is only a question of whether you can make yourself aware of it.

When this young man sat beneath a big spreading Bodhi tree in approximately 500 B.C. and vowed not to get up again until he had cut through all illusions and come to a clear understanding of what lay under this anxious, fearful, constantly traveling self, he was trying to close the same gap that Job attempted to close when he pleaded with God to explain the meaning of his suffering.

THE BIG QUESTIONS

A few of the big questions might be: Why do I feel different from everything else I see? Why does everything I hold in my hands constantly slip through my fingers, and *why* can't I live forever? Siddhartha would get to an answer through watching his thoughts and being utterly present. He would watch those thoughts eventually disappear as a primary means of identifying himself and see something more immediate and quite extraordinary take their place.

You could say that meditation or silent prayer is the practice of dwelling in this underlying un-anxious all-seeing, all-appreciating un-defensive self that does not care whether it lives or dies, while not taking our eyes off the world. It can be done by disciplined sitting and breathing; it can be achieved by arranging to get completely, life-threateningly exhausted in the Himalaya and having two people hold open a large pair of doors in a mountainside. It seems it can be glimpsed by being abandoned in a marriage. The big, big question is: Can you cultivate a daily discipline that simply doesn't need all this trauma in order to open the door and keep it open?

Shakyamuni practiced holding these doors open through a fierce kind of attention in which he refused to ascribe names to what he saw until he came to realize, that in effect he wasn't this self or this otherness he was witnessing but a living, constantly changing conversation between the two.

Finally, standing up and walking away from the Bodhi tree under which he had sat, the Buddha summarized his insight in what became known as the Four Noble Truths. In effect, he said, these are the rules to follow if you want to have a bigger life than the part of you that worries; if you want to have a life bigger than the part of you that is afraid of death. It was the Buddha's to-do list for finding the self.

The first, the one whose faint echo reached Deirdre in the front seat of the pickup truck, the one she was waiting to hear, was: *There is no life without suffering.*

Which could also be translated as: There is an absolute universality to suffering; that is, there is no way for any human being, no matter how successful, no matter how wealthy, no matter how blithe of heart, to arrange circumstances such that they will be exempt from the emotional and physical hurts common to all people who have ever lived. This is a given: a foundational reality. It was a foundation that Deirdre came to rest on when she leaned across and saw Trungpa's interpretation of the Buddha's original words.

The Buddha used the word *Dukka*, which meant not only physical suffering, but also and even primarily mental and emotional suffering. The word conjured a constant sense of dissatisfaction, a perpetual uneasiness, a persistent and often very subtle sense of anxiety. It was as if someone had spoken to Deirdre in a language she could understand and pointed at something completely obvious, which some reluctant part of her had hoped was not true: her suffering was real and it was an absolute foundation to being human, to being fully herself. It wasn't a mistake, a wrong path she had taken. It deserved to exist like everything else in creation and it could lead her to a sense of home in the world.

Dukka is universal, it is present in a bag lady on the streets of Berkeley or in a Rupert Murdoch closing a deal on Wall Street: it is the sense that, no matter how full your shopping cart, things are not exactly as they should be and there is something more to be done to make that cart fuller. The bag lady moves her shopping cart to the opposite corner of the intersection, Rupert Murdoch looks for the next acquisition, and we ourselves witness them both, thinking, like them, that there surely *is* something strangely wrong with the world. But there are no exceptions, including ourselves; the first noble truth says we all have a little of the bag lady and a little of the Rupert Murdoch in us, in our own very lovable and very unlovable ways.

We can sense Deirdre's sense of release even in the first sentences of the magazine article. She must have been ripe for it, of course, but it is a freedom in itself to see that there is no way to live without at some time suffering. It enables us to watch our worries arise and go away almost independent of whatever actions we take on their behalf. We could say that for Deirdre it was love's first glimpse of the self. With this glimpse she actually became intrigued and even excited by her predicament. Like Romeo seeing Juliet, she saw a possibility for happiness across a previously uncrossable divide and between previously warring parts of herself; it was a glimpse she turned very quickly into a pursuit.

The interesting point is that if we continually watch our worries and turn ourselves into witnesses to their constant coming and going, and if we turn that self-observing faculty into a continuous exercise of attention, we are well on our way to becoming a Buddhist without having to bother with robes, shaved head or incense. To begin with, we just watch our thoughts and their constant attempts to keep us safe, and by doing that we have a possibility of living without being ruled by the worries we are observing. With daily practice a space seems to open up between the thoughts in which we get a glimpse, an intuition, a gravitational tug toward something else, something both emboldening and frightening.

SHY AND UNWILLING: CATASTROPHES, COINCIDENCES AND COMINGS TOGETHER

One of the first dynamics we run into when we have glimpsed this elusive deeper self is the realization that our everyday surface self, the one who walks around, getting things done, is most often terrified of the meeting that has taken place. It starts to become deeply nervous. It acts as if the contact will bring about its own disappearance. Its fears may be justified. Fighting for its own survival, it is not only shy of the contact it has made; it may work hard to cover over the fact that any meeting has actually taken place. It may also work even harder to describe the meeting in language that can dismiss and belittle the experience. What we are confronted with in the initial stages of the pursuit of the deeper self is the beginning of a long rear guard action by the surface self to preserve its life.

Little wonder, then, that throughout human history many of the stories that tell of this pursuit of the self, have in the beginning, to do with a kind of subterfuge, a tricking of the personality into unconscious recognitions. Like the initial stages of a love affair, the attraction is often subliminal, not to be spoken of and happening just below the radar screen of a busy, I-don't-have-time-for-all-this existence. It must happen, in effect, almost against our will. It is full of the coincidences, multiple accidental meetings and the sudden recognition of the potential lover's face in surprising places.

Falling in love with the self is like falling in love with a person: a deeply illogical experience that goes against all our surface attempts to plan. A friend of mine met her future husband by arriving jet-lagged in Los Angeles from London, determined to do nothing but go home, shower and sleep. She called a friend to come and pick her up, misdialed the number and got an ex-boyfriend who was very surprised to hear from her but very excited about a theater event for which he was setting off at that moment. He insisted she come with him. My friend ignored the invitation, said thank you but no thank you and went home. Twenty minutes after she got in the door, the bell rang, and her ex-boyfriend turned up and with great good humor insisted it wasn't about starting their relationship again; he asked her to get her things on and come. Tired but beautifully dressed in a subtle green robe that her husband still remembers to this day, she walked into the reception line at the event and fell in love with a man she had never seen before who turned to watch her walking past, with whom she now has two children and with whom she has just celebrated her twentieth wedding anniversary. One tiny conscious *no* on the surface could have closed off that path into her future marriage and parenthood forever.

Deirdre Blomfield-Brown was in this shy but beautiful stage of unconscious subterfuge, a stage of tricking the conscious self into thinking it is doing something else when in fact it is arranging for its own demise. It is a stage in which we start to hear themes and people being mentioned by strangers, seemingly on a daily basis, where until now we had never heard of them before. A time when books seem to fall off shelves open to specific references that remind us of something we have to follow. It is as if the conscious mind cannot fully come to terms with it all on its own, and if it did, it would probably grow afraid and quash what was happening. It relies on the coming together of circumstances in ways that cannot be easily labeled and dismissed. We do not know the basis of these coincidences: the lama on the snowy trail, the old woman at the bottom of the slope—perhaps we are just alert to things in the extremity of our attentions which before, during an ordinary day at the office, we would have passed by. We see them because now we want to see them. They seem to leap out at us. Some part of us knows they are going to help us find the way; they are going to help us find a shelter that cannot be taken away. Perhaps we are part of an invisible web that our surface mind cannot fathom, but looking back at those accidental meetings with the deeper self, it can all seem as fated as those first unlooked-for meetings we had, years before, with a lover or a spouse.

One book that Deirdre sought out was Trungpa's *In Tibet*, which she read to her students, thinking it would broaden their minds. They were so taken by the book that they wanted to meet this man from such a far-off, exotic land with such a strange religion. She had them all write letters to him inviting him to come. It wasn't long before Deirdre heard that in fact Trungpa was coming to her area. Under the excuse of a good broadening education for the children, she went along. Before the event she had the schoolchildren think of questions to ask and had them all make presents. One of the children, the daughter of a potter, made a mug that said "Trungpa" on it. Years later, Deirdre was to wonder whatever happened to that amusing gift. No matter the gifts, all of the children were very excited to meet this exotic man with such a distinctive name.

Appropriately enough for a Tibetan teacher, the seminar was held at the top of a mountain, and even more appropriately, there was a huge snowfall, which Deirdre and the children had to first drive in and then walk through to get to the center. The first meeting was reassuring, not with Trungpa, but with a messenger from him, to tell the children to treat Trungpa as they would anybody else and not to glorify him or make a fuss of him in any way.

The session with Trungpa took the form of a question-and-answer session, with the children in Deirdre's class taking the lead. One story stayed with Deirdre. A child asked if Trungpa was afraid of anything. He said that his teachers had taught him how to be fearless; he followed it with a story from his youth in Tibet. He had journeyed with other monks to visit a neighboring monastery in the mountains, where they had found a fierce dog chained up outside the entrance. This dog was extremely vicious, foaming at the mouth and straining at its leash to get at them. The party he was with tried to gingerly creep around the dog, to get through the door of the monastery, but the chain suddenly broke and the dog went for them. Trungpa told them that all of his attendant monks ran off . . . but he ran straight at the dog. . . .

Deirdre looked at all the children with their mouths hanging open and watched Trungpa wait a moment for dramatic effect. Then he said, "And the dog was so shocked that it put its tail between its legs and ran away."

Deirdre was not so courageous to begin with. She found herself in an interview with Trungpa not many weeks later and set the defensive tone with a constant chatter that allowed nothing serious to arise in the conversation. Trungpa listened to the chatter for a while and then made a motion to signal the conversation was over. He stood up and she stood up and then something erupted from far away inside her. She started with humiliating, runaway blubber, blurting out her woes and her sense of depression and abandonment. Deirdre remembered Trungpa's patience and kindness to her, but she also remembered his advice in these words:

> *It's like being in the ocean when the waves are really rough and high. They knock you over and you find yourself on the floor of the ocean with your face in the sand. The sand is getting in your nose and your mouth and your eyes and the waves are holding you down. But then the wave recedes and you stand back up and you walk until the next wave comes in and knocks you down and the same thing keeps happening. And each time you just stand back up and after a while it seems to you that the waves are getting smaller and smaller.*

First Conclusions on Suffering and the Self

The pursuit of the self is the pursuit of that part of us not defined by our worries and anxieties. But this pursuit begins only by admitting that human anxiety is endless and to be expected. These waves of existential anxiety may knock down the surface self, but there is another, deeper self with a larger perspective that was never knocked down at all. The pursuit of the self is the pursuit of this non-self, one large enough to hold the necessary losses of a human life.

Second Conclusion

The pursuit of the self is also the pursuit of that part of us that is untouched by our successes and accomplishments. The marriages of relationship and work may bring us tangible outer gains, wonderful sex (at times), children, a house, money, recognition and the ability to help others through our actions, but the marriage with the self is the pursuit of a way of being that is so alive to all the phenomena of existence that it stops distinguishing so much between what is winning and what is losing.

Hard Conclusion

The pursuit of this super-self is difficult exactly because we cannot imagine what it would be like to be beyond winning and losing. In the pursuit of the self we cannot get there from here. We get there to begin with by stopping.

Conclusion on Stopping

Stopping is not passive; stopping allows us to look at the world as if we have seen it for the first time. Stopping stops us from keeping things alive beyond their appointed time. Stopping makes us realize everything is going to disappear, including ourselves, and enables us to stop trying to act as if we were immortal. We begin to realize that disappearance can be as miraculous as appearance. We can also read questions like this one by the poet David Ignatow with some patience and new understanding.

I wish I knew the beauty
Of leaves falling
To whom are we beautiful
As we go?

BOOK FOUR

Engagement: The Dramas and Disappointments Immediately Prior to Marriage

CHAPTER 8

Have Nothing,
Dare Everything

From a swaying railway carriage somewhere between Pitts-
burgh and Chicago, Robert Louis Stevenson wrote a letter to a
friend, saying: "I reached New York Sunday night; and by five
o'clock Monday was under way for the West. It is now about ten
on Wednesday morning, so I have already been about forty
hours in the cars. It is impossible to lie down in them, which
must end by being very wearying. . . ."

It is hard to fathom, looking from our era of fast transcontinen-
tal air travel, that after a full forty hours traveling west, Stevenson
had not yet even reached Chicago. He was traveling as cheaply as
he could and the carriages were crowded, hot and unbearably
uncomfortable. He could barely nod off, and he wrote the above
lines while keeping one tired eye on a neighboring child as the
mother slept and the other, equally tired eye on his writing pad.

He finished the letter with a flourish even as he half wrote,
half babysat in the swaying carriage. "No man is of any use until

he has dared everything," he scrawled at the end. Stevenson's *everything* had nothing to do with money, though he was penniless, and everything to do with his health and happiness. He was daring all in an area where he had little in the way of reserves.

It is not known whether Stevenson had the early stages of tuberculosis or was simply suffering from constantly recurring pleurisy brought on by the contagious fevers of his childhood. But his letters, as he traveled west across the plains, convey a sense of animal spirits and at the same time profound, enervating sickness.

> *What it is to be ill in an emigrant train let those declare who know. I slept none till late in the morning, overcome with laudanum, of which I had luckily a little bottle. All today I have eaten nothing, and only drunk two cups of tea, for each of which, on the pretext that the one was breakfast, and the other dinner, I was charged fifty cents. Our journey is through ghostly deserts, sage, brush and alkali, and rocks, without form or colour, a sad corner of the world. I confess I am not jolly, but mighty calm, in my distresses. My illness is a subject of great mirth to some of my fellow-travellers, and I smile rather sickly at their jests.*

As he looked out of the window in his sickly state, the open spaces of the American West seemed empty, barren and grey. He reached bottom looking out at an infamous stream of stomach-curdling alkali waters that had sickened those who had come this way by covered wagon a generation before. It was as if he were drinking from it himself: "We are going along Bitter

Creek just now, a place infamous in the history of emigration, a place I shall remember myself among the blackest. I hope I may get this posted at Ogden Utah." He did indeed post his letter, and from Ogden, the train wended its slow way through the high barren deserts of Nevada, over the Rockies and down into California and the busy port of San Francisco.

Why come all this way for one woman? Why risk ridicule from his friends (they were not impressed), why endanger his career, his health and ultimately his life? Why dare everything? Why do we see Stevenson's journey as being both crackpot and incredibly emboldening and admirable? It is probably because we recognize in his journey the fact that real courage always takes the form of particularities. It is not courageous to decide to marry in the abstract; it is not brave to find someone generally suitable. In Jane Austen's *Pride and Prejudice*, we are moved by Charlotte Lucas' dire need and not by her courage when she tells Elizabeth Bennet she will marry the awful Mr. Collins.

> *"I see what you are feeling," replied Charlotte,—"you must be surprised, very much surprised,—so lately as Mr. Collins was wishing to marry you. But when you have had time to think it all over, I hope you will be satisfied with what I have done. I am not romantic, you know. I never was. I ask only a comfortable home; and considering Mr. Collins's character, connections, and situation in life, I am convinced that my chance of happiness with him is as fair as most people can boast on entering the marriage state."*

> *Elizabeth quietly answered, "Undoubtedly;"—and*
> *after an awkward pause, they returned to the rest of the*
> *family.*

To marry in the abstract is to marry for form's sake, for money, for security, for an heir to our name, or so that we will not be left in our own irredeemable loneliness. Charlotte Lucas negotiated the future knowing full well what she was doing, carving a life of her own inside Mr. Collins' life. But more often, marriage in the abstract usually leads to a great deal of collateral emotional damage along the way to those who are mere stepping-stones to our ideas about how things should be, especially the person we might have chosen as a mere vehicle for our unacknowledged desires.

Could logic have helped Stevenson at this time? Logic would only have returned him home to look in the abstract. It would say that there were thousands if not tens of thousands of women in the world with whom he could have chosen to marry: plenty of female Mr. Collinses: women in Scotland with a heritage similar to his own; women in England with literary connections, houses, land and money; women especially who were not already married; women who did not have children already; women who could say yes a little sooner in the process and not have him travel an ocean and a continent to find them.

Stevenson's courage lies in the specific recognition of a specific woman in a specific place with no other life than her own, children and all. He had come to this very strange and very specific place to find her. Far inside him lies some internal symmetry to the outer form he sees in her, the form he first recognized with such longing through that lit, evening window in France. He intuits that when those two inner and outer images come together, something extraordinary can happen. At least one thing in the world will be whole.

THE TESTING

In following Stevenson's journey we find ourselves with wonderful troubling specific questions for ourselves. His *dare everything* asks us not only to be courageous in the abstract but also to ask ourselves about specifics. Do I really believe I can get there from here as he did? No money, no job, only the sense he could do it without money, could write his way into his career no matter whether he was traveling or destitute. Or do I believe I need to be a different person, have more money in the bank, a solid writing desk and not move until I have enough in my pocket for first-class travel?

These questions extend into other questions. They serve to put us on watch. For instance, to write, do I really need the perfect studio in which to write in comfort? To fall in love, do I need the perfect person, unencumbered by any other priorities than me? On the subject of the first question, it is astonishing to see the sheer number of letters and manuscript pages of *The Amateur Emigrant* that Stevenson wrote and continued to write through his sickness and heartbreak. He was someone who had an intuitive grasp of that first noble truth my snowy, accidental Tibetan lama friend had studied all his life. There was no getting around suffering; the only question was, Could you still live your life, pursue your love, in the midst of life's determined onslaught?

On the second question, of the perfect unencumbered object of desire, there is something deeply touching about Stevenson's love for a very encumbered, outspoken, older woman who had bouts of prolonged sickness as frequently as he did. This being California to which he travels, we are tempted to run ahead in the story, write the script, make the film and have one of her friends take her firmly by the shoulders and say, "This guy's for real, and he's on his way. What are you waiting for?" The scene could take place on a promontory over the open strait of water where the Golden Gate Bridge now stands. The unbuilt bridge standing for their two as yet untied lives. We must close the scene, however. At this stage, Fanny in her wisdom almost certainly still wanted to wait.

We want to write the script of their meeting that way because there is some deep form of recognition that Stevenson's sincerity is worthy of acceptance or belief. All paths to authenticity lead through the doors of humiliation, and we are impressed by this wild Scotsman's ability to put the taste of absolute, nose-in-the-turf, single-malt humiliation in our mouths. It is this taste of adventured groundedness, this willingness to sacrifice everything for the glimpsed possibility, that is so deeply satisfying about Stevenson. No matter where the path leads him, he follows it, further into the West, further into poverty, further into heartbreak. All the time writing, looking, noting and celebrating through letters to his friends the very latest, most amazing low to which he has sunk.

We are not sure exactly what kind of welcome Stevenson

received when he arrived in San Francisco, but it did indeed bring him to touch an even lower low. If we read between the lines, it seems that Fanny had not yet found the courage to ask for a divorce from her husband, and through her real happiness at Stevenson's arrival she would have no doubt felt enormous guilt at having brought him so far. Her husband was a charismatic, sociable man like Stevenson himself, and though he had supported a mistress for years, we cannot underestimate the hold he had over Fanny, or the enormous power of societal shame and reproof that surrounded divorce at that time. Divorce is a difficult personal door to go through at any time; it is hard to imagine adding the sense of being a fallen woman and the way that would redound on her children to the emotional difficulties she would have to encounter in any case, on making the separation.

Stevenson's anticlimactic arrival serves to encourage us to make clear distinctions about different stages of an engagement. An engagement may be official and trumpeted to the world or unofficial and underground, unable to fully speak its name, like Stevenson's declaration of intent, but every serious engagement brings its participants beyond the original private understanding to the threshold of a crucial public testing.

The early stage of a commitment may take spontaneous daring, but this spontaneity must just as spontaneously end and be replaced by the necessity for a different and more sober form of courage, more adapted to the long haul. As we will see later in Jane Austen's life, the acceptance of a proposal, or a delay in acceptance, plunges both sides into a more rigorous examination of what is being offered or withheld from each party. In a strange way it opens each side to the underbelly of the relationship, the essential aloneness of an individual, no matter the outer committed state. Perhaps we are visiting the particular *kind* of aloneness we will experience in the relationship, and finding out in detail whether it is one we can live with.

Stevenson took off into the hills south of Monterey to leave Fanny alone, to lick his wounds and no doubt to try to get a little perspective. He camped out under the trees, marveling at the landscape of the Santa Lucia Mountains and the waters of Monterey Bay in the distance. The journey to get to this point, however, had taken whatever strength he had and his last disappointment had probably siphoned off the rest. He fell into a semi-comatose state, barely able to look after himself in the wilds. In this semi-delirious state he was found by two goat farmers, who recognized the seriousness of his condition and, almost against his will, took him in.

> *I was pretty near slain: my spirit lay down and kicked for three days; I was up at an Angora goat ranch in the Santa Lucia mountains, nursed by an old frontiersman, a mighty hunter of bears, and I scarcely slept, or ate, or thought for four days. Two nights I lay out under a tree in a sort of stupor, doing nothing but fetch water for myself and horse, light a fire and make coffee, and all night awake hearing the goat-bells ringing and the tree frogs singing when each new noise was enough to set me mad. Then the bear hunter came round, pronounced me "real sick" and ordered me up to the ranch. . . . One is an old bear-hunter, seventy-two years old, and a cap-*

tain from the Mexican war; the other a pilgrim, and one who was out with the bear flag and under Fremont when California was taken by the States. They are both true frontiersmen, and most kind and pleasant. Captain Smith, the bear-hunter, is my physician, and I obey him like an oracle.

It was an odd miserable piece of my life and according to all rule, it should have been my deathbed but after a while my spirit got up again in a divine frenzy, and has since kicked and spurred my vile body forward with great emphasis and success.

This encounter with mortality seems but a mere interlude to Stevenson, who cannot help himself but follow this near-death experience with the real point. "My new book, *The Amateur Emigrant*, is about half drafted. I don't know if it will be good, but I think it ought to sell in spite of the [devil] and the publishers; for it tells an odd enough experience, and one, I think, never yet told before."

But one experience about which he was telling very little in his letters had to do with his relationship with Fanny. He probably found it difficult to know himself how the future would fall for them both and he would have been constrained by a natural nineteenth-century reluctance to speak to others about a private relationship. Stevenson decided to make the best of his life as he had found it in this odd corner of the world, and became a part of the fledgling Monterey community for a while, writing for the local paper, hanging out with the good ol' boys in the saloon and nursing himself back to health with the aid of a local doctor.

October saw him moving to San Francisco, no doubt to be nearer Fanny, though she was still across the as yet unbridged bay in Oakland. October also brought him nearer to penury. He rented digs in the city and lived on increasingly little through the winter while he wrote. His daily budget at one time dropped to forty-five cents a day, his letters to friends in the British Isles were rarely answered, and his orbit between bouts of writing and sickness was reduced to a daily walk to a coffee shop, where he ate carefully and drank sparingly on his meager outlay.

Stevenson's claustrophobic immersion in a poverty-stricken daily round in the streets of San Francisco reminds us of the way most relationships seem to have a testing, hermetic period before any final public commitment. As if we must become engaged not only to the sense of togetherness in the future relationship, but also to an early sense of solitude and loneliness that can lie at the center of even the happiest marriage. It is as if a sense of trial is a necessary human ingredient to any committed life to come. This trial seems to be necessary not only in the puritanical sense of being seen to earn the object of the quest, but also in a purifying sense of being stripped down to some kind of essence which we must visit and stay in for a long period. In this immersion it is as if we are building a memory bank for the future, a memory of how much we wanted the marriage in the first place and of exactly how we felt when we wanted it. It may be that we need to have this prior solitary confrontation with commitment so that we can keep close to something that, in the future of an ordinary, taken-for-granted married day, we can remember something we might be in danger of losing.

Fanny must have also been distilling some essence of her relationship with Stevenson. The evidence says she was certainly going through a form of emotional breakdown herself. Breakdown or not, if she was like most of us, she would be rehearsing in her mind what it would take to send him back to Scotland and leave her to her familiar misery, while simultaneously going through her speech to her husband declaring she was leaving him and his mistress forever. Perhaps, in her private rehearsal room she was practicing to see which part she might like to play for the rest of her life.

Many engagements that seem to proceed to the altar with barely a ripple to disturb the surface arrangements can be fraught with self-doubt underneath: the handwritten vellum invitations hiding panicked feelings of entrapment or the not-to-be-looked-at possibility of having taken a wrong turn. My own sister waited until the church was booked, the reception arranged, the flowers ordered and dozens of presents had arrived at the door before announcing to a startled world that it was all off, she had changed her mind, she didn't want to marry the man. I was aghast at the time, not with the minor scandal, but with her absolute, unblinking courage in the face of money spent, relatives astonished, flowers withering and mounds of presents to send back. I am sure if she had only come to the decision halfway down the aisle she would have turned around and told everyone to stop gawping and go home. They breed them that way in Yorkshire. True to herself, she changed her mind again two years later and married the same man with no regrets, no doubt much surer of what she was doing, though I am sure not without some tension in the groom and the assembled guests as to whether the ceremony would reach its natural conclusion.

The nearer we get to the actual time of commitment, the nearer our private hopes and imaginings are to being examined in public. In a strange kind of internal parallel, we start to make our thoughts and doubts on the matter more conscious to ourselves. Stevenson, the future author of *The Strange Case of Dr. Jekyll and Mr. Hyde,* must have gone through both the light and dark of his sentiments toward Fanny and marriage many times. In many ways, as these doubts and questioning voices become louder, we have to hold tightly and unremittingly to the unspoken vow to which we are bound.

THE WORLD'S WARNINGS

Since one of the other core competencies of human beings, beside constantly worrying, is giving unasked-for advice to others, each of us on the threshold of commitment is surrounded by a swirl of warnings, advice and rules to follow around the public act of marrying. This is always distressing to the lovers involved who see themselves part of a unique universe of private affection untouched by the general experience of others. There is always at this point a rising sense of disquiet about the way a privately held love becomes the subject of public speculation.

As we approach marriage we find we become a kind of public property, open to other people's thoughts on a relationship we feel they know nothing about. We can look down on Stevenson as he makes his way from tiny apartment on Bush Street to humble restaurant on Powell Street. He thinks he is alone, but as he walks, we see him as but one of a long line of people holding hidden, unspoken hopes for marriage. We imagine Fanny Osbourne, across the bay in Oakland, wondering if all marriages are equally as unhappy as her first one. As each of them comes to ground in the reality of their situation, they are faced with the particular practicalities surrounding their future together. They would have inherited from human history a long list of warnings and public pronouncements on the matter of marriage.

Below, a selection of warnings to those who wish to marry, written before Stevenson's time and after, followed by a single note of encouragement.

WARNINGS TO STEVENSON

Those marriages generally abound most with love and constancy that are preceded by a long courtship.

JOSEPH ADDISON, *The Spectator*, December 29, 1711

Men marry because they are tired; women because they are curious. Both are disappointed.

OSCAR WILDE, *A Woman of No Importance, 1893*

I have always considered marriage as the most interesting event of one's life, the foundation of happiness or misery.

GEORGE WASHINGTON, May 23, 1785

All tragedies are finished by a death, all comedies by a marriage.

LORD BYRON, *Don Juan, 1819*

Love is blind, but marriage restores its sight.

GEORGE C. LICHTENBERG

Let men tremble to win the hand of woman, unless they win along with it the utmost passion of her heart.

NATHANIEL HAWTHORNE, *The Scarlet Letter*

WARNINGS TO FANNY

Any one must see at a glance that if men and women marry those whom they do not love, they must love those whom they do not marry.

HARRIET MARTINEAU

When poverty comes through the door, love flies out the window.

ANONYMOUS ENGLISH SAYING

If you are afraid of loneliness, don't marry.

ANTON CHEKHOV

Keep your eyes wide open before marriage, half shut afterwards.

BENJAMIN FRANKLIN

Before marriage, a man will lie awake all night thinking about something you said; after marriage, he'll fall asleep before you finish saying it.

HELEN ROLAND

The total amount of undesired sex endured by women is probably greater in marriage than in prostitution.

BERTRAND RUSSELL, *Marriage and Morals*

WARNINGS TO BOTH
FANNY AND STEVENSON

Love, the strongest and deepest element in all life, the harbinger of hope, of joy, of ecstasy; love, the defier of all laws, of all conventions; love, the freest, the most powerful molder of human destiny; how can such an all-compelling force be synonymous with that poor little State and Church begotten weed, marriage?

EMMA GOLDMAN, *Anarchism and Other Essays*

To tie together by human law what God has tied together by passion, is about as wise as it would be to chain the moon to the earth lest the natural attraction existing between them should not be sufficient to prevent them flying asunder.

HERBERT SPENCER, *An Autobiography*

It is not a lack of love, but a lack of friendship that makes unhappy marriages.

FRIEDRICH NIETZSCHE

Courtship to marriage is a very witty prologue to a very dull Play.

WILLIAM CONGREVE, *The Old Bachelor*

TONGUE-IN-CHEEK WARNING

Happiness in marriage is entirely a matter of chance. If the dispositions of the parties are ever so well known to each other or ever so similar beforehand, it does not advance their felicity in the least. They always continue to grow sufficiently unlike afterwards to have their share of vexation; and it is better to know as little as possible of the defects of the person with whom you are to pass your life.

CHARLOTTE LUCAS in Jane Austen's *Pride and Prejudice*

WARNING FROM STEVENSON TO HIMSELF IN AN ESSAY HE HAS NOT YET WRITTEN

Marriage is like life in this—that it is a field of battle, and not a bed of roses.

ROBERT LOUIS STEVENSON, "Virginibus Puerisque"

SINGLE NOTE OF ENCOURAGEMENT
AND SUPPORT TO MARRIAGE;
WRITTEN IN THE NEXT CENTURY BY
SOMEONE NEVER ALLOWED TO ENTER
THAT STATE BECAUSE HE WAS GAY

Like everything which is not the involuntary result of
fleeting emotion but the creation of time and will, any
marriage, happy or unhappy, is infinitely more
interesting than any romance, however passionate.

W. H. AUDEN

A WAY ACROSS THE BAY

Stevenson's sense of being trapped by present outward circumstances was always leavened by a sense that there was a bridge
somewhere across to the other side, which as yet he could not
see. This motif of escape by finding a hidden pathway appears
again and again in Stevenson's later fiction, and an allegorical
version of this time in San Francisco seems to appear in *Kidnapped*, written five years later. Stevenson's abducted hero,
David Balfour, is shipwrecked off the west coast of Scotland. He
can barely swim and struggles ashore on the small island of
Erraid. Though he can see the main island of Mull and houses
and turf smoke across the small strait, he is too wary of the
depth of the sea and the power of the currents to cross the short

body of water to safety. He spends four days on the island wondering why the passing local Gaelic fishermen only laugh and shout at him in incomprehensible Gaelic, refusing to pull in to take him to safety.

All the ingredients of Stevenson's time in San Francisco seem to be accurately represented: near starvation, ever-present sickness, the sense of isolation with Fanny so near and yet so far just across the bay, the constant walking backward and forward, the incomprehension of the locals and finally, even a hole in his pocket through which his money had drained. All of this combining to remind him how far he was from his rightful inheritance as the son of a wealthy Scottish family.

> *It seemed impossible that I should be left to die on the shores of my own country, and within view of a church-tower and the smoke of men's houses. But the second day passed; and though as long as the light lasted I kept a bright lookout for boats on the Sound or men passing on the Ross, no help came near me. It still rained, and I turned in to sleep, as wet as ever, and with a cruel sore throat, but a little comforted, perhaps, by having said goodnight to my next neighbours, the people of Iona. . . .*
>
> *Not that ever I stayed in one place, save when asleep, my misery giving me no rest. Indeed, I wore myself down with continual and aimless goings and comings in the rain.*
>
> *. . . A little after, as I was jumping about after my limpets, I was startled by a guinea-piece, which fell upon a*

rock in front of me and glanced off into the sea. . . . I
carried my gold loose in a pocket with a button. I now saw
there must be a hole, and clapped my hand to the place in
a great hurry. But this was to lock the stable door after the
steed was stolen. I had left the shore at Queensferry with
near on fifty pounds; now I found no more than two guin-
ea-pieces and a silver shilling.

It is true I picked up a third guinea a little after, where
it lay shining on a piece of turf. That made a fortune
of three pounds and four shillings, English money, for a
lad, the rightful heir of an estate, and now starving on an
isle at the extreme end of the wild Highlands. . . .

This state of my affairs dashed me still further; and,
indeed my plight on that third morning was truly pitiful.
My clothes were beginning to rot; my stockings in partic-
ular were quite worn through, so that my shanks went
naked; my hands had grown quite soft with the continual
soaking; my throat was very sore, my strength had much
abated, and my heart so turned against the horrid stuff I
was condemned to eat, that the very sight of it came near
to sicken me.

But on the fourth day, our marooned hero sees a local fishing
boat once more heading his way. He dares not allow himself to
hope they are coming for him, but eventually he cannot help
himself and runs toward the boat. The fishermen do not come
ashore to take him off, but in their attempts to communicate
with him he finally discerns a shouted word in Gaelic he can

recognize. *Tragh*, tide. They are pointing toward the other end of the island and he realizes at once what a fool he has been. He is on a tidal islet, and they are telling him he could have walked off at low tide anytime over the last four days. He charges across to the other side of the island to find that the stretch of water is now a small trickle through which he can wade.

A sea-bred boy would not have stayed a day on Erraid; which is only what they call a tidal islet, and except in the bottom of the neaps, can be entered and left twice in every twenty-four hours, either dry-shod, or at the most by wading. Even I, who had the tide going out and in before me in the bay, and even watched for the ebbs, the better to get my shellfish—even I (I say) if I had sat down to think, instead of raging at my fate, must have soon guessed the secret, and got free. It was no wonder the fishers had not understood me. The wonder was rather that they had ever guessed my pitiful illusion, and taken the trouble to come back. I had starved with cold and hunger on that island for close upon one hundred hours. But for the fishers, I might have left my bones there, in pure folly. And even as it was, I had paid for it pretty dear, not only in past sufferings, but in my present case; being clothed like a beggarman, scarce able to walk, and in great pain of my sore throat.

I have seen wicked men and fools, a great many of both; and I believe they both get paid in the end; but the fools first.

Stevenson asks us not to rage against our fate but to look at the tidal flow of events surrounding us with a keen eye. Only those who put more energy into self-pity than into paying attention are truly marooned.

It is an encouragement to think of Stevenson's increasingly concentrated bearing down on the single issue of marriage to Fanny. He is demonstrating what most human beings recognize as implicit faith. A faith all the more admirable for the isolation, poverty and ill health to which it had condemned him. But Stevenson had an eternal and internal sense that something was always around the corner. It was an irrepressible optimism that even Fanny would have cause to complain about later. He saw these difficulties not as unending but more as a conundrum to be solved, a certain geography through which you had to navigate to escape imprisoning circumstances. There was a bridge across to the other side; it was just a matter of time before he found it.

Sobering Conclusion

We may be gladly abducted by our enthusiasm in the early stages of a relationship, but in a full sober assessment of what we have committed *to*, we almost always come to feel as if we have actually been *kidnapped* by circumstances. The sense of being trapped, we realize, is also a presentiment of what is to come, and something we must learn how to live with. The time of engagement, official or not, is a time for serious questions and sometimes a serious falling-out. How did we get to this point? Is there a way out of the quarrel and into the marriage? Is there a way out of the engagement and the marriage altogether? Is this the right man or woman for me? Our previous life lies in ruins or is about to be reduced to its foundations.

Before our consecrated togetherness, we each find ourselves on a kind of Magic Island of aloneness, experiencing the first pangs and the first difficulties we will encounter in the marriage itself. Being tempted to pull out, to send back the presents, to run screaming in the opposite direction is an entirely appropriate dynamic. The coming to ground, the necessary self-examination, will either give us a good realistic foundation for the marriage to come or bring us to our senses and allow us to escape from the misery that lies ahead.

Conclusion on Stevenson's Admirable Lack of Balance

Stevenson does not try to balance his writing with his pursuit of Fanny. They are both nonnegotiable; they occur in parallel and feed each other. Stevenson can no more stop writing or stop loving Fanny than he can cut off his own right arm.

Through all his trials and tribulations, in sickness and

in health, he keeps writing; in fact, one of the difficult facts about Stevenson for Fanny, the mother of two children, with no means of supporting herself, was that she would be marrying a writer who at the time was not a success. Stevenson's honesty in the relationship came through his cheerful insistence in refusing to hide this fact, in effect saying it is a writer who has fallen in love with you and it is a writer who will marry you, will you accept me? His lack of hiding or subterfuge is indicative of an admirable sense of integrity.

Though he may be daring everything and indeed losing everything for this first marriage, he refuses to lose his commitment to not only his work marriage but also his marriage to his self.

Stevenson's marriage with the self glows most forcibly through his relationship to death. He is not afraid to risk all in living an uncompromising conversation with the future. He is courageous enough to risk himself in that ultimate conversation with his own disappearance. Though he is knocked down by the waves of circumstances, he keeps getting up again, looking for the gap opening steadily between disasters and ready for the path across the waters to Fanny.

Conclusion on Risk

What we see as risk and foolhardiness on the outside can seem more like a constant cohesive drive on the inside that holds to priorities that cannot be discerned by others because they reside in a far too private chamber of personal experience to be shared easily. To dare everything is not necessarily to travel off, but often the opposite, to have faith in a foundation you have discovered in life and which, though it is difficult to describe, even to yourself, you refuse to relinquish.

CHAPTER 9

Jane Austen:
Despite All

ENGAGING WITH WORK THROUGH
DIFFICULTY, DOUBT AND DISTRACTION

Sometimes the choices we make around relationships and work seem to have no choice in them at all. Each of us grapples with forces far larger than our goals or ourselves: each of us wrestles with our family inheritance, our educational possibilities, the lucky or unlucky DNA that ordains our health and, especially, the fateful time in history into which we were born.

There are other powers we like to forget. Nature can be a deadly arbiter of our future, independent of our human need to plan. Nature's winds can drive us out of a city, destroy our schools and undermine a health system for years to come. A tsunami can devastate a thousand miles of coastline, and constant rain may inundate half a nation. As human beings, we have a necessary conceit about our own ability to influence events. The truth about our own modest contribution might immobilize us: much easier then, to tell ourselves a story about how much we make our own reality. The United States, that supposed bedrock home of upward mobility, is actually one of the developed industrial nations where people are most likely to live and die in the class to which they were born. We are creatures who like to believe our own publicity, and we do not like to face powers that can easily surpass and encompass our best hopes. We hope always for a free pass to circumvent forces that humble us on a daily basis.

Although we can never escape these overarching powers and difficulties, it can be instructive to look to those who have made sense of their life or their work in the midst of overwhelming circumstances, circumstances where we would have every reason either not to try or to look the other way and pretend they did not exist.

Shakespeare's sonnet 64 is unstintingly courageous in this regard: it demonstrates the kind of courage needed to look the leveled World Trade Center towers in the eye, to survey a devastated New Orleans or to say goodbye for the last time in the face of a loved one's death.

> *When I have seen by Time's fell hand defaced*
> *The rich-proud cost of outworn buried age;*
> *When sometime lofty towers I see down-razed*
> *And brass eternal slave to mortal rage;*
> *When I have seen the hungry ocean gain*
> *Advantage on the kingdom of the shore,*

And the firm soil win of the watery main,
Increasing store with loss, and loss with store;
When I have seen such interchange of state,
Or state it self confounded to decay,
Ruin hath taught me thus to ruminate
That Time will come and take my love away.
This thought is as a death which cannot choose
But weep to have, that which it fears to lose.

We do not need to understand the meaning of every line, we do not need to know that Shakespeare is standing among stately funeral monuments, where even the solid brass depicting the noble dead is worn by age, to know he is looking at the passing of all he loves and all he wishes to preserve. Shakespeare's ability to face death does not have to depress us; it might make us want to work less and spend more time with a daughter; to walk out of the house and into the fields while we still have the legs, the breath and the ability to do so. Sonnet 64 looks at the need to catch the tide while the tide is in and travel out with it as it ebbs. There is no other choice of course. Sonnet 64 looks at forces greater than the human mind can countenance. There is nothing personal about death taking us away; it is simply the ebb and flow of a tide beyond human understanding. But Shakespeare's full appreciation of the unremitting nature of time brings us alive to both the vulnerabilities and opportunities of the present.

But weep to have, that which it fears to lose.

We weep to have what we most fear to lose. All the most precious things in a human life are the very things to which we find it most difficult to make ourselves vulnerable and open. To feel a joy in life is also to know it is fleeting and will pass beyond our grasp. Best, then, not to make ourselves vulnerable in the first place, to protect ourselves by looking for neither the consummation of our hopes nor their raw disappointment. Best to be just a provider to a daughter so as not to feel later, as she grows away, as Shakespeare said again, in *Hamlet,* "the pangs of disprized love." Best not to look life's possible losses full in the face. Best to live in a bland middle that knows nothing of either.

It is difficult at first to put Jane Austen's novels in the same category of courageous confrontation as Shakespeare's unblinking sonnets and tempting to think that she looked mainly out of life's bland middle, especially life's bland middle class. Yet a close understanding of her life and the books that came out of that life find her looking straight at those portions of life to which she was most vulnerable; which frequently overwhelmed her and which prevented her from obtaining many of the states of existence she dearly wanted: love, courtship, engagement and marriage.

These overwhelming powers were problematic not only for Jane Austen but for numberless other women of her day, rendered helpless by a lack of money, authority and personal power. She lived in a time when the circumstances of an individual woman's life could completely overwhelm any sense of personal will or volition; a time when it was much easier to be rendered powerless by a sudden disappearance into a man's life or a child's life than to find a place to make a stand, a work or a life. But she also lived in a time when all of these dynamics were coming to light and being examined and spoken about out loud, almost for the first time.

JANE AUSTEN QUOTE ABOUT HISTORY

The quarrels of popes and kings, with wars and pestilences in every page; the men all so good for nothing and hardly any women at all—it is very tiresome.

Though Jane Austen never entered into a physical marriage, she was wedded in a powerful imaginative way to the minutiae of a woman's everyday experience and especially the way a woman besieged by those minutiae could, with a step-by-step courage, find a life she could call her own.

Jane Austen never did marry. Why does that statement call for such reflexive pity? It carries a different meaning if we follow it up: *Jane Austen never did marry, and therefore she was given the time and perspective to produce books as well written as those by anyone who ever lived.*

There is a general human intuition that if marriage is refused in practical, physical terms it must then be lived out imaginatively. A Catholic sister, taking religious vows, refuses marriage to a man but says she is married *in Christ.* We constantly speak of being married to a job, to the mob, to an idea of the future. Saying yes to one subtler form of marriage, we are understood to have said no to the other, more obvious one.

The refusal can be less dramatic than religious vows. A woman may be married to her art, her dogs, her peace and quiet or her sense of independence over the demands of actual physical commitment to another person. Marriage to another person may rightly be refused forever or for a time, in order to keep open other possibilities. Possibilities perhaps for a way of being in the world, and out of that way of being, a way of doing certain work that marriage, with its close physical and emotional commitments, would not allow.

Often, the refusal to marry on the surface happens without our conscious consent. We think we want the outer marriage, but all the time our behavior is telling us, and the world, that we actually want something different from what our society demands we take so gladly. We seem frustrated on the surface, but from another perspective, other opportunities are beckoning. The pressure to fall into marriage can be immense and unconscious and is not necessarily suited to us as particular individuals. We live in the midst of currents and pressures that are immense in guiding our expectations toward certain norms that may be good for humankind in general but deadly for us as specific individuals.

JANE AUSTEN QUOTE ABOUT MARRIAGE

Human nature is so well disposed toward those in interesting situations, that a young person, who either marries or dies, is sure to be kindly spoken of.

Death was perhaps the only alternative. For a young middle-class woman like Jane Austen coming of age in the 1790s, the whole of her surrounding social conversation was geared toward one thing: the hoped-for *marriage*. Work and career for a woman of her class were inconceivable: inheritance descended through the male line, money was doled out to unmarried female members of any family reluctantly, if at all. Any money was hard to come by in the first place. The incredible choice of careers and multiplicity of endeavors that today, we take for granted; and for which we can be well paid, simply did not exist at that time. Most streams of money came from agricultural rents; belonged within jealous, watchful families and were passed from generation to generation. Capital of any kind was so rare and hard to come by it was almost worshipped, and was almost never spent, but its interest was used to support houses, marriages and children, who were in turn to keep it sacrosanct for the next generation.

JANE AUSTEN QUOTE ABOUT THE ABOVE

People always seem to live forever when there is an annuity to be paid to them.

There was not just a pressure to marry then but to marry well; to marry someone, not necessarily with opportunities in an unspecified future, but with a guaranteed inherited income. No wonder Jane Austen's first lines in *Pride and Prejudice* became instantly famous.

JANE AUSTEN'S MOST FAMOUS QUOTE

It is a truth universally acknowledged, that a single man in possession of a good fortune must be in want of a wife.

However little known the feelings or views of such a man may be on his first entering a neighbourhood, this truth is so well fixed in the minds of the surrounding families, that he is considered as the rightful property of some one or other of their daughters.

Jane Austen's tongue-in-cheek assessment of a rich prospect arriving in the neighborhood cannot hide the sheer acquisitive aggression that would have accompanied being introduced to such a man. In such circumstances Jane would have found herself with not only her own hopes on display but also those of her family and relations, and must have wondered at times how to separate them.

Our image of Jane Austen is often influenced by her stately appraisal of others' behavior—the way she chronicles and choreographs her characters' movements through relationship and engagement with minute detail. It is surprising, then, that in Jane's early letters to her sister, Cassandra, we find an almost giddy sense of excitement about the prospect of balls, social gatherings and the opportunity for rampant, if tongue-in-cheek, flirtation.

JANE AUSTEN QUOTE ON GETTING
TO KNOW SOMEONE

*It is not time or opportunity that is to determine intimacy;
it is disposition alone. Seven years would be insufficient to
make some people acquainted with each other, and seven
days are more than enough for others.*

But there was one eligible stranger who came into the neighborhood who stood out in particular, and whose disposition Jane found immediately attractive: Tom Lefroy, a quiet, serious graduate of Trinity College, Dublin, who came to stay with his aunt, Jane's friend and mentor Anne Lefroy. He was known to have a "kind disposition and affectionate heart" but he was also a man of long and diffident silences that Jane seemed to have found strangely attractive and a perfect foil for her quick and lively mind. It was said at the time that Jane made all the moves, but the relationship does not seem to have been all one-way, as there are memories of a sudden visit by him, which surprised Jane. There is also note of a long private conversation about the risqué and erotically charged novel *Tom Jones* that must have been full of possible signs and portents for both of them.

Readers of Jane Austen will be familiar with the assiduous way in which her female characters add up the mounting evidence that an offer of marriage is about to be made. In the run-up to a ball, after which Tom would go back to Dublin, Jane was so sure of Tom's intent that she wrote to her sister: "I rather expect to receive an offer. . . ." She covered up the out-loudness-of-it-all only by saying, "But I shall refuse him unless he promises to give away his white coat."

Jane had no possibility of changing Tom's habits of dress; his aunt Anne Lefroy, though a close friend of Jane's, spirited him out of harm's way. Tom was the great hope of dozens of poorer Lefroy relations who hoped to rise with him into his glittering legal future. Anne Lefroy knew that in their eyes, Jane was a perfect nobody, bringing little in the way of dowry or prestige; the Lefroy family would be scandalized at the match. Too much was at stake to allow mere love and affection to undermine it.

JANE AUSTEN QUOTE
SHOWING HER DEPTH OF FEELING

At length the day is come on which I am to flirt my last with Tom Lefroy and when you receive this it will be over. My tears flow at the melancholy idea.

Looking back over Jane Austen's life, we see in Tom's appearance and disappearance, a high-water mark of her prospects in marriage. Her letters from then on show a gradual acknowledgment of her increasingly slighter prospects for a match.

JANE AUSTEN QUOTE
SHOWING LACK OF SELF-PITY,
DESPITE PREVIOUSLY FLOWING TEARS

Next week I shall begin my operations on my hat, on which you know my principal hopes of happiness depend.

Looking back over her life, we can also be thankful from our perspective that Jane was able to work not only on her hat but on her novels. There is little chance we would have a word of her in print had she gone off and married the then young, but, we are sad to hear, soon to become very boring Tom Lefroy. There is also little doubt that a marriage with a man would have smothered the second very important marriage with her work.

A DIFFERENT CONSUMMATION

Had Jane Austen married Tom Lefroy, we might very well be living in a world in which *Pride and Prejudice* would never have seen the light of day. We would be without the scintillating, intelligent vivacity of an Elizabeth Bennet and the smoldering, aristocratic eroticism of a Darcy and his unfathomable wealth. We might be unable to recognize an obnoxious Mr. Collins when we see one, or the snobby condescension of a Lady Catherine de Bourgh.

JANE AUSTEN OBNOXIOUS MR. COLLINS
QUOTE AFTER ELIZABETH BENNET'S
REFUSAL OF HIS HAND IN MARRIAGE

You must give me leave to flatter myself that your refusal of my addresses is merely words. . . . My reasons for believing it are briefly these:—It does not appear to me that the establishment I can offer would be any other than highly desirable; and you should take it into farther consideration that in spite of your manifold attractions, it is by no means certain that another offer of marriage may ever be made you. Your portion is unhappily so small that it will in all likelihood undo the effects of your loveliness and amiable qualifications. As I must therefore conclude that you are not serious in your rejection of me, I shall chuse to attribute it to your wish of increasing my love by suspense, according to the usual practice of elegant females.

Besides her appetite for comic relief, in all her novels, we would be bereft, of a particularly fierce examination of human foibles put to the test in marriage and relationship. Women of the nineteenth century would certainly have lost a powerful spokeswoman for the enormous emotional and physical costs and humiliations of being born into their sex. We do not know how many innumerable Elizabeth Bennets have recognized themselves in her pages since that time and gained confidence in their choices because of it.

JANE AUSTEN QUOTE TO INSPIRE
THE INDEPENDENCE OF THE FUTURE
ELIZABETH BENNETS OF THIS WORLD

You are very kind in planning presents for me to make, and my mother has shown me exactly the same attention; but as I do not choose to have generosity dictated to me, I shall not resolve on giving my cabinet to Anna till the first thought of it has been my own.

Without Jane Austen's depiction of feminine self-preservation, Hollywood would be poorer, publishers would certainly be poorer, but we all would be unknowingly impoverished without *Pride and Prejudice, Sense and Sensibility, Emma, Mansfield Park* and *Persuasion.* In short, we should be very happy that Jane Austen had no first marriage that might have given her a temporary conjugal happiness but then dissipated her powers to work and influence the future fate of her sex.

We must also pause to reflect that we would also be disappointed if she had not put the powerful, concentrated sense of disappointment at not marrying and the imaginative sense of what she might be missing, into her novels.

Upon the whole, therefore, she found, what has been sometimes been found before, that an event to which she had been looking with impatient desire did not, in taking place, bring all the satisfaction she had promised herself.

It was consequently necessary to name some other period for the commencement of actual felicity—to have some other point on which her wishes and hopes might be fixed, and by again enjoying the pleasure of anticipation, console herself for the present, and prepare for another disappointment. . . .

In marriage, it was the familiar, eternal fate of a woman not only to have her life and art smothered by the priorities of a man, but also to experience the consequences of constant childbearing and the complete subjugation of her own time and thoughts to the rearing of children and the running of a house. Certainly we know that Tom Lefroy turned into a somewhat tedious, somewhat self-righteous, high court judge (an inescapable fate of all judges) and pillar of Dublin society in later years. Perhaps Jane might have goaded him out of that fate, but most likely she would have done it to the detriment of her work as a writer.

As it was, Jane Austen was to spend enough years in exile from her writing through the natural twists and turns of her own life. Once her household tasks were done, her single life may have given her some freedom to write, but she was still, as a single unmarried woman, in the thrall of her parents. One other day that marked Jane Austen's life, besides the one that saw the disappearance of Tom Lefroy, was the day she came home to find that her parents had decided to forsake her childhood home and move them all, with or without Jane's consent, to the distant, fashionable city of Bath.

The village of Steventon that Jane was forced to leave was

everything Bath was not: quiet, spacious, deeply communal, familiar, and close to well-loved wooded paths and fields. Bath was bare stone surfaces, outward slightly faded glitter, posturing and more of that jostling, aggressive maneuvering for marriage of which Jane did not need reminding. As a writer, she fell as silent in that confined city exile as she might have done in a busy, childbearing marriage. It was only after eight long years, first in Bath and then Southampton that fate swept her back to the Hampshire countryside and she could begin to write again.

She had been forced to negotiate one other last traumatic difficulty in order to clear the way for a real engagement with her work. The negotiation began with a first yes that was a yes to a surprising proposal of marriage, followed by a final courageous and necessary no that closed the door to marriage forever and prepared the way for the life and work for which we remember her.

It is instructive to see how much of Jane Austen's work had to do with acute observation. She teaches us to see and hear and to understand the undercurrents and crosscurrents that often contradict a surface meaning. She is constantly moving from depth to surface and back again. Between the surface of life and its depths she looks at the way we also constantly search for symmetries of completion in love and marriage. Elizabeth Bennet sees in Darcy the outer representation of something she finally agrees she wants to make complete inside herself. Yet, as Jane Austen was at great pains to tell us, the inner shape of the character we seek is not often represented in its outer form. Yet a woman will seek and find, seek and find, will be discerning or not, will marry happily or tragically. All the time drawn by a flame she has fed herself. Her future happiness depends on how much the desired outer form is balanced by an internal counter image she has established inside her, how much faith she has in her own judgment. How will she be able to discern that symmetry inside herself and then find it inside another, how much can she see beneath the surface?

JANE AUSTEN QUOTE ON EXTERNAL AND INTERNAL SYMMETRIES

Vanity and pride are different things, though the words are often used synonymously. A person may be proud without being vain. Pride relates more to our opinion of ourselves, vanity to what we would have others think of us.

In 1802, at twenty-seven, in the sunset of her eligibility for marriage, visiting from Bath and staying at the grand country residence of nearby family friends, Jane Austen was shocked by a sudden and disturbing proposal of marriage from the son and future heir of the stately house.

Harris Bigg-Wither was not an impressive sight; six years her junior, he shambled about the house, hardly daring to make eye contact. Even more seriously, he had almost no conversation, never mind the witty, rapid exchanges Jane was used to with her sister. Somehow he brought himself to propose. She was aghast, but she could not easily say no. Describing herself long past romantic notions of marriage, there was much to be said in the way of mutual advantage. She would be mistress of an imposing residence, with any future money worries cleared away. She could, like Charlotte Lucas in *Pride and Prejudice*, probably create separate living quarters. To be a spinster, after all, was to be irrelevant and disappear from others' eyes.

JANE AUSTEN QUOTE ON THE FEAR OF SOCIAL DISAPPEARANCE

Everybody around her was gay and busy, prosperous and important; each had their object of interest, their part, their dress, their favourite scene, their friends and confederates. . . . She alone was sad and insignificant; she had no share in anything; she might go or stay; she might be in the midst of their noise, or retreat from it to the solitude of the East Room, without being seen or missed.

In an earlier private letter, lamenting the lack of opportunity for women at that time, she had said there was "nothing more to be pitied in the world than an old unmarried woman of little means." In the vulnerability of simply being wanted, she said yes. She must have gone away from Bigg-Wither wondering what she had done. After perhaps the worst night of her life, awake for hours alone, then waking her sister to talk it over, she summoned the strength to go back and say no. There followed a sense of scandal, shame, embarrassment, and a swift collective leave-taking from a house to which they could not now return.

One of the greatest and most discerning minds with regard to the perils of hasty marriage, the woman who would later write *Emma* as a kind of literate warning to other young undiscerning women, had got it very wrong, caught herself and pulled back from the very brink.

JANE AUSTEN QUOTE
TO HER SISTER, CASSANDRA

To be so bent on marriage—to persue a man merely for the sake of situation—is a sort of thing that shocks me; I cannot understand it. Poverty is a great evil, but to a woman of education and feeling it ought not, it cannot be the greatest. . . .

One can only imagine, at that brink, the sense of dread she must have had in the pit of her stomach. The sense of absolute entrapment we all have experienced when we commit to something to which we cannot ultimately belong, and realize from that moment on time will begin inexorably to slide right by us. The consequences of a wrong marriage are understood in our literature, our mythologies and our personal biographies to be enormous. It is not only the entrapment of being with the wrong person, but the sense of another possible parallel life slipping away while we are occupied with a person and a life we know is not good for us.

Bigg-Wither does not seem to have been unduly disturbed. He married two years later and managed to keep the wife he found very busy by producing a family of ten children—a parallel life that Jane Austen, despite some parallel regrets, would not have wished on herself.

But in many ways, the years in Bath and Southampton, away from the Hampshire countryside, were like an interminable and unhappy marriage with the wrong person. As many of us do not need telling, prolonged unhappiness is not a passive state but one in which our best energies and strengths are slowly eroded by a constant emotional toll. The exile did finally come to an end. The family returned to Hampshire, but without their father who had passed away in Bath. Once Jane was firmly ensconced with her mother and sister in a comparatively spacious house owned by her wealthy brother in the Hampshire village of Chawton, she found the breadth, silence and security to begin writing again.

Not that she even had a room of her own in which to write. She shared a bedroom, as she had her whole life, with her sister, and the frugal manner in which they were forced to live meant that servants were at a minimum and everyone's help was needed with the physical tasks of the house.

What surely must have made a difference was a new sense of internal psychological space, a realization that she could be happy now in the circumstance in which she found herself. She had found a home she could marry and settle down with. One of the more restful achievements of having found the right partner in life is that we suddenly realize how much effort has previously gone into all the searching. Finding a mate takes enormous amounts of physical and emotional energy—dressing, comings and goings, and endless drama—which is why it can be so difficult to look again in midlife if we lose that happiness and must seek anew.

JANE AUSTEN QUOTE SHOWING HER LACK OF PATIENCE WITH RUNNING AFTER LOVE

Our ball was rather more amusing than I expected.... The melancholy part was, to see so many dozen young women standing by without partners, and each of them with two ugly naked shoulders! It was the same room in which we danced fifteen years ago! I thought it all over, and in spite of the shame of being so much older, felt with thankfulness that I was quite as happy now as then.

In committing to a new, more spacious way of life we find the same dynamic as in committing to a person; our energies are now concentrated on this place, this time, this house and in Jane's case, this time in her life, this village, this mother and sister and their community. The outer satisfactions of being engaged to a work or a person release all forms of creative energies that before were involved with constantly articulating our previous unhappiness. Happily engaged, a sense of timelessness begins to appear again and in that experience of timelessness a real sense that there is endless opportunity for the tasks at hand.

"There is a moment in everyday that Satan cannot find,"

said the engraver and visionary poet William Blake, who lived not far from Jane in the fast-growing city of London. In 1809, when Jane Austen moved to Chawton, Blake was having an exhibition of his engravings at the Royal Academy in London: a brief moment of fame from which he was to sink back into obscurity. But success or failure, Blake never stopped writing, drawing and engraving, exactly because he seemed to have a daily experience of timelessness from which all of this endeavor came. The moment that Satan could not find was the moment you seized against the odds amid the besieging commitments of the day to write, to paint, to think and to imagine. On one level you were caught in the snares of incarnation; on another level, part of you was free, with a much larger horizon than the one just before your face.

The greatest, most prized excuse for a writer is the lament over our lack of time in which to write. It is a false and paper-thin defense against another more difficult, underlying dynamic: the inability to have the will to find the time. It is quite sobering to find with experience that if we write only a hundred words a day—a normal paragraph—we will have a book of ninety thousand words in three years. Three years is about the average time for a good prolific writer to produce a new work, given that the first year is often spent not writing at all, the second year telling ourselves that we must write, and the third in a gradually increasing frenzy building up to perhaps three or four thousand words a day.

The sober truth is that any of us can find the time to write a book, no matter the schedule of unstoppable events in our life.

Finding the part of us that wants to write the book is a different matter altogether.

From the outside, especially to those who long for a more artistic life, a writer looks to be involved in what looks like unscheduled imaginative adventure, but what she needs above all else is structure and a goodly amount of space within that structure. It takes a good, settled sense of what we are about, first to think that we deserve the time and then to arrange our day so that what we want comes about.

Engaged and committed at last to the hidden marriage for which she had been preparing all her life, Jane Austen found in the private cottage at Chawton the structure and the tiny increments of space she would use to widen out into a world that would have room, not only for her self, and a sense of satisfaction in the present, but for uncounted millions to whom she would never be introduced, living in the future.

Conclusion: On the Nature of the Time in Which We Are Born

We live out our three marriages according to the nature of our biological, cultural and political inheritance. These forces are generally larger than any personal hope we have of overcoming them, although we may have a chance to move history along and give those in the future a little more sense of choice and possibility.

In very exceptional circumstances we may even get

enough help to be an exemplary exception to our times, but we do not in the end know what kind of exception we will be.

Though we must live according to the nature of our times, the death of our hopes in one marriage may lead us to live out those same hopes with other imaginative vows. We do not know in our youth which marriages we are destined to live out literally and which we are meant to hold in a different, more allegorical way. We must find out as we mature the marriages we are able to bring to life physically or imaginatively.

Alone in the Struggle:
Turning to Face the World

I returned to the village on a clear summer's day. Wild hya-
cinths dotted the high green alpine meadows, and the light
reflecting from the glaciers on the heights of Manaslu was ach-
ingly bright. As we approached the flat stone houses stacked
against the mountainside, it was difficult to believe that this
was the same village into which I had stumbled seven years
before, descending from the ridge and appearing out of the falling snow. That day had stayed in my mind in such an indelible
way that it was hard to connect this calm blue June sky with
that freezing grey windswept March of long ago.

I was arriving with eight or nine others, none of whom had
heard the story of my previous, winter arrival, or of its drama.
The outline of that day had been dramatic, but the true internal drama was hard to convey and so I had kept it to myself. In
any case, I wasn't sure I had kept the flame of that experience
properly alive. I was afraid of discovering that it was something

I had completely made up and I did not want to disappoint myself with that discovery—better to be silent and see what the intervening years had brought.

In the people themselves, the years had wrought enormous changes. The intuition I had first felt, meeting the lama in the snow, that in effect, I was the harbinger of a wave of travelers to come, had proved to be all too correct. The trail in the valley below was well trekked now, though perhaps not so many would have come in March, even after all these years. Teahouses had sprung up along the trail, and although the way was still arduous and the weather as fickle as ever, the sense of edgy exploration and immense collision of the present with the past had almost gone.

As if to emphasize the difference, our entrance into the village this time, even as a group of nine, went unremarked. I looked at passing villagers going about their daily tasks, chopping and hauling wood on metal-runnered sledges, plastering the outer walls of houses, and wondered if any of them would remember that cold day in winter seven years before, when a stranger had come down out of a blizzard from the ridge above and collapsed on the cliff path in front of their Buddha. Perhaps it seemed to belong as much to a mythological past to them as it did to me.

My present companions had no such comparisons to make, however, and to them the village must have looked as exotic as anything they had looked for when they signed up to join me for my return to this high Himalayan valley. They were looking forward very much to seeing the village, but especially the interior of the temple, an interior that I had not seen myself and which I had discovered later, was famous for the carved statues that filled its main hall.

Despite having spent three whole days in the village, I had never visited the statues. Being so sick after my collapse, I had spent my time lying in a horse manger, mostly convalescing, barely able to stand upright and not interested in getting up to walk the steep street to the white, piled height of the monastery that stood over the village. Besides I had had a searing singular experience with one particular statue that had me very perplexed and it seemed irrelevant at the time to look for more.

Only afterward, when I had returned to Katmandu, had I heard about the carvings inside the monastery—how famous they were in the Tibetan Buddhist world, how very, very special and beautifully wrought they were supposed to be. I had marked the village and the temple as a place to return to when I was fit and well. But these seven years later, as we entered the village, I realized I had also brought this little knot of people to see it because I myself wanted to see if there was anything left of that day that could speak to me. Special statues or not, I wanted to be in this place and breathe the air again as a way of measuring myself against the young man I had been those seven years ago, at the edge of my strength, on that fateful day in March.

The reception was certainly disappointing. The people were well used to visitors by now, and we had to work very hard to rouse out an old monk from his midday nap and persuade him to find the large brass key for the door. This key seemed to have migrated from one flat-roofed house to another and after a good while trying to track it down we seemed to be deep into the politics of the mountain village but no nearer finding it. At last, whatever political barrier was preventing us from seeing the temple fell away, the key was found—back at the very first house we had gone to—and we started up toward the temple. As we walked I looked out to my right where I could see the path leading out onto the cliff face. I was momentarily tempted to walk out along ledges again, but I kept my face turned toward the monastery, not wanting to try to emulate such a unique, hard-won, not-to-be-repeated experience.

In front of the worn doors to the monastery, the old man bent, as old men are wont to do, toward the keyhole as if looking right through it, slowly turned the key and smiled as we all heard the satisfying click of the lock. He swung his prayer beads high as the doors opened and we followed his beckoning hand into the vestibule.

Entering the hallway, we were immediately immobilized by the blank darkness of the interior. The high, piercing mountain light outside had been so intense that this somber interior cut off our ability to see almost immediately. We felt our way along the walls, spreading out in the entrance hall and eventually stopped, unable to go farther. One of us suddenly remembered we had a flashlight in one of our packs, and the old monk waited in the dark while we tried to find it. There was a little moment of controversy while the group established who indeed had the precious light and whether it would have any working batteries if we were able to find it.

I was standing next to what I thought was a friend, talking, beginning to mumble perhaps the first few words about having visited the village before, when suddenly my eyes, getting used to the dark, caught a first glimpse of the person to whom I was actually speaking. It was no person at all, but a grim, grimacing pair of eyes and aggressive mouth leering at me in the dark, a skull cup pressed to its lips. I just about leapt out of my skin and into the dark, dusty air with surprise and fear.

In a moment I went from being in a state of absolute relaxation to a state of complete panic. Another moment and I realized that I was looking straight into the formidable eyes of a carved Vajrapani figure, one of those set up as a guardian in almost every Buddhist temple I had seen.

Roughly translated from Sanskrit, *Vajrapani* means "the one who carries the thunderbolt," which conveys an accurate idea of how I felt when I saw the creature in the first place. As an electric sweat broke out on my forehead, the hair on my neck began to subside and my autonomic nervous system slowly returned to normal, I was very glad of the enclosing darkness and its ability to hide my momentary panic from the rest of the group. I was a little embarrassed. "What was that fear?" I asked myself. "The old bogeyman in the dark?" It had certainly taken me by surprise. I had seen the guardian figure, by sheer luck in effect, as the carver wanted me to see it, in absolute innocence. In the complete darkness, the part of me that would classify it as a certain kind of artifact representing this or that was in complete abeyance, my underlying reptilian mind instead looking for threats and unknown possibilities in the artificial night of the hallway. In an unguarded moment the guardian figure had sought out and found the part of me that was ready to be afraid.

The figure was certainly one to put me on my guard, half woman, half man, in one hand carrying a thunderbolt-spear, in the other a skull cup from which it drank blood. It seemed to represent the part of the world that can easily kill us without thinking: the tsunami, the earthquake, the fallen tree; that part of the world that doesn't care about our personal biography or what we have done to deserve mercy. In other representations, the left hand of the Vajrapani holds a lasso with which he binds demons. He may wear a skull crown beneath which his hair stands on end. His expression is most often wrathful and he is given an all-seeing third eye. Around his neck weaves a serpent necklace and his loincloth is often the skin of a tiger. Despite all this, it is surprising to find that he can actually be a good friend, someone meant to help you locate and bind the particular demons that make us so easily afraid of the world.

The accepted, unthinking interpretation of these figures is that their presence at the temple entrance was meant to ask you to leave your fears outside the door. This figure had given me the exact opposite experience. It was as if the Vajrapani had skewered and identified precisely those fears that lived right below the surface and exactly those fears most liable to irrupt in me when irrationally disturbed. In effect it asked me to bring in with me the very fears I had felt when I first saw it, innocently and terrifyingly, in the dark.

I felt an invitation to bring everything into the temple precinct, not just the part of me that was spiritually presentable.

Whether I was spiritually presentable or not, the flashlight had been found, and we were ready to move farther into the temple. Down a long corridor I could see up ahead in its glimmering light, a seated Buddha, holding his hands in a gesture of beckoning. Our guiding monk raised his prayer beads over his bent back and led us down the corridor, bowing slightly as he passed the seated figure and turned left in the darkness into the temple. The light followed him, as did the individual who held it and the rest of the group. We stood behind the monk as he bowed again in front of the main altar, lighting the dozens of yak butter lamps that stood on the broad stone surface. The oblong hall filled with thick smoke and incense from the candles and we bowed, as he did, toward the altar. After a moment we looked up together, and there, on a high shelf running around the upper edges of the room, were dozens of the statues I had heard so much about, looking down on us through the thick, rising incense.

We all looked up at once. We were all affected at once. It seemed as if a wave or tremor of recognition passed through the group and there was an audible sigh as we all saw the faces at exactly the same time. It was as if we were all being made suddenly welcome to a surprise party by a crowd of happy, hospitable strangers. In the midst of this welcome I was having a very private, internal experience as I looked up astonished with the rest of the group. What was immediately evident was not just the sheer artistic beauty of the statues but more especially their faces, which seemed to look down on us, standing below, with confident, knowing smiles. They seemed to welcome us not only in the normal human way to a house, a meal, a home, but to an experience of life we all wanted and from which the glow in their faces seemed to emanate.

The carved faces were welcoming strangers but also intimately familiar. Looking up at them was like looking into memorable human faces I had seen all my life: My aunt beaming down at me as a child before she pulled out a surprise from behind her back. My father's face on first seeing me walk up the road after an absence of years. My mother's eyes looking at me over a late-night glass of wine, as she told me stories of her own mother. These were faces that looked at the world not only in delight but with a sense that they were experiencing an eternal, ever present form of happiness that was larger than any sorrows they might see.

It is rare to visit a place and have it live up to any expectations we have secretly built up before the moment of arrival. Human beings are moody creatures; the slight irritation of an uncomfortable left shoe can overwhelm a view of Michelangelo's David and make us want to retreat across the piazza for a cappuccino or a gelato, a coffee or ice cream we could easily have bought back at home in our local shop. It is hard for human beings to pay attention to anything other than the minutiae of their own physical world, to lift themselves from everyday concerns they have brought with them from one end of the earth to the other. All the more powerful, then, for us to have had not just an individual response, but a spontaneous communal appreciation of this astonishing collective welcome.

DAVID WHYTE

THE NEED FOR HOSPITALITY AND WELCOME

What we were recognizing was a particular kind of face and a particular kind of invitation that human beings unconsciously look for all their lives. A welcome we are especially reluctant to give when looking in our own mirrors. I was struck especially by the irony of the situation. The carver had caught a very familiar yet unfamiliar love and compassion in the human face in very solid, immovable wood. I wondered how it was possible to create such lifelike caring qualities in such a hard medium when here we were, standing below, with such soft, malleable faces, but faces that were so often in our daily lives, closed and set firmly against the world.

We do not often admit how much the shape of our face can be an invitation to others or a warning to keep away. Our face influences our future by what it invites or disinvites. The way we *face* the future actually creates our future as much as our individual actions along the way.

I remember holding an afternoon drinks party at our home near Seattle, where two very different faces attending the event stood out clearly and illustrated this point. It was a glorious winter afternoon; our kitchen was full of people with a fire blazing on a raised hearth at one end of the room. My daughter and I were welcoming people at the door as they arrived. My daughter, being an eight-year-old who was very shy with strangers, would hide behind me as I greeted each guest and wave her hand from behind my legs.

This shy, hidden welcome on my daughter's part was the cause of smiles and laughter for everyone who turned up. But it was entirely natural on her part. The shyness ended, however, as soon as one particular stranger turned up. Satish Kumar is an old friend of mine, but I had not seen him for years. He grew up as a Jain monk in India, then, as a young man, he walked around the world purposefully without a penny in his pocket, found a home in the British Isles and then over the last thirty years or so had become one of the prime movers behind a successful educational center. At sixty, his face was so full of life and happiness and welcome that my daughter ran out spontaneously from behind my legs and held her hands out toward him. I was taken aback by the sudden courage of my hitherto reluctant daughter, but I could see what she was running toward. Satish's face was an invitation to happiness itself. Seeing him always makes me want to practice the set of my own face as a kind of daily discipline. I only have to see him and I want to be as naturally happy and appreciative as he is, and more important, he makes me want to show it.

A very disturbing, very undisciplined face appeared in the doorway a moment later. A man whose face seemed to carry not only past disappointments, but also a sense that it was only a matter of time before it was disappointed again. This man's face seemed almost hungry for circumstances to betray him. My daughter stayed firmly behind my legs; not even a waved hand appeared by way of welcome.

By sheer coincidence, Satish and this gentleman were placed sitting on either side of the raised hearth with the blazing fire between them. From my station at the back of the kitchen I could see them both clearly and in contrast. From this angle the difference between the two faces seemed absolutely staggering. As if I was gazing upon two different species of human being, I looked at them both and could see with absolute clarity that these two faces had radically different futures in store for them independent of anything they actually did.

Satish's face brought things running toward him, especially that part of the world that might be shy and innocent; might be reluctant to trust itself in the world. This was true in a very practical way. Satish, who had hardly a penny to his own name, was famous for attracting willing hands and willing money to everything that was needed for his beautifully produced magazine, his experimental primary school and his environmental college. His charm and his ability to persuade others to help were not knowing, or forced or strategic; they were an invitation to a way of seeing and appreciating. They triggered that longing, in everyone he came across, for the way of life that stood behind such an engaging smile.

The existentially disappointed gentleman on the other side of the fire had no idea how much his defensive posture reinforced his notions of the world, what he had driven off or what had not even come out of hiding to be driven off in the first place. He did not meet my daughter, because he did not even know she was there. How many other possibilities in life had hidden or run the other way at his appearance? To him the world constantly withheld itself from him and that was another piece of evidence pointing to the equally awful way the world was made.

In that mountain temple, under the gaze of all those faces, we were being welcomed by a hundred Satishes, all asking us to run out and greet them. It was remarkable to feel the sense of absolute contentment and almost bubbly happiness as we stood beneath them, talking in a low hubbub of reverence, not wanting to be anywhere else but here in this semidarkness, in this candle smoke, seeing and appreciating what we were seeing. The old monk beamed with us, our full appreciation of his statues making him proud and happy, making him feel that perhaps, after all, he hadn't been wasting his time with these so easily dissatisfied, ever-wandering Westerners.

ENGAGING THE DEMON, ENTERING THE TEMPLE

There is something pleasing about the way that day in the village progressed from disappointment on first returning, to befuddlement looking for a key, to fear in the dark, to revelation in the temple. Many of the motifs human beings have described over the centuries looking for a closer engagement with the self are compressed into those hours: curiosity, followed by puzzlement, followed by apprehension and darkness, followed by insight and revelation. Followed, I might say, by an even more difficult task of sustaining the insight and revelation.

It also recapitulates the journey Deirdre Blomfield-Brown made once she had resolved to follow the life represented by the magazine article she had discovered not in a Himalayan temple but on the front seat of a pickup truck. Once she had the initial

life-changing encounter, she had had to return to the experience, with others, by taking her school class along to see the
man who had written the article. It is as if a crowd represents
the surface rational mind to which we look for corroboration,
but also to which we look for a kind of witness to something
that seemed at first, intensely private. As with my return to the
mountain village, Deirdre revisited a breakthrough experience
by going to hear the lama who had written the article, and she
brought a crowd with her, as I did, for psychological safety. On
the outside she came for a visit marked only by curiosity. On the
inside she came to see if what had happened to her was real.

Finding the key is a very old human motif. Again and again,
we have to find a way in through the door, and again and again,
the stories say that the key is always right under our noses. It is
so much under our noses, in fact, that in the end we are always
told we *are* the key, we each of us, as a foundational dynamic of
life, have to find all the ways we fit in the lock. We are the ones
who turn in the door and open it.

We have to look for the key by looking at the way we are
made to open the great conversation of life. What am I naturally drawn to? How am I made for the world? What is my
essential nature? Deirdre found that despite her 1950s Catholic
midwestern upbringing, she seemed to have an unconscious,
underlying recognition of all things Tibetan, but more especially for the life that stood behind all the robes and the incense.
After her first personal encounter with Trungpa, she moved up
to a center for Tibetan studies in northern New Mexico.

One day a very well-known figure of the early 1970s arrived

at the center, but Deirdre was much more interested in the woman who had accompanied him: "I remember seeing (the poet) Allen Ginsberg drive up with Tsultrim Allione, who was then a Tibetan nun. When she got out of the car I was struck by her robes and by everything about her. It was almost a physical shock. . . . I remember thinking to myself, 'What is this?' I hardly remember Allen at all."

Her attraction to teachers in the tradition was visceral and unconscious, almost defying her surface puzzlement as to what they were actually saying. "A Tibetan Buddhist lama came to the camp. His name was Lama Chime. When I saw him, I had the same experience that I'd had with Tsultrim. His talk didn't make any sense to me, but the minute it was over I went up to him and asked, 'Could I study with you?' . . . He lived in London and said if I came there, he would give me some instruction."

Deirdre found that her personal key fit this old Tibetan lock; she could see it would open the door to the underlying truths of Buddhism and perhaps, more important at that time, her possibilities for happiness. She turned the key and walked right through. "After I'd been with Lama Chime for two weeks, I took refuge, a vow through which one formally enters the Buddhist path. Then I took the bodhisattva vow, a personal vow to seek enlightenment and help others do the same. Two years later I was a nun. I thought I was so worldly-wise. I was only thirty-six years old." Deirdre was also no longer Deirdre; as a mark of her dedication she took the Tibetan name by which she is now known, Pema Chödrön.

As we find out later, getting through the door is never really the hard part, although we may think so at the time. Though we may have expended a lot of effort to get to the entrance itself, to find the key and go through the door, the real difficulty in engaging with the self lies on the other side, waiting in the darkness. All disciplines have crucial testing thresholds, thresholds that ask us if we are serious or ask us if we want to turn back and do something else. If we are equal to the test, it is also a time when we realize the greater import of what we have dedicated ourselves to. At this threshold we find that there are dimensions that have absolutely nothing to do with our particular comfort or happiness, that in actual fact we are involved with others as much if not more than ourselves and that this takes an ability to actually get beyond that small self that first searched for the key and turned it in the door.

A TERRIFYING STEP

The key to my own young adulthood turned in the door of mountaineering and rock climbing. All of my young masculine needs for danger; robust physicality, older male companionship and visible accomplishment were taken care of by my happy discovery of that sport. All of my daydreams during school class time were for the weekend, the high cliffs and visions of myself conquering another steep line up a limestone, grit stone or granite crag. Find me, then, one cold spring day, in the granitic wilds of Scotland, following a climbing club elder up a climb far beyond my powers. We were near the top of the cliff; the man had led the next-to-last, most difficult pitch: a frightening overhanging crack followed by a real overhang, a resting ledge and then a blank wall.

He secured himself and then brought in the rope until it was tight on me. "Climbing," I shouted into the wind. I soon found myself in desperate straits, ascending that strenuous crack and going over that overhang in such a panicked sweat that I bypassed an item of gear a few feet beneath the overhang that I should have taken out, and ended up flopped onto the ledge with the rope pulling tight from below me, instead of above. I lay there panting, looking at the rope looping down beneath the overhang, into the void.

The item of gear was made up of a sophisticated chunk of metal that was made to catch in the back of cracks and then hold, attached by a short length of Perlon rope through a metal gate. This metal gate opened and closed around the climbing rope itself. I called up to the man above and told him of my predicament. He was unmoved. I had to go back down and get the gear, thus freeing the rope and climb up again. I protested that it was impossible, it was too difficult, I would gladly buy him a new item to replace the old if I could just untie, secure myself, pull the rope through, retie and leave the gear in the rock.

"You will do no such thing," came the reply from above.

I remember sitting on that ledge at fifteen years old almost weeping at my predicament. The man seemed merciless, insisting not only that we might need the item on the last pitch above, but that it was against all principles to leave anything behind that had to do with safety; for good measure, and true to his essential Englishness, he said it would detract from the experience of other climbers who would come and find a piece of litter on the cliff. I had to go back down.

Because there was a loop down through the gear, it meant that if I came off the cliff I would fall the distance to the gear and then the same distance below the gear before it held— about twenty feet. Four hundred feet above the ground this was not a happy thought, even though the rope without doubt would hold me. But even if I got down to it, could I climb the desperate overhang again?

The whole drama on the cliff stays in my mind because my climbing elder was absolutely right. He was initiating me into the necessity of doing the right thing, no matter the outward circumstances, no matter how difficult it looked. As he carried on insisting from above in a loud but steady voice, the man kept addressing me in North-of-England fashion as *youth.* As in, "You have to go back down and get it, *youth.*" Whenever this mode of address is used in Yorkshire, it means you are being taught something you need to know and that you certainly need to remember into the future. It wasn't just this climb or the fact that we might need the gear on the next pitch, but for longer, more serious possibilities to come: in the Alps, in the Himalaya, places where every item of gear was precious and could not be lightly forsaken. My future was in this moment as well as my awful present. There was a certain unmerciful economy to the necessities of climbing and I was going to learn it in this terrifying place, all the better so that I could remember it in equally terrifying places in the future.

I did retrieve the gear, and I did make it back over the

overhang with only a little help from a very tight rope because of my drained arm strength. What I remember most, and what has stayed in my bones, is how any difficult, seemingly terrifying situation just necessitates a step-by-step, concentrated approach; an absolute presence for the next move, the next arrangement of the ropes. Each step taken opens up the next step and the next. A little like writing this book, in fact. Freedom comes through a persistent, all-encompassing tenacity. My concentration had to be total and absolute. Step by step, handhold by handhold, I did everything I needed to do. I was being shown, hanging four hundred feet above the ground, that I could do this when it was necessary. I would remember that calm, fixed necessity in similar frightening situations through the years to come. I had faced the Vajrapani at the door to my future climbing career. He would be my fearsome friend, waving that item of gear like a thunderbolt at me, whenever the need arose again.

Pema Chödrön's moment of initiation and confrontation came in a subtler but equally fearsome way. As a dedicated Buddhist nun, she had given herself to the disciplines of meditation, looking at those constant anxious thoughts, those constantly arising senses of lack and trying to see to their roots. This seeing to the root is in effect the Buddha's second item on the to-do list, better known as the second noble truth: that our sense of lack, our sense of worry and inadequacy, has a root and a cause. This root is our desire to have any other reality than the one we are confronted with in the moment. The wish to be helicoptered off the cliff face, to have a climbing partner who doesn't care so much, to have anything other than this underlying sense of divine discontent at what we have to do and who we seem to be in the face of immediate circumstances.

STALKING THE DARKNESS

One of the roots of Pema Chödrön's discontent at the time became concentrated on a person with whom she was working very closely. It was a person who she felt did not like her very much, and it was a relationship from which she felt she could not escape. Though by now, through the door and years into the practice she was well versed in getting into the entrance, the real confrontation with the Vajrapani, the guardian to her practice, was just about to happen.

> *What's more, this person was inaccessible and wouldn't talk to me about the problem. That combination of feeling disliked and having no chance to discuss it made me feel there was something terribly wrong with me, that I was a bad person.*
>
> *I tried all the meditation techniques that I had been teaching people, but nothing would relieve the pain I was feeling. It was similar to the pain I'd felt when my husband had left me. So I went up to the meditation hall where I was practicing at the time, and I just sat there. I did not do any particular meditation. I just sat there in the middle of this pain, bolt upright, all night long.*

One of the diagnostic features of an initiation is the sense of absolute aloneness, on the cliff face or in the meditation room, as if our ability to converse with the otherness of the world is going to be experienced through an absolute concentrated, compacted sense of being utterly by ourselves. The first experience is often a childlike sense of helplessness: my temptation to weep on the ledge, to go back to the mothering part of the world that doesn't want you to live with the consequences of a full participation in life. To be a child is to be exempt from consequences, to hide out of sight and let another, more adult world explain us to a world that seems to threaten us.

This concentrated sense of the self and its need to hazard itself in the world brings us to a difficult, fully adult understanding of existence that may come like a physical shock, that this self is not exempt from the fiercer aspects of mortality, that it can cease to exist, can die and pass away.

> *I had an insight. The first thing was that I felt physically like a little child, so small that if I'd sat in a chair my feet wouldn't have touched the floor. And then there was a recognition that I needed to relax into the pain. Until then, I had avoided going to this place where I felt bad or unacceptable or unloved. No language could express how awful that place felt. But I just started breathing into it. I realized that this was a pivotal moment. Somehow, even with the divorce, I had never quite hit the bottom. And that evening, I did. I was seconds away from experiencing the death feeling.*

To Pema Chödrön the death feeling was a collapsed, hollowed-out feeling of absolute dissatisfaction: a sense of not wanting to go on, and not needing to go on. But in the midst of that giving up she felt as if she could look at this part of herself as if it was almost separate from her. Being "bolt upright," being completely attentive and completely aware of it, she could open up to it, "relax into it," as she was to say, a way of saying, I suppose, that she could make herself much larger than this primary fearful dissatisfaction and then operate from this greater identity. Suffering, dissatisfaction, Dukka, was inevitable, but there was a way of paying attention to difficulties that made you larger and wiser than all those lifelong worries and anxieties.

THE QUICKENING

What Pema Chödrön was experiencing was also a kind of quickening, an acceleration of difficulties that occurs when we start to become serious about self-knowledge. The fragile surface self begins to fragment and to slough off like an outer skin. The newly emerging larger identity is not yet here but the old is not yet gone. In self-exploration we can find ourselves in stages where we approximate to a gangly adolescent who suddenly doesn't like anything or anyone, including themselves. It is a concentrated bitterness that medieval Christian monks described with the Greek-derived word *accidie*.

Accidie is a crucial and difficult threshold, where everything seems to recede like a tide, including our own willingness to go on. Everything seems to fall apart, including our own application to the task. Like a writer who will not write, it can signify laziness, weariness, listlessness and that marvelous word *sloth*. But because the application in religious life is not just to writing, but to the existential ground of our life, the consequence of feeling inadequate to the task can seem multiplied and magnified. Pema Chödrön experienced it as a spiritual desolation, an emptiness that clouded her mind and dulled her heart. It is what Psalm 91 refers to as "the pestilence that walks in darkness" or "the destruction that wastes at noonday."

Stalking the darkness might be a good description of what occurs when we start to look beneath the surface of the particular marriage to which we have dedicated ourselves. It appears like a guardian figure seeming to threaten and frighten us, seeming especially to ask us if we are worthy enough to enter. It is a doctor losing her first patient, an ambulance driver failing to arrive at the accident in time, but it is also Stevenson in the isolation of San Francisco, totally engaged in that isolation to his love across the bay; it is Jane Austen beginning to write again, out of her unmarried state, about the foundations of commitment.

THE FOUNDATIONS OF SELF-COMPASSION

But as Pema Chödrön discovered, the Vajrapani is not asking us if we are worthy enough—that is our problem in the first place. That is where most of us go wrong. The Vajrapani is simply asking us to bring the parts of us into the temple that arise in us when we see its fearsome challenge in the dark. It wants all of us, not just the perfectionist. The figure at the entrance is asking us to be just as aware of our self-sabotaging propensities as we are of our virtues, to give them equal attention; to understand how terrified we are as much as how confident we can be. It is there to make sure we bring all of us into the temple, to be authentic and to be tenacious in that authenticity.

Making room for our own fears, we suddenly have room for the fears of others. Once we have renounced the need to live without suffering, to be special, to be exempt from the losses and doubts that have afflicted all people since the beginning of time, we can see the difficulties of others without being afraid ourselves. Our fearful, disappointed surface face starts to fall away. We can welcome other people into our lives because no matter their fears, they do not make us afraid. Suffering is the natural cyclical visitation that comes from being alive. We can be present, we can give them a listening ear; we can even be helpful and useful to them.

Engaging with the self, starting to treat ourselves as if we were a living, learning surprise, worthy of existence despite our constant fears, enables us to engage in a real way with others, to see others as possible surprises and even gifts. When anxiety falls away, appreciation and gratitude seem to naturally take their place. We can suddenly see a larger person than the one in front of us who is afraid, but we understand that misunderstanding and that disconnect—we have traveled that way ourselves. We have compassion, and as that word suggests, we can *suffer with*.

There is no way of living without anxiety, but there is a way of holding ourselves that is larger than any particular worry and allows our constant sense that something is wrong to fall into a natural hierarchy of experience. Our worries fall down this hierarchy of experience until they become like an eye or an ear or an arm or a leg or an idea, not ourselves, but a way of perceiving the world, not a description of who or what we are, but a means of paying attention. Our anxieties become good servants to some other faculty of belonging waiting inside us, ready to engage in a way that surprises and emboldens.

Conclusion: On Being Utterly Alone

Engagement with the self reaches its climax with the sense of being utterly alone with the struggle. There is a peculiar quality to the distilled essence we imbibe when we come to this sense of complete isolation. Ironically, our sense of communion with others is enhanced when we understand how completely alone people feel when confronted by the forces that surround them.

Our ability to receive help in that isolation comes from our ability to *ask* for help or to be someone others *want* to help. Our faces are a measure of our willingness to join the conversation and to invite others into the particular world we inhabit. To close the face to others is to lose a sense of kindness and mercy for others. As a direct correlation, our own world then begins to seem isolated and merciless itself. We decide not to choose that way, but to go in the opposite way, to face what must be faced.

Poetic Conclusion: Or What Really Happened in the Mountain Temple

THE FACES AT BRAGA

In monastery darkness
by the light of one flashlight,
the old shrine room waits in silence.

While beside the door
we see the terrible figure,
fierce eyes demanding, "Will you step through?"

And the old monk leads us,
bent back nudging blackness
prayer beads in the hand that beckons.

We light the butter lamps
and bow, eyes blinking in the
pungent smoke, look up without a word,

see faces in meditation,
a hundred faces carved above,
eye lines wrinkled in the handheld light.

Such love in solid wood—
taken from the hillsides and carved in silence,
they have the vibrant stillness of those who
　　made them.

Engulfed by the past
they have been neglected, but through
smoke and darkness they are like the flowers

we have seen growing
through the dust of eroded slopes,
their slowly opening faces turned toward the mountain.

Carved in devotion
their eyes have softened through age
and their mouths curve through delight of the carver's hand.

If only our own faces
would allow the invisible carver's hand
to bring the deep grain of love to the surface.

If only we knew
as the carver knew, how the flaws
in the wood led his searching chisel to the very core,

we would smile too
and not need faces immobilized
by fear and the weight of things undone.

When we fight with our failing
we ignore the entrance to the shrine itself
and wrestle with the guardian, fierce figure on the side
     of good.

And as we fight
our eyes are hooded with grief
and our mouths are dry with pain.

If only we could give ourselves
to the blows of the carver's hands,
the lines in our faces would be the trace lines of rivers

feeding the sea
where voices meet, praising the features
of the mountain and the cloud and the sky.

Our faces would fall away
until we, growing younger toward death
everyday, would gather all our flaws in celebration

to merge with them perfectly,
impossibly, wedded to our essence,
full of silence from the carver's hands.

from D.W., *Where Many Rivers Meet*

BOOK FIVE

Living Together:
The Art of Marriage

The Art of Marriage: The Disappearance, Reappearance and Dissolution of the Self

If we feel we are being tested during the engagement period, then marriage itself is a fearsome examination during which we are almost always found wanting. It is interesting to discover, in a search through all periods of literature and culture, that happy marriages are seldom depicted. If they are depicted, it is usually as a prelude to a story of a happiness soon to be disturbed or destroyed.

This may be not because there are no happy marriages but because what defines happiness in marriage might look so different from the inside that we cannot recognize it or describe it from the outside. Most marriages are dynamic moving frontiers, hardly recognizable to the participants themselves; moving frontiers that occupy edges of happiness and unhappiness all at the same time.

There is also the phenomenon of disappearance, in which personal happiness suddenly loses a fixed meaning, where a period of misery or sacrifice for one of the individuals may, in a sense, be a help to the other partner or especially a help to the infant children of the partnership. What is defined as "I" before the relationship does not seem to survive its encounter with the other "I," and to begin with, the new "we" seems to offer little in compensation.

We often enter a marriage with images of how it will enhance our sense of self, increase the happiness we already possess and end a sense of aloneness. After the initial euphoria, we just as often find that in the marriage itself our sense of self is obliterated, our previous sources of happiness disappear and our sense of isolation is made more acute through the constant proximity of the other, their never-ending presence suddenly seeming to give us no time to think or gain a larger view.

What is difficult about the imagined happiness of marriage is the hard reality that both sides of the partnership have to rebuild their lives from the razed foundations of their former individual existences, and faced with this discovery we cannot really believe this radical rebuilding from scratch is necessary. We want to remain intact and untouched, and we soon intuit it is impossible. The temptation at this point is to hold our selves back from a full participation. Ironically, if we want to preserve ourselves we have to make a new home for that self and not retreat into the old house. Marriages often begin to fail when one side or the other refuses to begin building from this new, joint foundation but wants all the development on their previously planned side of the street.

What is fascinating and almost existentially mischievous about marriage is that whatever one side of the partnership wants will not occur; whatever the other side of the partnership desires will not occur, and the whatever that does occur is the combined life that emerges from first, the collision, and then the conversation between the two: a conversation that may seem foreign to both to begin with; something they might not recognize or even think they want.

We stand outside the rectory of St. Andrew's Presbyterian Church on busy Post Street in San Francisco on May 19, 1880, and watch Robert Louis Stevenson and Fanny Osbourne, now Mrs. Stevenson, emerge into the city, newly married. Knowing what we do about what it took to bring them together, we are intrigued at these two extraordinary lives coming together at last. Why does the coming together of two people made for each other give such pleasure to other human beings? Do we see ourselves in them? Do we hope they will be exempt from the pains that have accompanied all other marriages? Throughout human myth and story, two people committing against all the odds and against all the difficulty that lies ahead of them has always been a source of admiration, misty eyes and celebration for all but the most hard-bitten, bitterly disappointed witnesses.

In the wedding ceremony, two become one in public and thereby, represent all the inner private portions of us that have lost each other and wish to be in some kind of earnest conversation again. The dedication of a human being to any kind of deep-seated belonging in human life seems to be a moving thing for others to witness, and it may be that this first exterior marriage ceremony is an outer representation, not only of the other two marriages, but also of every other kind of dedication that a human being can make. The wedding vows say that if this promise can be fulfilled, all kinds of other, more private promises, some never spoken, some not even yet imagined, might be possible, too.

The vows a couple speak out loud somehow affirm that it might be possible to be courageous no matter the way ahead, that it doesn't matter if the promises are forgotten and remembered, forgotten and remembered so long as they *are* revisited and kept alive, not only for themselves but for every other witnessing marriage and every other kind of partnership that exists in society and perhaps for the onlookers, every other deep-seated coming together that exists in the depths of the human psyche.

If marriage is an overt opportunity for conversation, generosity and self-improvement, it is also a battleground for all of the unspoken, underground streams that are brought together beneath the steady flow of arrangements. In some interior place, while the vows are being spoken out loud on the surface there is a mingling of unspoken, unresolved difficulties from the background of each partner. There is a way in which we are marrying the mother, the father, the cousins, the whole inheritance of a family, including the exiled black sheep who hasn't even turned up for the ceremony. These collateral marriages to others occur whether we see any of the individuals on a daily basis or no. They are firmly inside the psyche of the individual we are marrying, and they will play a part in the drama to come.

In a very personal way we are marrying not only a person's ability to love and take care of us, but also that person's particular species of selfishness and particular form of egotism. It is only a question of time before these appear. One of the tests of finding the right person is to ask ourselves if this is the particular form of selfishness and egotism we can live with. Considering the difficulties of marriage we might pose the question on a grander scale and ask if this is the particular form of insanity we can live with. A sign of possible success is our ability to answer in the affirmative. It means the chemistry is right, and also that we are looking not for perfection in our partner but for a mutual exploration of imperfections.

MARRIAGE: THE SPIRITUAL NECESSITY FOR A GOOD LAUGH

One of the absolute necessities for sanity is a sense of humor: the ability to laugh at our attempts at dignity and control in the midst of the uncontrolled indignities of relationship. Humor is a faculty that acknowledges our multilayered identities: that whatever context you have arranged for yourself on the surface, there is always another context that makes that original idea of your self, absurd. The promise to live with one other person for the rest of our lives is a very particular form of insanity itself from many perspectives. Weddings themselves often demonstrate their dark underpinnings through black humor: the bride's dress shredded by a car door, the father-in-law marooned in a jammed elevator, while the bemused congregation waits. I remember acting as best man to a good friend's wedding in Scotland. After a quiet drink the night before the ceremony, I took a walk with the bridegroom-to-be along a cliff above the waters of Loch Lomond. I was talking companionably and philosophically about the life that lay ahead of him when I realized all at once that I was talking to the night air. My friend the groom had disappeared; had fallen actually, down the thirty-foot cliff. As he survived the fall and in fact was completely unhurt, eventually laughing out of the darkness below, we can see it now as the perfect metaphor for what he was doing. Falling to a ground beneath the ground he stood on now, falling into parenthood, falling into unknown waters: helpless in the void that had now appeared beneath his unthinking feet.

All marriages have a kind of trapdoor quality to them—a trapdoor that seems to open up only after the commitment has been made. Every newly committed couple find themselves in a powerful gravitational field pulling down their surface lives into all the other unspoken lives they represent. In that field they find not only the virtues and flaws of their upbringing but the tensions behind entire family histories. The presence of this dark underside to human relationship often finds expression at weddings in unconscious ways: the slightly tipsy relative whispering too loudly the past sins of the bridegroom, the bride's parents surveying with deep suspicion the demeanor of the opposing family; quiet, vehement arguments about who sits where and who pays for what. At the blandest suburban wedding we can often see the person playing out the part of the good fairy, blessing all she sees, and the one consciously or unconsciously attempting to curse the proceedings and all who attend. The inclusion of a crowd at a wedding lets us know that our kitchen discussions and bedroom arguments will be equally well attended. The ceremony itself involves the past as well as the future; the conjoining of two often turbulent stories with all their dramatis personae, not just the two standing at the front, going through the ceremony.

WELL MATCHED

At the Stevenson wedding, this underground parallel reality found expression in Fanny's former husband, Samuel Osbourne. Though the divorce from Osbourne had been finalized only in December, he appeared at the wedding immaculately dressed and with a woman on his arm, a woman he introduced to everyone as *Mrs.* Osbourne. Samuel Osbourne had quickly and quietly married his mistress as soon as the divorce was granted. No doubt Stevenson found it both highly amusing and a great relief, perhaps, to feel that portion of Fanny's past closing so quickly and so firmly.

But it would have been hard to close the door on Fanny's story so quickly. Her story is more than a match for Stevenson's. Every marriage is probably the meeting of two equally compelling stories, if they can be but told properly, but this youthful forty-year-old woman walking out of the church door with him had in many ways seen as much, lived as much and demonstrated as much hair-raising bravery, artistic endeavor and adventure as Stevenson.

Born Fanny Vandergrift in the Indiana of 1840, she grew into a dark, curly-haired tomboy who married, at only seventeen, a charismatic Kentuckian, Samuel Osbourne. The following year, 1858, she gave birth to a daughter, Isobel. The Civil War took Samuel away, not just to battle, but on, to California and Nevada, where he joined the craze for silver mining. At the height of the conflict between the Union and the Confederacy, Fanny traveled alone with six-year-old "Belle," first by ship to Central America, then, long before the famous canal was built, through malarial jungle across the Isthmus of Panama. Arriving on the Pacific side, mother and daughter took a ship to California. The final epic leg was by stagecoach and wagon train to the mining camps of Nevada.

Fanny then, may not have been too impressed by Stevenson's journey from Scotland to Oakland using such a luxurious means as boat and train. In Nevada, she had found herself one of the few women in a very rambunctious society; she learned to shoot a pistol very straight and began rolling her own cigarettes.

Samuel took up with local saloon girls, and Fanny may have been relieved when rumor had it that he had been devoured by a grizzly bear in faraway Idaho. Unfortunately, this proved unfounded, and a boy, Lloyd, the future inspiration for the writing of *Treasure Island*, was born in 1868. Fanny moved away to Indianapolis, reconciled with Samuel again, then moved back to Oakland and gave birth to a second son, Hervey, in 1869.

Samuel did not change his ways, but Fanny did. She had taken up painting, studying with Virgil Williams, the founder of the San Francisco School of Design, under whose inspiration she developed an ambition to study abroad. Independently and heroically, she decided to move herself with the three children to Europe to study art. Fanny and Isobel enrolled in the Académie Julian in Paris in 1875. Hervey died in France at the age of six, of tuberculosis. The following year Fanny was eating dinner with her daughter, her surviving son and a circle of friends in the artists' colony at Gretz when a strange young Scotsman startled them all by entering through the window and introducing himself.

The biography of Fanny Osbourne is worth as much effort and study as any of Robert Louis Stevenson. They were two, very individual, very headstrong characters come together out of two twisting, turning, difficult stories, two stories coming together to make another difficult but very worthwhile story: their marriage.

The recipe for what we might call *happiness* was not simple.

WAYS THEY WERE ALIKE

Stevenson	*Fanny*
Brave, foolhardy.	Brave, almost foolhardy.
Headstrong; knew what he wanted.	Headstrong; knew what she wanted.
Loyal in love and friendship.	Loyal in love and family.

Unremitting application to his art under all circumstances.	Unremitting application to a sense of personal freedom. Art as a metaphor for freedom.
Sexually compatible (intuitive guess).	Sexually compatible (intuitive guess).
Extraordinarily good writer.	Fine writer (evidence of diaries).

WAYS THEY WERE NOT ALIKE

Stevenson	*Fanny*
Often indifferent to his own health.	Careful of her health, the health of her children and Stevenson's health.
Liked to carouse with friends.	Enough experience of this with Samuel Osbourne.
Could be a snob about his education and manners.	Could be sensitive about her education and manners.
Difficult relationship with his parents.	Developed very good relationship with Stevenson's parents.
Money: £250 per year promised by his parents, a sum that enabled the marriage.	Money: None.
Later earned large income from *Treasure Island, Dr. Jekyll and Mr. Hyde*, et al.	Income: None.

The interesting thing about a marriage is that the ways in which we are alike can be just as difficult for us as the ways in which we differ. If we are brave ourselves, there can be nothing more irritating than the other person's bravery, which wants to take us off in a direction that we don't think is interesting at all; if we are foolhardy we might be resentful of our partner's competing foolhardiness, particularly if it uses up the patience of friends and relatives that up to now it has been our exclusive right to draw on. Some attributes balance with a partner's attributes, some do not. Some initial incompatibilities are later seen to be complementary strengths. The tidal exchange of positive and negative attributes moves also according to the demands of work, child rearing, mood, inclination and fatal, passing remarks in the kitchen.

Because each marriage is such a mystery to its self, it is even more of a mystery to those who look from the outside. There are also the factors of time, tide and the inevitable transformations in the person to whom we have committed. What makes our relationship tick in our twenties may be very different from what we need in our thirties, and radically different from what we ask for in our forties and fifties. A marriage is a mystery in the present but also wrapped in the enigmas of time and transformation over time. The pressure of marriage may be unrelenting and awkwardly present every hour of the livelong day but it is at the same time almost intangible and untouchable in the sense of our being able to understand how it "works." It is this unworkable aspect that makes most marriages resistant to mere strategy as a way of improving them or saving them.

Something more alive, more essential needs to be fed at its center.

What is called for is an ability on the part of the couple to "see" each other, to constantly apprehend the essence of the other. This ability makes no sense to us at first when we realize that essence is so often a mystery even to the person who is supposed to possess it. What is even more difficult is that this essence is no set of facts and figures about the other person but has more to do with their hopes, desires and imaginings for themselves.

Perhaps there is nothing more essential about individuals than the desires they hold for themselves. In courtship we may discover that the chief desire of our partner is a Porsche, in which case we can be horrified by the boring, narrow nature of their hopes or happy that they are just as shallow as we are and therefore bound to get along famously. More seriously, the essential desire of a person always matures and changes, through a Porsche to a porch and a house attached to it and a life attached to the house that possesses much larger horizons than any the sports car traversed when we first imagined ourselves in the driver's seat.

To find out our partners' desires, we must sustain a conversation with them that helps to bring those wants and desires to light. Sometimes we have to do this even when they are afraid of discovering them themselves. The deep, abiding fear is that we will stumble across the desire in them that wants a life different from the one we are capable of giving them. Essentially, we are afraid that they may find that their desire is to love something or even someone else—one of the most painful discoveries a partner can make. The crux then, the most difficult ground in the relationship, the portion of a relationship that elevates it to the level of a religious discipline or practice, is that I must "love," must *see* the very part of my partner that could take this person away from me. I must keep contact with the part of the person that is pulling him or her into the future, though I risk not participating in that horizon.

It can be painful for us even to imagine our partners enjoying themselves without us, either after we have gone or actually and quite often, while we are still alive. In fact the most generous portion of a marriage might be where one partner actually risks and hazards the other in letting him or her go off at times on these psychological travel excursions. The fear of infidelity is of course deep-seated and almost impossible to erase from the human heart. The ability to let a person live his or her own life must include this very difficult conversation in order to reassure one or the other that they are not undermining a sense of togetherness. There are other fears. This radical and cyclical giving away of the other partner may not survive the discovery that one of the partners made a mistake and should not have married in the first place. Infidelity may be opportunity—for a relieved escape—but so may a retreat in the mountains or a journey undertaken alone. The courage in giving the other away is in being willing to find out along the way how real and on what foundations the relationship actually exists. It is certain that we will discover that even in their fidelity, the other's love is not completely constant, that in fact no human being can sustain the expectations of another in the areas of love and intimacy and for that we must look to the other, third marriage with the self. No matter how suited we are to our partners, in a marriage, we will always discover the part of us that feels betrayed by the other, no matter the protests, promises and declarations made along the way.

The women of early-nineteenth-century Nantucket had a very disturbing but enlightening song for the masculine psyche to hear and learn from. Though no doubt it was sung only when their whaling men were safely over the horizon.

THE NANTUCKET GIRL'S SONG

I have made up my mind now to be a Sailor's wife,
To have a purse full of money and a very easy life,
For a clever sailor husband is so seldom at his home,
That his wife can spend the dollars with a will that's all
    her own,

Then I'll haste to wed a sailor, and send him off to sea,
For a life of independence is the only life for me.
But every now and then I should like to see his face,
For it always seems to me to beam with manly grace.
With his brow so nobly open, and his dark and kindly
    eye,
Oh my heart beats fondly towards him whenever he is
    nigh.
But when he says goodbye my love, I'm off across the sea
First I cry for his departure, then laugh because I'm free.

The women of Nantucket were indeed free and ran the family business affairs while their husbands were hunting whales in the South Pacific. Men were ever so slightly more expendable to the ongoing health of the Nantucket community than the women.

In relationship our deep-seated anxieties about whether we are really wanted or not are almost always reinforced and brought up for a deeper examination. The phenomenon of the woman who is released, by the death of her husband, from all kinds of daily checks, balances and inabilities to explore is also a familiar dynamic. The Merry Widow, happy as a lark, using the family fortune to really enjoy herself and just as often, to really help others enjoy themselves, appears in many cultures as a warning to the controlling, masculine psyche about how his contribution to the marriage might be interpreted. Of course, a man can feel just as released from a marriage by a partner's death as can a woman. Though it may be a painful love of independence that may never breathe its own name aloud.

What the Merry Widow phenomenon tells us is that each of us longs for that equivalent freedom while we are still alive; while we are still married, while we are paying the mortgage and while we are raising the children. It might be a central discipline of relationship for the couple to cyclically help each other through windows of freedom no matter where they are in the chronology of family life. The understanding that we are not the be-all and end-all for our partners, nor should we be, helps us to grant ourselves and the other person freedom now rather than later. In giving away the personal conceit of wanting to be the entire source of their happiness, we give them away generously in the process. In the great Murphy's Law of Relationship, we then find that we have more of them present; actually enjoying our company, that they volunteer to stay with us exactly because we have tried, against a natural selfish undertow, to give them a sense of choice.

I have a good Irish friend who always says, when I have a troubled question about marriage and relationship, "Go against yourself." It is very sound advice, well worth being calligraphied, framed, and placed on the kitchen wall above the scene where many of our attempted conversational breaks for freedom take place. To go against our selves in a relationship is to find another form of self that can grow without destroying the growth of the other.

The French philosopher Simone Weil had this to say about this fierce nexus of difficulty at the heart of "love," this Vajrapani figure, standing fiercely at the entrance to love, fidelity and happiness in marriage and relationship: "What we love in other human beings is the hoped-for satisfaction of our desire, we do not love them for their desire. If what we loved in them was their desire, then we should love them as our self."

When a relationship stifles individual and essential wants and needs for too long the conversation always ceases to be real. The relationship also ceases to be real, the couple begins to dance ghostlike on the grave of their initial attraction to each other, an attraction that becomes increasingly abstract and increasingly built on the momentum of memory. We stop telling the story of our original meeting with any delight because it ceases to have any real bearing on our day-to-day reality. Not that we can easily stop those ghostly dances and be paragons of truth and insight. But the very attempt to continually find out what the people might want for themselves is a generous and beneficial act that can often heal any previous neglect or undo the harm inflicted through a thoughtless dismissal of their desires.

Add to this the fact that most human beings, whether they be tycoon or trash collector, walk around feeling inadequate to circumstances or comparing themselves unfavorably with others and constantly attempt to make up for this inadequacy by establishing themselves as kings and queens of their own domestic space and that the domestic space of the marriage is the place where these hidden dynamics of competitive inadequacy are played out in the full light of day, and we can begin to have a little appreciation for the kind of maturity, sense of humor, self-knowledge and generosity called upon to make a marriage even approach the door of happiness.

This internal sense of inadequacy that Deirdre Blomfield-Brown discovered in her first brush with Buddhism and studied closely as Pema Chödrön is a constant companion to human relationship. It is one of the reasons that every relationship has at its heart a battle for moral ascendancy. This daily, often amusing struggle takes place in the kitchen; in the car and in the psychological direction the couple is taking together. This seems to be a very old dynamic, the great battles in Ireland's ancient epic the *Táin* began with idle bedroom chat between a king and queen that swiftly turned competitive. The bloodshed is often more subtle in our own relationship. The attempt for moral superiority is more often than not an attempt to be the one who is right and who therefore is still themselves inviolate, not compromised by the other's constant subversive presence.

Moral superiority is also an attempt at personal freedom. When I am sure I have contributed more to the relationship than my partner, I am equally sure I deserve a break in another area commensurate to my efforts. The ironic unspoken need is to be appreciated and thus be given time off from the relationship, so I can go for a jog, play the violin, read in peace or have an evening with old friends. I have done this; therefore, I deserve that.

It can be very shocking to suddenly agree with your partner and say that the person does actually do more and should take all the time he or she wants. The admission is so against the grain that it almost always leads to consternation, an equal compliment and an attempt to create time for the other too. It also, almost always leads to laughter, which is the only remedy for the eternal battle for the moral high ground. It can be instructive and hilarious to track together as a couple the endless voyage through the day looking, like Noah and his wife, for the moral high ground. My wife and I find that this monitoring of our speech makes not only for insight and harmony but for constant visitations of hilarity. We deconstruct our speech this way to take apart our conceits of superiority, though of course nothing stops us from believing that we really do, after all, contribute more than the other.

PROBABLE *BALANCE OF MORAL SUPERIORITY* BETWEEN FANNY AND STEVENSON

Fanny	*Stevenson*
Looks after health of self, family and Stevenson.	Devil-may-care "brave" attitude to own health.
Provides sense of home wherever they are.	Pays for home wherever they are.
Discriminates between friends who help and those who do not.	Loves a rogue.
Invaluable partner, supporter and editorial contributor to fame of famous man.	Famous man.
Does not stand on ceremony.	Inherited sense of good manners.
(*Guess*) Like most women: the probable arbiter of the frequency of their sex life.	(*Guess*) Like most men: God's gift to women and a sense that the wife should feel privileged.
Indispensable editorial consultant to *Treasure Island.*	Indispensable author of *Treasure Island.*

Underneath the hilarity is serious intent to admit our flaws and put them in conversation with one another. There is no real conversation without vulnerability, and many times the only way of showing vulnerability at the beginning is through developing, as a couple, a robust sense of humor. The more sober, life-changing assessments can come later, when we have become used to looking underlying dynamics in the eye.

Stevenson was able to see one underlying dynamic of his relationship beneath all surface struggles with Fanny almost immediately and in a very generous way.

"As I look back, I think my marriage was the best move I ever made in my life. . . . It was not my bliss that I was interested in when I was married; it was a sort of marriage *in extremis;* and if I am where I am, it is thanks to the care of that lady, who married me when I was a mere complication of cough and bones, much fitter for an emblem of mortality than a bridegroom."

We might begin the marriage as a mere complication of cough and bones or we might more likely end it that way, but the understanding is that the other you have married will see something beyond and beneath the all-too-mortal surface and be by that bedside at the very beginning or the very end. In committing to all the vitality in the other, we must commit to something larger than the eventual loss to which we know we are being introduced. Fanny must have known by the state of Stevenson's lungs and the fact she had lost a child to a similar disease that she could lose Stevenson any moment after leaving the church door. Little wonder marriage has been seen by many religions as a form of apprenticeship to a greater generosity we must learn in giving, receiving and letting go. Marriage is a long slow-motion goodbye, occurring even as the introductions are being made and the spark is being lit. It is a door into a much larger world than the couple, ducking beneath the arch amid rice and confetti, can yet appreciate.

When Stevenson and Fanny left the door of St. Andrew's Church and stepped into busy Post Street, they were stepping into a very large world indeed. They were beginning a marriage that would involve a great deal of difficulty and a remarkable amount of happiness but also a really remarkable amount of travel. If we tend to think of marriage as a time of settling down, we might be surprised by Fanny and Stevenson's interpretation of the institution.

ITINERARY OF
FANNY–STEVENSON MARRIAGE

Place	*Reason for Going*
Napa Valley, California	Health/Honeymoon
Braemar, Scotland	Writing
Westbourne, Dorset, England	Writing
Davos, Switzerland	Health
Hyères, France	Health
Saranac Lake, New York	Health/Writing
Yacht *Casco*, Pacific Ocean	Health
Honolulu, Hawaii	Health
Vailima, Samoa	Health/Writing

We can see in Fanny and Stevenson's travels an overt way of underlining different stages and epochs of their relationship: epochs that in other relationships might be represented by subtler milestones. The Stevensons' newly blended family sailed to England in 1880 and found his parents and his friends waiting for them all on the dock at Liverpool. Little by little Fanny repaired the relationship between the father and the son that had been severed so completely on his departure. Stevenson's father and mother grew to love Fanny very deeply as the years went by, seeing in this strong but charming character an apt partner for their wayward son.

Stevenson and Fanny's relationship grew over the years, as they moved from property to property, country to country, through all their travels, to include their melded families, the authorship of dozens of volumes of prose and poetry, a wide circle of friendship and a transpacific voyage that most couples would have been proud to have completed in their early twenties. The extraordinary years through which they were to travel together tell us that our outer foundations of home and mortgage, settled community and recognizable, readily explainable career, are not strictly necessary to have a good marriage. The foundations may be in the adventured conversation itself, wherever the couple or the family find themselves.

Furthermore, this was not a hermetically sealed relationship out of touch and out of conversation with their times, traveling in a little self-made bubble of their own. Fanny Stevenson was never content to remain on the outside when it came to her husband's writing; she combined the role of a nurse with collaborative editorial duties. They faced the literary world together and Fanny often worked hard at being a gatekeeper, keeping away those of Stevenson's friends who kept him up late drinking, and admitting those such as Henry James, who combined an appreciation for Stevenson's work with a care for his health.

Stevenson both resented and greatly admired his interventionist wife. He saw marriage as a battleground, not only between the individuals involved but also like his character in *Dr. Jekyll and Mr. Hyde*, a fateful battle for good and evil occurring inside the heart and mind of each individual. To Stevenson this struggle with the soul was a battle worth choosing and continually worth fighting. A partner in marriage was a partner in self-revelation. His books may be full of what looks like escapist adventure, but he saw the longings of the reader and the longings of the husband as one and the same. He saw the realist writer as being one defeated by his subject, someone who downgrades reality in order to participate in it; he saw the so-called realist in marriage as equally overcome, someone trying to protect themselves, someone who has downgraded a long, surprising adventure to a series of economic and emotional transactions.

> *But we are so fond of life that we have no leisure to entertain the terror of death. It is a honeymoon with us all through, and none of the longest. Small blame to us if we give our*

whole hearts to this glowing bride of ours, to the appetites, to
honour, the hungry curiosity of the mind, to the pleasure of
the eyes in nature, and the pride of our own nimble bodies.

(from "Aes Triplex")

It might have been exactly because Stevenson had the scent of death in his nostrils for most of his life that he was unwilling to compromise his ability to live. He was larger than life, like many of his characters, whether in his writings or his marriage. One thing Stevenson knew, in a real way, as most of us know only in the very far-off abstract, death was sure to come; to him it was only a matter of when. In the end it came swiftly, far from his wintry, native Scotland, in Western Samoa on December 3, 1894, at the age of only forty-four, from a cerebral hemorrhage. When he died, surrounded by his wife, his mother and his step-children, Lloyd and Isobel, he was working on what many consider his finest work: *Weir of Hermiston.* As ever, Stevenson was in the midst of literary endeavor up to the moment of his death. He was also, as this letter from his mother shows, in the midst of his family and his marriage, giving a helping hand in the kitchen. We do not know who, in that marriage, had the high, moral ground at the moment of his going but it was almost certainly soon forgotten.

How am I to tell you the terrible news that my beloved son
was suddenly called home last evening. At six o'clock he
was well, hungry for dinner, and helping Fanny to make
a mayonnaise sauce; when suddenly he put both hands to

his head and said, "Oh, what a pain!" and then added,
"Do I look strange?" Fanny said no, not wishing to alarm
him, and helped him into the hall, where she put him into
the nearest easy-chair. She called for us to come, and I was
there in a minute; but he was unconscious before I reached
his side, and remained so for two hours, till at ten minutes
past 8 p.m. all was over.

Fanny Osbourne buried Stevenson on the mountain of Vailima. She grieved for her husband, did all she could to keep his legacy alive and also went on to live another robust twenty years. Her travels took her to France, Spain, Portugal and back to San Francisco, where she became something of a celebrity hostess, representing the Stevenson literary legacy at a substantial house on Russian Hill. She then took up with a man many years younger who seems to have adored her, and passed her last years in Santa Barbara, California, where she died in 1914, swiftly, like her husband, of a cerebral hemorrhage.

In keeping with her wishes, her ashes were taken by her companion and daughter Isobel to be laid alongside those of Stevenson in the mountain plot at Vailima, looking over the broad ocean they had explored together so many years before.

Conclusion: On the Art of Marriage

The consummation of our hopes in marriage happens not only through the daily testing of our ideals and our ability to bring those ideals alive in the partnership, but in the collision between the part of us that has great difficulty sustaining conversation with anything other than ourself. Marriage is where we realize the other person actually is alive and has notions and desires that have very little to do with our own hopes and dreams. Marriage is where we have to be larger than the self who first made the vows.

Marriage is where we realize that we have also married a stranger whom we must get to know. Marriage is where we learn self-knowledge; where we realize that parts of our own makeup are stranger even than the stranger we have married and very difficult for another person to live with. Marriage is where we realize how much effort we put into preserving our own sense of space and our own sense of self. Marriage is where we realize how much we want to be right and seen to be right. Marriage is where all of these difficult revelations can consign us to imprisonment or help us become larger, more generous, more amusing, more animated participants in the human drama.

A Long List and a Self-Evident Conclusion from Stevenson's Literary Output

A courtship and marriage that includes long separation, near starvation, near death, ill health, disappointment, age disparity, alienated parents, a blended family, being a stepparent, constant travel and constant cultural adjustment is no excuse for not paying attention to the other two marriages of work and self. A good central conversation can bring all the other conversations alive.

Below is a list of Stevenson's works completed *before, despite, because of* and especially *during* all the above.

BOOKS

The Pentland Rising. Edinburgh: Privately printed, 1866.

An Appeal to the Clergy. Edinburgh and London: Blackwood, 1875.

An Inland Voyage. London: Kegan Paul, 1878; Boston: Roberts Brothers, 1883.

Edinburgh: Picturesque Notes, with Etchings. London: Seeley, Jackson & Halliday, 1879; New York: Macmillan, 1889.

Travels with a Donkey in the Cévennes. London: Kegan Paul, 1879; Boston: Roberts Brothers, 1879.

Virginibus Puerisque and Other Papers. London: Kegan Paul, 1881; New York: Collier, 1881.

Familiar Studies of Men and Books. London: Chatto & Windus, 1882; New York: Dodd, Mead, 1887.

New Arabian Nights. London: Chatto & Windus, 1882 (2 vols.); New York: Holt, 1882 (1 vol.).

The Silverado Squatters. London: Chatto & Windus, 1883; New York: Munro, 1884.

Treasure Island. London: Cassell, 1883; Boston: Roberts Brothers, 1884.

A Child's Garden of Verses. London: Longmans, Green, 1885;
  New York: Charles Scribner's Sons, 1885.

Macaire. Edinburgh: Privately printed, 1885.

More New Arabian Nights: The Dynamiter, by Stevenson and Fanny
  Van de Grift Stevenson. London: Longmans, Green, 1885;
  New York: Holt, 1885.

Prince Otto: A Romance. London: Chatto & Windus, 1885; Boston:
  Roberts Brothers, 1886.

Kidnapped. London: Cassell, 1886; New York: Charles Scribner's
  Sons, 1886.

Some College Memories. Edinburgh: University Union Committee,
  1886; New York: Mansfield & Wessels, 1899.

The Strange Case of Dr. Jekyll and Mr. Hyde. London: Longmans,
  Green, 1886; New York: Charles Scribner's Sons, 1886.

The Merry Men and Other Tales and Fables. London: Chatto &
  Windus, 1887; New York: Charles Scribner's Sons, 1887.

Memoir of Fleeming Jenkin. London and New York: Longmans,
  Green, 1887.

Memories and Portraits. London: Chatto & Windus, 1887; New
  York: Charles Scribner's Sons, 1887.

The Misadventures of John Nicholson: A Christmas Story. New York:
  Lovell, 1887.

Underwoods. London: Chatto & Windus, 1887; New York: Charles
  Scribner's Sons, 1887.

The Black Arrow: A Tale of the Two Roses. London: Cassell, 1888;
  New York: Charles Scribner's Sons, 1888.

The Master of Ballantrae: A Winter's Tale. London: Cassell, 1889;
  New York: Charles Scribner's Sons, 1889.

The Wrong Box, by Stevenson and Lloyd Osbourne. London: Longmans, Green, 1889; New York: Charles Scribner's Sons, 1889.

Ballads. London: Chatto & Windus, 1890; New York: Charles Scribner's Sons, 1890.

Father Damien: An Open Letter to the Reverend Dr. Hyde of Honolulu. London: Chatto & Windus, 1890; Portland, Maine: Mosher, 1897.

Across the Plains, with Other Memories and Essays. London: Chatto & Windus, 1892; New York: Charles Scribner's Sons, 1892.

A Footnote to History: Eight Years of Trouble in Samoa. London: Cassell, 1892; New York: Charles Scribner's Sons, 1892.

Three Plays: Deacon Brodie, Beau Austen, Admiral Guinea, by Stevenson and W. E. Henley. London: Nutt, 1892; New York: Charles Scribner's Sons, 1892.

The Wrecker, by Stevenson and Lloyd Osbourne. London: Cassell, 1892; New York: Charles Scribner's Sons, 1892.

Catriona: A Sequel to Kidnapped. London: Cassell, 1893; New York: Charles Scribner's Sons, 1893.

Island Nights' Entertainments: Consisting of The Beach of Falesá, The Bottle Imp, The Isle of Voices. London: Cassell, 1893; New York: Charles Scribner's Sons, 1893.

The Ebb-Tide: A Trio and a Quartette, by Stevenson and Lloyd Osbourne. Chicago: Stone & Kimball, 1894; London: Heinemann, 1894.

The Body-Snatcher. New York: Merriam, 1895.

The Amateur Emigrant from the Clyde to Sandy Hook. Chicago: Stone & Kimball, 1895; New York: Charles Scribner's Sons, 1899.

In the South Seas. New York: Charles Scribner's Sons, 1896; London: Chatto & Windus, 1900.

A Mountain Town in France: A Fragment. New York & London: Lane, 1896.

Songs of Travel and Other Verses. London: Chatto & Windus, 1896.

The Strange Case of Dr. Jekyll and Mr. Hyde, with Other Fables. London: Longmans, Green, 1896.

Weir of Hermiston: An Unfinished Romance. London: Chatto & Windus, 1896; New York: Charles Scribner's Sons, 1896.

St. Ives: Being the Adventures of a French Prisoner in England. New York: Charles Scribner's Sons, 1897; London: Heinemann, 1898.

The Morality of the Profession of Letters. Gouverneur, N.Y.: Brothers of the Book, 1899.

Essays and Criticisms. Boston: Turner, 1903.

Prayers Written at Vailima, with an Introduction by Mrs. Stevenson. New York: Charles Scribner's Sons, 1904; London: Chatto & Windus, 1905.

The Story of a Lie and Other Tales. Boston: Turner, 1904.

Essays in the Art of Writing. London: Chatto & Windus, 1905.

Essays of Travel. London: Chatto & Windus, 1905.

Lay Morals and Other Papers. London: Chatto & Windus, 1911.

On the Choice of a Profession. London: Chatto & Windus, 1916.

Poems Hitherto Unpublished. Ed. G. S. Hellman, 2 vol. Boston: Bibliophile Society, 1916.

Records of a Family of Engineers. London: Chatto & Windus, 1916.

The Waif Woman. London: Chatto & Windus, 1916.

New Poems and Variant Readings. London: Chatto & Windus, 1918.

Confessions of a Unionist: An Unpublished Talk on Things Current, Written in 1888. Ed. F. V. Livingston. Cambridge, Mass.: Privately printed, 1921.

Robert Louis Stevenson: Hitherto Unpublished Prose Writings. Ed. H. H. Harper. Boston: Bibliophile Society, 1921.

When the Devil Was Well. Ed. William P. Trent. Boston: Bibliophile Society, 1921.

The Best Thing in Edinburgh: An Address to the Speculative Society of Edinburgh in March 1873. Ed. K. D. Osbourne. San Francisco: Howell, 1923.

Castaways of Soledad: A Manuscript by Stevenson Hitherto Unpublished. Ed. G. S. Hellman. Buffalo: Privately printed, 1928.

Monmouth: A Tragedy. Ed. C. Vale. New York: Rudge, 1928.

The Charity Bazaar: An Allegorical Dialogue. Westport, Conn.: Georgian Press, 1929.

LETTERS

The Letters of Robert Louis Stevenson to His Family and Friends. Ed. Sidney Colvin. London: Methuen, 1899.

CHAPTER 12

A Sweet Prison:
Living with the
Work We've Chosen

Writers may seem the ultimate imaginative travelers, but like most of us in work, what they crave most of all is a settled rhythm and a place they can call their own in which to get things done. Though the run-up to a marriage needs the drama and passion of courtship, the tone and atmosphere of the marriage itself is almost always understated, the magic more subtle.

Equally with the marriage with work: almost all human endeavor needs a cradle to hold it and carry it along, particularly in its early stages. The act of creating a place in which to work: a desk with a pleasant aspect, by a window if possible; a corner where we can see our coworkers but still have a sense of privacy can create a sense of buoyancy and current that can float us through very difficult days. But because work, like a marriage with another person, demands this daily psychological cradle to hold it and make it real, it can also suffer from the same twin maladies of confinement and boredom. We long for the everyday with a partner of desire, we long for the everyday with a work we can love and have and hold, and then we find that it is a rare living art form to keep either a marriage or a work fresh and alive.

I am rarely jealous of anything posessed by others, but quite recently, while visiting a friend in a very quiet corner of the West of Ireland, I discovered the demon of envy living quietly in my breast. I entered his study and found myself in a little working paradise that made me almost giddy with desire. The center of attention was a beautifully organized desk, which sat level with a window that gazed out onto a wild acreage of grass and meadow that rose and rose into the mountains of Connemara.

The mountain landscape seemed to offer an invitation to horizons as yet touched; as yet unbroached. Not only was this desk the meeting point of an incredible outside with a beautiful inside, but it was also the place where finely constructed bookshelves gathered at either side of my friend's shoulders and curved off into the room. The shelves were filled with first editions and manuscripts: objects of love and constant examination.

The room had an atmosphere of enjoyment, inquiry and study that filled the air almost like incense. I gazed upon that meticulously put togther and maintained study as a motorsport aficionado might gaze openmouthed upon a racing-green 1959 Jaguar XK 150 roadster, in gleaming concours condition. I wanted to turn the key and drive this study off into my literary future. On the surface, I sat in a chair talking to my friend, drinking tea; chatting about Irish poets and poetry, but inside I was seasick with longing for a place like this, a space like this and the days of work that could come from being seated in the very chair he was occupying.

But would it be good for me? In this study, as in the Jaguar, I imagined the wind in my hair as I threw the gear changes through page after page of uninterrupted writing. The glittering object of desire is often seen as the answer to all present difficulties. The natural thought is that with this incredible thing, with this woman, with this car, with this work space, I will be different; a person without the problems I possess now. But there are manifold drawbacks to the mistake of actually purchasing the 1959 Jaguar XK 150 roadster that I longed for so mightily at the classic car rally. Could I maintain it? Could I even afford to maintain it? Do I have the day-by-day energy and character to keep it in the manner to which it is accustomed? Would my drives in the countryside be flawed with worries about paint work, insurance, an irreplaceable part about to go in an inaccessible place? The outer show is often a precious conceit. It is a want that may actually be a way of stopping real things from happening.

My friend's desk and study might be just as problematic for the simple reason that they are not mine. I did not build them from the ground up, they are not a natural outcome of the way I work. I did not grow in that particular community and that landscape where he did; the logistics of life, cultural adjustment and travel might overwhelm any ability to work for a good while. I would be ruling someone else's kingdom and the truculent nobles might rebel; conspire to depose me and get me out. Even the effort to create in my own home a study like the one he possesses may dispossess me from the actual act of working.

My own kingdom is always more austere, my own arrangements never completely messy but never completely tidy. I always put the act of work before the act of arranging things so that the background to whatever foreground I may be involved in at the desk very quickly disappears. If I look closely at what I need for work, the prized, internal possesion of focus is much more important than the external environment that I might lust after in the abstract.

The interesting dynamic about human happiness in the marriage to work is that we can glide down the road in the metaphorical Jaguar XK 150, having a completely miserable, blazing argument with our partner while the wind is blowing unheeded through our hair. I can also find myself in the aptly named Ford Focus, laughing my way into a marvelous excursion. But neither Ford Focus nor Jaguar can guarantee us a place in the kingdom of happiness. It is the one in the driver's seat, setting the destination and the attitude for the journey of work and vocation, who seems to make up our real possibilities for satisfaction over time.

The difficult truth is that our kingdom does not have to be very big at all in order for us to do good work: what is difficult is simply starting the work and carrying on with it day after day. My work space can be a small corner of a table on a train or if we are really, really focused, a knee on which to balance a writing pad.

I once stood in fascination over a man crouched on the scruffy floor of a swaying London Underground carriage. He was furiously scribbling paragraph after paragraph as we hurtled along through the black dark of the Bakerloo Line. Nothing stopped his work—not the accidental kick of his pad by passengers getting on or off at the stops, not his falling back onto his bottom when the train halted in the tunnel. He simply picked up his pen again in whatever position he now found himself in and carried on writing energetically. My first guess was that he was a journalist with a deadline and an irate editor had just shouted at him over the phone. But there was something about the man's utter concentration, his almost pleasurable forgetting of the squalid world around him and the determination that drove him on, line after line, that made him seem free in his intensity from outside pressures.

The memory of that man has stayed with me year after year, reminding me that I could work wherever there was a corner, wherever there was a knee or a pen or a pad, wherever there was a pause in the besieging clamor of the world. I didn't need a paradise in order to work, but work itself, given focus and given time for that focus to blossom, could open a little Eden of its own.

Most work is done in the midst of a host of other clamoring, crowding priorities. The great swaying underground carriage of life. The other two marriages do not go away just because we have a boss shouting back at the office. Leave the first marriage to a real person alone for too long, and our partner will have far more searching things to say about us than our employer. Lose a sense of self in the process of working, and we very quickly begin to hate the person at the center of the struggle.

WORK AND PARENTING: THE SHOCK
OF THE CHILD'S ARRIVAL

One of the most difficult pulls in this constantly pulling world is the pull of parenting. There is no more clamoring and necessary distraction than the needs of a child. For most of us there is no dispute about whose needs come first. The infant is king and queen of our days and extends its reign far into the night. There is a psychological shock to the system confronted with the enormous amount of time and worry a child can take out of two healthy people, never mind a single struggling parent. Our pre-child imagination has no comprehension of the way an infant can drain twenty-four hours of any time to rest and recuperate let alone turn our minds to the joys of creation. For many, a child's youngest years, though filled with other rewards, can be a kind of panicked exile for parents at least as far as their work is concerned. The equivalent of Jane Austen's wilderness years in Bath and Southampton when she felt completely at the behest of others' needs with no place to call her own in which to think or rest or build a life she would want for herself.

The psychological shock wave of parenting almost always passes through a woman's psyche with far more power than a man's. Though the male psyche may feel devastated and exhausted by a child's arrival; though he may feel marginalized in the sexual affections of his wife; though he may scour the shops for diapers, breast pumps, bottles and the latest in baby transport; though he may wake as many times in the night, his mode of thinking, his ability to split and compartmentalize his life, and above all, his biological and inherited excuses to go out the door to earn the bread in the early days of the child's infancy, give him a powerful pivot from which to keep his ambitions and his work alive in his imagination.

Many women are not only overwhelmed by the mighty and often beautiful sense of connection with the newly arrived being just plucked from their person, but often have secondary health difficulties that come with the physical experience of the birth. It is hard to really comprehend how much physiological capital our bodies put into the necessity of giving birth. The evolutionary powers playing through our psyche place the preservation of the human race through reproduction far above the need for a good job or satisfying work. That part of the world that is behind our procreation doesn't really care if we drag our last burden of nourishment for our infant through the frozen wastes and die in the snow outside the cave door, as long as that burden gets to the child and allows it to survive until the other parent or the grandparent or the tribe can take over and see it through to adulthood.

There are two possibilities, perhaps we can call them necessities, for keeping the marriage with work alive through the difficult years of childbearing and child rearing. The first is to reimagine the way we have named our work and defined its success. We may find that our priorities have been erased and redrawn by a birth or an adoption; that we don't care for the corporate world's priorities anymore and that mothering or indeed fathering is now our central work.

We may come to the reimagination of our work through the gladly received, genuine revelations of parenting or especially for women, with difficulty, through a rueful acceptance that the months or years with a child have taken us off the career track and that the sacrifices needed to get back on that moving stair are not worth what it would take. Even if we find that circumstances allow us both to be a good parent and to follow a brilliant career, the moral basis of the brilliant career hinges on not neglecting or abandoning our children at crucial times in their growing, and demands that we reexamine the basis of our marriage with work and many of the outer rewards of prestige we demanded up to the moment we became parents.

OPENING A SPACE

The second necessity is to find a rhythm, often with the help of our partner or our family or our friends that enables us to make short visits to that kingdom of silence and creativity. These short visits on a regular, rhythmical basis may not further the work very much in the early days, but they are essential to keeping it alive in the heart and mind of the struggling parent until time begins to open up as the child grows and goes off to school.

As this window begins to widen and allow fresh air into the life of the besieged parent, the work also slowly begins to resuscitate itself and come back to life. Our vocation starts to pick its feet out of the mud and move onto higher, drier ground.

J. K. Rowling famously wrote large portions of the first Harry Potter book in the midst of this caked, slow-moving, mud-walking, desperate parent stage. "There was a point where I really felt I had 'penniless divorcée, lone parent' tattooed on my head," she said in one interview. Living alone with her infant daughter, Jessica, in an unheated Edinburgh flat, she would trudge through the streets wheeling Jessica to a local café and snatch moments at her writing between feeding and comforting her child. It's a help to know that Rowling felt a general hopelessness during much of that time, and a further encouragement to know that she kept on moving through the mud, kept on writing despite her quiet, private despair.

The café in Edinburgh where J. K. Rowling wrote now has a small plaque on the wall outside to explain who sat there with such private, unsung courage. Most likely the place in which we sit and struggle to bring our work back to life will have nothing to commemorate it except a little window in our own memory that opens onto the small stage on which we appeared during difficult times.

Perhaps each of us should go back with actual plaques and place them in cafés, on walls or in office cubicles with little notes of private courage for the inspiration of others. "This is where I kept my faith alive during very dark days," "This is where I found the courage to leave my marriage," or "This is where I realized that I couldn't have everything I wanted and so felt the freedom to request what I needed." Such puzzling, intriguing and inspirational signs everywhere might bring us to an understanding of the constant enacted dramas occurring around us. How every chair and every corner holds a possibility for redemption. The plaques that said things such as "This is the table where I gave up on my ideals and took a very large bribe" would be equally instructive for the reader.

What J. K. Rowling and the Jaguar XK 150 tell us is that what human beings need around them to do good work is always less than they think. What is difficult about sustaining a close, intimate relationship with our work is what is difficult in the other two marriages—the willingness to give ourself to its underlying priorities and to do it wholeheartedly, for even just a snatched half-hour, day by day. What is required is to dig deep emotionally, conversationally and thematically, however slowly and however incrementally, in one area. It is something we can return to from powerful evolutionary forces such as child rearing or from other, more seductive but surface distractions that are less overwhelming yet more insidious than the demands of raising a child.

We could describe the inability to focus in our work as a kind of vocational promiscuity—an unwillingness to be faithful to a central theme, an indication either that we have chosen the wrong work just as we might have chosen the wrong partner, or that we are afraid of the deeper context to which it is leading. We may be afraid of living up to that greater context. The intimacies that come with giving ourselves wholeheartedly to a

relationship have always been acknowledged as being frightening, but there is also a deeper intimacy and a certain kind of
risk that comes with giving ourselves wholeheartedly to a work.
Like a good relationship, a good work followed for a goodly
amount of time always opens up our own character: our virtues
and our many, many flaws; a good work like a good relationship
always eventually asks us to be bigger than our own wants and
desires, to see ourselves in a much larger context than the self
that thought it had gained everything it wanted to keep itself
safe.

One of the central disciplines of work is also one of the central disciplines of relationship: not getting caught in abstracts
and outer forms but staying close to the internal ground, the
sure foundation upon which the work or the couple stand. It is
this central foundation where our possibilities of happiness are
to be found. This foundation is almost always a place of radical
simplicity, unlike many of the towering, tottering, Dr. Seuss–
like structures we raise above it.

Though we must have vision it is important not to overbur-
den our work with abstract expectations. My exploration of far
horizons may not need a Jaguar XK 150 to find satisfaction in
the world. My desperation for peace and quiet in which to do
my work may not need a view of the mountains of Connemara.
My expression of love and affection for my partner may not
need a balcony in Hawaii on which to do it. The relationship
depends not only on romance in the Tropics but on daily affections in the grayer climate of the everyday. We may be lucky
and find both, but I may be able to enrich the marriage without

straining it with extra debt for the hotel and meals in Honolulu. By accident or luck, the work I have chosen may get me the mountain-view study and the Jaguar to drive there, but more likely I will be deflected by those attainments if they were not natural to my interests in the first place. The marriage of work has everything to do with the romance of the everyday.

If we feel we need a perfect partner or a perfect house in which to live out a marriage or a perfect study to do our work, or the perfectly perfect car to feel good about ourselves, it is instructive and humbling to see the conditions under which Jane Austen revised *Pride and Prejudice* and *Sense and Sensibility* and then wrote from scratch three very "big" novels, *Mansfield Park, Emma* and *Persuasion*. Her center of operations would have put most writers to despair.

Jane's study, once she was finally settled into the cottage at Chawton, was no real study at all, but a small family living room constrained by being set in the midst of all the daily activities of the house. Her desk was a small table on which perched a sloping writing bureau under which she seemed to have been able to put away quickly any fresh manuscript page whenever anyone entered by the door, which seems to have been quite frequently. One of the well-loved stories at Chawton that modern-day guides tell visitors is that Jane specifically asked for a squeaky hinge on the door to be left unoiled so that she would have a warning anytime the door was about to open. As the house was filled with the constant bustle of three women—her sister, her mother and a close friend of the family—the squeak must have been a constant annunciation of interruption. All this seems to have provided her, against the odds and against our needs for perfection, all the room and time enough for her to write and revise five classic novels.

The small desk must have constituted an incredibly tiny lens for her to bring such a large world into focus. It must, at the same time, have felt absolutely essential to her happiness as a writer. It was her far-off island, her mountain cabin and her own kingdom all at once. It was to this small desk that Jane Austen returned again and again, living out the settled marriage to her work.

In retrospect, looking back over any marriage, there is an intensity to the days we fill with children, meals, arguments, hilarity and exhausted floppings into bed. Yet as we look back over the procession of days, most of those days seem inseparable from one another; very few particular days are actually preserved unique unto themselves in the amber of memory. In many ways the settled intensity of a good work is very similar. From the outside very little seems to be happening, but in good work we return every day to the desk or the workbench to push it along a little further. We inch along or fly along, depending on what part of the cycle of endeavor we have entered. What we remember looking back, is the rhythm and constant sense of returning to the frontier we have just established. Like the hundreds of times we enter a kitchen in our marriage to make another meal, or join the morning frenzy to get the kids out the door to school, we are in a particular time, but we are out of it at the same time, in a kind of eternity, where time does not seem to have touched us in the same way. Where, if the intensity of focus is deep enough, we seem to feel as if time is actually radiating out from the place we stand. In good work we occupy a frontier between what has been done and what is about to be done, both giving almost an equal sense of satisfaction. Each time we return to the work, that frontier is a little further out and a little nearer to accomplishing what we first set out to achieve. Like being in the midst of a growing family, we can sense the steadily growing satisfaction of a work slowly beginning to form: the coaxing of that work through all the setbacks and the dead ends, the final ability to bring it to a conclusion, and the sense of satisfaction we feel in finally sending it out in the world for others to examine and use, is one of the great privileges of having found a vocation to which we want to give ourselves wholeheartedly.

Jane Austen's wholehearted return to writing soon had her bringing out manuscripts she had written years before, which had lain in packets during the years of exile in the Bath and Southampton. She worked intensely at the little desk, "lopping and chopping," as she described it, until she had resuscitated both *Sense and Sensibility* and *Pride and Prejudice* and, we must imagine, her own lost, exiled self at the same time. In the process she must have healed that marriage with the self, which had lapsed over the previous years; she must have brought to a halt the flow of corrosive shame we have about our selves when we cannot get to a work we know we were made to do.

There must have been a curious parallel in bringing the younger self who had written the first draft all those years before into conversation with the person she had become. She was bringing that younger person back alive and at the same time bringing the text up to the standard her mature sensibilities could live with, shading and lightening her characters and her plotlines.

Jane Austen had a great deal of light and dark in her life. The patterns and the crosscurrents of aloneness and community forged her sensibilities as a writer. As a woman she was unlucky to be exiled from the mainstream experience of marriage and as an author very unlucky to be kept from publication and writing until her mid-thirties, though, as with Rowling, one of her manuscripts had lain in a publisher's drawer for years.

But as a woman who was a serious writer, she was also very, very lucky to have never married. Childbearing and the overwhelming identity of wife and mother at that time might have buried her talent as a writer for good. As an author she was also very lucky not to have been published so early. Her early ability to play the giddy flirt may have taken a young and successful Austen into the shallower end of literary London; may have dissipated her judgments and her sense of distance. There is something unmistakable about Jane Austen's voice as a writer. Her individual form of narration, had become over the years of isolation, that of the consummate outsider but that of the outsider who knows how the inside works. Exile, unhappiness and invisibility gave her a place at the edge of the crowd from which to sit and watch, and from that place she steadily unveiled the structures of everyday life that had been so readily taken for granted by those who were so constantly up on the floor, dancing.

Her close relationship to her work was echoed also by her very close relationships with her sister and her mother. She had a busy, affectionate family around her that also had plenty of what we might term today "dysfunctionalities." But far more important, no matter the cyclical round of affection and tension with mother or sister, was the fact that they were *her* family. This was *her* home, *her* study, *her* family, no matter how eccentric or strange.

LIVING WITH FAMILIAR DIFFICULTIES

A marriage with a work, like a marriage with a person, has its particular miseries no matter what the balance of happiness may be. But we know we are right for the work when we feel big enough to live with the particular difficulties it entails. One of the ways we recognize we are married to the right person is that we find not only that we can live with the person's particular foibles, but also that we can live with the particular form of insanity we create together as a couple. Like a particular marriage, every work has its own particular rhyme and reason but also its strange epiphenomena. As with the strange baby language some couples create to form a private brand of communication, we find ourselves with a particular and sometimes peculiar grammar to our work. This grammar can take very interesting forms. On launching my own career as a writer I had no idea that poetry would take me so firmly into the world of international air travel. I spend as much time in airplanes and airports as I do actually speaking and reading at the end of the journey. To negotiate the air with at least a semblance of dignity it is necessary to become something of an expert on air mileage plans and upgrades, to know the preferable seats on particular aircraft, to join airline lounge clubs and to become knowledegable about the effects of jet lag, diet, sunlight and exercise on a body that must arrive fit and intelligent enough to speak—a skill I did not have the faintest idea I would need when I first gazed at the portrait of Keats staring dreamily off into an imaginative space I would negotiate at least partly by jet plane.

One of the most tempting abstracts of work is also at first sight its prime reality, the earning of money and prestige. There is no doubt that work should keep us from starving and our children from want, but there seems to be more possibility of genuine happiness in life if we let our wants grow naturally along with our income, rather than let it pull us away from the next natural steps in our progression and on into an artificial abstraction conjured from equally abstract wants—wants that may avalanche and overwhelm our commitment to the present.

Work is too easily connected in our mind to money, without our thinking hard enough about what the money actually allows us to do or whether the money itself is poisoning the soil in which the work is rooted.

The most successful novelist of Jane Austen's time was Sir Walter Scott, who combined his love of the written form with the ability to earn enormous sums of money for his historical novels. His first impressions of Jane Austen's writing as work-manlike and pleasing soon matured into a broad and deeply puzzled admiration.

> *We bestow no mean compliment upon the author of "Emma" when we say that keeping close to common incidents, and to such characters as occupy the ordinary walks of life, she has produced sketches of such spirit and originality that we never miss the excitation which depends upon a narrative of uncommon events. . . . In this class she stands almost alone; . . . the author of "Emma" confines herself chiefly to the middling classes of society; her most distinguished characters do not rise greatly above well-bred country gentlemen and ladies; and those which are sketched with most originality and precision, belong to a class rather below that standard. The narrative of all her novels is composed of such common occurrences as may have fallen under the observation of most folks; and her* dramatis personae *conduct themselves upon the motives and principles which the readers may recognize as ruling their own, and that of most of their own acquaintances.*

Scott was slowly coming to understand that this obscure woman might have a foundation to her writing that he himself struggled to find. He seemed to intuit that she was working with a territory that underlay the workings of the human psyche in a way that he himself had missed or had had difficulty reaching; as if he understood that the outer abstracts of adventure and derring-do in his novels had overwhelmed something far more important that Jane Austen had caught and displayed.

Scott was an exceedingly generous and openhanded man, as virtuous in life as many of the historical figures who filled his books, and his generous character shines through in this journal entry from March 1826.

> Read again, and for the third time at least, Miss Austen's very finely written novel of "Pride and Prejudice." That young lady has a talent for describing the involvements and feelings and characters of ordinary life which is to me the most wonderful I ever met with. The big bow-wow strain I can do myself like any now going; but the exquisite touch, which renders ordinary commonplace things and characters interesting, from the truth of the description and the sentiment, is denied to me.

There is something instructive and vulnerable about Scott's admitting to himself that he might have missed the forest for the trees. Whether it be in marriage or work or in our sense of personal happiness, we are constantly looking for the big answer, the big bow-wow strain, that will elevate or eliminate the tiny steps we have to take every day to keep the conversation alive and put us into a world where these little acts of vulnerability and frustration do not affect us. The temptation is to look for a kind of virtual existence, a Second Life where we are not touched by grief or age or a realization that our particular individual powers are so dependent on another.

The act of keeping close to the marriage with our work and vocation is the act of returning day after day, not only to the workplace, but to the physical and philosophical foundations that keep it alive in our hearts and minds as we grow and mature and even as we age and die. To be faithful to a work, we must welcome its vulnerabilities and difficulties as well as the many gifts it bestows. We must find the foundation upon which the marriage of work stands and grows and then through the difficult cycles of a human life constantly tend it and nourish it. At the end we may have to have the courage to tend it only through memory, but that memory will be rich with remembered voices and shared endeavor. If we push away the difficulty in work while young or never turn to face it in midlife and hope for safety in the abstract, we will find, as we do in a real marriage, that we are left deserted in our old age, by memory, by those who were never touched by our generosity. We will find ourselves in the company of abstracts, those merely being paid to sit by our bedside, and very far, physically and imaginatively, from those to whom we should have given ourselves more readily.

Though she died at only forty-one, Jane Austen must have known that her particular way of seeing had been passed on to many thousands of people. She would be astonished to know two centuries later how many millions had shared that seeing: she, who felt most at home in a village of "four and twenty families." She would also have had the satisfaction of knowing that her "children," in the shape of her characters, were alive and well in the imaginations of others and making their way in the world entirely on their own.

Many of us will have a less public satisfaction from our accomplishments, and many of us will never have our contributions acknowledged at all, but the knowledge that we have affected others and will be remembered even indirectly through our work seems to be a powerful arbitrator of human satisfaction. When we find a real vocation we "marry" our work but we also commit beyond the immediate work to a legacy we will leave behind us; we make vows to an invisible future that will somehow be sustained by an equally invisible harvest somehow gleaned from all the very, very visible effort. In work we marry a hoped-for future as much as we do when we marry a person. The memory and the hoped-for legacy is with us "till death do us part."

Conclusion: A Settled Marriage with a Work

Looking from the outside on a work is like looking from the outside on a marriage: on any given day, nothing much seems to be happening. J. K. Rowling working at her café table with a stroller at her side would have aroused very little comment; Jane Austen would have been difficult to catch in the actual act of working, particularly if we came in by the creaking door. The dramas and passion of courtship are replaced by what seems at first a hard-to-discern undercurrent. The progression of a settled work or a settled marriage is subtler, the magic being woven less overt. As it is difficult to explain the mechanics of a given marriage, so it is difficult to explain the mechanics of a vocation. Perhaps because it has less to do with mechanics than the slowly building, concentrated focus that gets the job done. The subtle joys of a steady application to a work yielding up its secrets and its subtle triumphs are hard to explain. Just as almost no one wants to know how happily married we are, almost no one wants to know the details of how we gain our sense of satisfaction in work.

We know we have the right vocation and are happily married to a work when we get a song in our hearts simply from doing the work itself, as much as from its rewards and its fruits.

Becoming visible to the world through our work seems to be a central necessity in a vocation. The more invisible we feel, the more unheard, unseen, unheeded, the more dissatisfied we seem to be and the more unreal we seem to ourselves. This attempt at visibility involves not just our effect on the present but also our effect on those yet to follow us. In the marriage with work, our legacy is our favored child, one we have made ourselves from our own body, one that for many years kept us awake at nights, a legacy through which we want to pass on our best hopes and dreams, something with a life of its own and something perhaps, just beginning to create its own future.

CHAPTER 13

Living with the Self:
Divorce, Forgiveness
and Remarriage

We were descending through darkness now: the trail following the endless wooded hillside down from the high mountains into the life-giving air below ten thousand feet. We had begun walking before dawn that morning but were still hours away from the flat, open valley bottom where we would pitch our tents at last. By now, many in our party were exhausted, tripping and falling frequently down the hellish, forest trail of liquid mud churned up by innumerable passing yaks. The rain had not stopped for the last week, and everyone was tired and by now, completely wet through. As leader of the group, however, I could not afford to be tired, though I had no choice about being wet. We had been walking for twelve hours now and along the way we had lost track of one of our number: a woman in our group who had disappeared during this long forest descent; every corner or rest spot on the trail offered me the possibility of seeing her, as I hoped, above all hope, she had merely gone ahead of us and found her way down.

But my suspicions that she had taken another route were growing by the hour. Our Bhutanese guide was a difficult character at the best of times, and even though his English was perfect, it was employed mostly in elaborate self-justifications, in telling us stories about how marvelous he was in every capacity and how any mistakes that had been made were someone else's. He had spoken to the group in the predawn darkness and told us all that there was only one trail down and that we could straggle out as much as we wanted because we could not get lost. My instincts had been to countermand the offer to straggle, but I had already been involved in a number of power struggles with this fellow, and in my hesitation the group was already off and away trying to gain as much distance as possible on what was to be at least a twelve-hour walk, the last walk of our ten-day trek through Bhutan.

By the time twelve hours had passed, we were still many hours from the valley floor, the constant rain of that day and the previous week having turned the paths into quagmires; we had also passed at least three places where the path bifurcated and where anyone straggling out in front could have taken a different path from the main body of the group, who by now were rightly staying close to the guide. When I looked the guide in the eyes as we sat beneath a large tree in the mud and told him that we could easily have lost a number of our group on the alternatives presented so far, he took it almost as a personal insult. It was a final confirmation, but too late now, that his priorities had nothing to do with the safety of the people in his care and everything to do with whether he was in the right.

I had only myself to blame. The clues had been there from the beginning. This fellow had puzzled me right from the very start. He did not strike me as being like any other Bhutanese I had met, nor was he like any Buddhists I had met in other Himalayan regions I had visited. On first arriving in Bhutan, I had spent an evening with him alone in the bars of Thimphu as an easy way of getting to know him and found myself, despite his wearing a traditional Bhutanese tunic, in the company of a coarse frat boy with reservoirs of resentment and a rampant sexual animus for any passing woman that completely floored me.

Late that night I heard his story and began to understand. When he was a child, Catholic missionaries had come to his family and offered to take him for schooling in northern India, free and clear, and all paid for. Under pressure from his family, he had gone, at six or seven years old, out of this high, poor but clear, inherited world and down into the foothills of India, where he had been thrown into a world where Catholicism met Hinduism and then met colonialism and it all combined in a Catholic, Hindu, colonial, repressed sexuality. It was a crossroads for which he did not seem to have received any proper guidance. No wonder he found it difficult guiding others. The move managed to uproot his Buddhist foundation without properly replacing it with a good Catholic one. What he had was the Catholic's appreciation of sin without the accompanying fear of its consequences and without a Buddhist's ability to watch those desires rise and fall away. More important, there was an almost physical sense of a split in this man's psyche, an irredeemable heartache and wound at having been rent from his family that was completely unconscious and driven out in pure resentment for a world that had exiled him. He was a man divorced from his inheritance, from himself and from those he was supposed to be guiding.

Ten days before this final muddy night, our first day's walk had ended in a debacle worthy of a Dublin Saturday night. We had come to a beautiful grassy shelf overlooking a river that our guide had told us would be our destination. But when we arrived at the place, we found it already occupied by another trekking group following the same river valley up into the mountains. What began as a robust argument, with our guide asking the other group's guide to move on, degenerated into a deadly face-off when our man drew the knife traditionally kept in the bosom of his very traditional tunic and threatened the other guide. Blood would have been spilled if we had not pulled our guide off and set up camp far enough up the river for the con-flict not to be resumed. Looking back, I see that I should have turned us around, marched back to Thimphu and replaced our guide. I prevaricated. We carried on.

Now, ten days later, after much damage control and contain-ment of this man, we had lost someone right at the end of the trek; again because of my hesitations in confronting my neme-sis. When we finally reached the valley floor and the end of the enclosing forest, the loss of the woman was confirmed. She was not there. There followed a very fierce argument about whether to alert the authorities in Thimphu so that they could send a search-and-rescue party, which I eventually won by simply going to the official who had greeted us at the end of the trail and telling him what had happened. I was beyond caring about this man's professional pride anymore.

Although I was told that the rescue party would be there by morning, I felt an overwhelming sense of responsibility for the woman and decided to set off back up the trail with a head torch and extra batteries to try to find her down one of the side branches where I had been told there was a woodcutter's hut. It was at least five hours back up to this branch of the trail through rain and mud. One of the yak herders who accompanied our group was chosen out to go with me, as I made it clear I did not want our egotistical guide along. Amusingly, this yak herder went by the nickname of "Superman" because of his distinctive blue-and-red-dyed robes. He certainly did not look the part of the superhero; he was very slender, with not an ounce of muscle on him, and he had obviously drawn the short straw amongst his fellow herders. I had no idea that Superman comics had even made it to these mountain regions of Bhutan, but Superman and I duly set off up into the dark, rain-soaked forest, where I soon found that despite his title he was terrified of the dark and very, very tired after his long day.

The job of yak herders is to run, and I mean run, behind the yaks as they carry their enormous burdens down the mountain trails, throwing sticks and stones and singing innumerable yak-herding songs to chivvy them along. With their throwing and running yak herders cover probably twice the distance of any trekker on the same trail. Yaks are by no means domesticated, but are wild and aggressive creatures that are barely tamed and that take an enormous amount of energy to keep them headed in the right direction. Each yak follows a strict hierarchy in the procession, with the leader carrying innumerable ribbons and bells hanging from its long and very dangerous horns.

The yaks would always set off late, with the camp on their backs, after the main group had left, and then around ten o'clock charge through our group of panicked trekkers, who at that time would be on eggshells listening for the daily cry: "The yaks are coming." Climbing a tree or a rock, or running at right angles at great speed into the bush was undignified but highly recommended. The sight of the herders themselves, singing, shouting and throwing sticks and stones after the hurtling, burdened beasts, was always a sign that peace would reign again until the whole process was repeated again the following day.

Now Superman seemed tired and bereft without the yaks as a focus for his efforts. We walked at a fast pace through the night, hour after hour, and all the while I ignored his obvious distress. As we walked, he sang an unending jabbering song, interspersed with blowing into the whistle around his neck. I finally stopped him and asked him what all the noise and hullabaloo was about. He stared into my face with a look of sheer terror and said that there were bears in every part of this forest and he must scare them away from us. I let him know that I was about to become more terrifying than the bears if he carried on with the racket. After this he settled down.

We carried on walking for about four hours, through the mud and the rain and the bear-filled woods. I thought of the woman with the bears and I thought of the fairy-tale nature of her being in the woodcutter's hut, if that was where she was.

We carried on walking. Finally we got to the crux of the walk, a liquid, mud path that negotiated a series of small cliffs up through the wooded slope. Superman looked up and slid to the ground with a moan. He lay spread-eagled in a puddle, almost sobbing. I knew he wasn't pretending. I sat down against a rock beneath a tree. The first rule of rescue is not to endanger the rescuers, something I had been pushing to the back of my mind for the last while. My Indiana Jones–style hat was pulled down over my forehead, and I watched the steady rain dripping off the rim as I gazed down at the sodden blue-and-red superhero.

In that moment in the pouring rain, sitting in the mud and wet as wet could be and realizing we had to turn back, I had a profound feeling of absolute, utter and complete tranquillity. It was, perhaps, the one time in my life when I could physically understand the sentence "The peace that passes all understanding." It came out of having absolutely no choice, but it wasn't just that we had done our best and there was no other decision but to turn back; it wasn't that I was thoroughly soaked and thus couldn't get any wetter. It was as if suddenly, everything in the world was in its right place. Every part of the earth and every part of the surrounding darkness of space was part of this concentrated experience happening here and now; as if a whole cosmos was radiating out from our little mud-spattered redoubt in the dripping woods: as if all events and characters in this play had conspired to this moment and there could be no other outcome. Adding to my sense of peace was a sudden, illogical but absolutely certain feeling that the woman for whom we searched was safe and that we would find her tomorrow walking into our camp.

If the story seems far-fetched, it proved to be doubly so when the woman did walk into our camp the very next day, having been found by another descending yak train negotiating the muddy trail. She had spent the night exactly where we thought she might be found, in that mythical woodcutter's hut. She had heard the bears shuffling about outside and been initially frightened, especially as she was menstruating and had heard the old stories about bears being drawn to the odor. But her agitation had also subsided in the night, as ours had, into a profound peace, and she had a dream of seeing the baby she was about to adopt in Cambodia immediately after our visit to Bhutan.

After the trip, when the woman did reach Cambodia to go through the legal process of adoption, she found that the very night she had spent alone in the hut was the selfsame night the baby she was to adopt had been born and brought to the orphanage.

All very far-fetched, all absolutely true. It is remarkable to think that from the perspective of the birth that night and her own impending motherhood, we were not meant to find that woman. She was to go through a form of childbirth herself up there alone in the woods with the bears. All the flawed decisions, the selfish egomaniac guide, my hesitations and lack of asserting myself as leader, the pouring rain; Superman's exhaustion, were all forgiven by the larger context into which we had all walked.

Until I heard that story, I had been prepared to teach our guide a lesson and put in a detailed report to the Bhutanese officials who ran the guiding program, asking them to fire him for a big catalogue of reasons. After I heard it and after my experience in the rain and after I saw the baby back in the United States, I let it go. I couldn't be so self-righteous, though I must admit to a certain sense of relief when I heard that he had got himself sacked anyhow and couldn't endanger any other group.

What is also remarkable is how much the drama of that night was constituted by individuals who did not know themselves very well or the larger story in which they were participating. The unreliable Catholic Buddhist guide, my lack of confidence and follow-through in confronting him were all forgiven by the bigger story. It seems to be that bigger story that the self must find and commit to in order to find happiness in the third marriage with the self.

Back from the Himalaya, home from the fairy-tale woodcutter's hut and away from babies being brought in the dead of night to Cambodian orphanages, back in our car or our workplace or our office cubicle, the marriage with the self can seem very difficult, very stubborn; the experience of profound peace like a magical falling in love that we now have to sustain in a serious disciplined follow-up, like a marriage following a courtship, but this time, a marriage with the self.

Spending any time at all in the day with that elusive entity called the self can be very, very difficult, let alone entering into anything we might describe as a real marriage. There is a sense of being put on trial in each of the marriages but particularly in this internal marriage. Silence of one kind or another is necessary to come to terms with that self, and at least a little of that peace that passes all understanding that I felt in the forest and yet silence seems to be the very thing that initially brings us out in an allergic reaction.

It is remarkable how deathly afraid we are of any real quiet that might start to open up a spacious noncoercive relationship with the self or the world. Much easier to turn on the iPod, the laptop, the BlackBerry. In unmediated silence we intuit all our flaws being made abundantly clear to us and all our previous actions being revealed in their true light. We would much rather stay on the surface, where our self-protections can be put into a virtual context, or laughed off, or seen as being a natural part of our character. What we do not understand is the self-forgiveness and the self-compassion that come along with all the inner and outer seeing.

With the larger picture, seen in silence, untouched by our particular anxieties, comes a possibility for freedom. We are creatures afraid of ourselves and afraid of what we will find at the center of our many outward manifestations of selfishness, big and small. It might be a comfort, then, to understand how much our happiness in the other two marriages of relationship and work depends on our having a settled marriage with the self. It might also be a consolation to follow those who have gone this way before us, who bore the same fears and allergic reactions to silence, to self-revelation and see what they might have found in building a steady relationship with the world that opens up in that silence.

A MANUAL FOR MARRIAGE WITH THE SELF

We might remember again the Buddha's to-do list for finding the self. He spent years deepening the state that I had just had a small glimpse of in the dark, rain-filled forest. His experience is that of the consummate practitioner who took my little fling, my lightning raid on peace and tranquillity, and made it into a settled relationship. It is worth looking at the jottings on that invisible yellow sticky pad that he passed on to others who came after him. It could equally be instructions for keeping a relationship alive. They are indeed the instructions Deirdre Blomfield-Brown took heed of and followed faithfully in her marriage to the self as the newly dedicated Pema Chödrön.

As Pema Chödrön, a dedicated Tibetan Buddhist, Deirdre found herself not only responsible for her newly disciplined life, but also, in recognition of her dedication, appointed head of a monastery built on the wild shores of Nova Scotia, Canada. In taking vows in the Buddhist tradition, she would have made an undertaking to follow the Buddha's to-do list, better known as the Four Noble Truths.

Other people's disciplines and rules always have a little of the insufferable about them, so we should read them, even if they are the Buddha's, with a great degree of skepticism. Here they are, including the ones we have encountered already.

ITEM ONE. *Of great help to those wandering wet, muddy forest paths in the pitch dark.*

Understanding that there is no life without suffering. It is impossible not to be visited cyclically by that quality; we should not waste our energy trying to keep the changes that discomfit us at bay. We should consider ourselves just as much alive and just as much our self in every part of the cycle, lost or found, whether the tide is in or out, whether the grand old duke of York is at the top of the hill, at the bottom or only halfway up or down. We should stay in the conversation whether we are happy or disconsolate. In other words, with regard to suffering, we might as well complain about the weather for all the good it will do.

ITEM TWO. *Of great comfort to those who have not achieved a specific outcome.*

Our suffering comes from the fact that we are attached to the outer form that something assumes in a given instant rather than the movable conversation that stands behind it. Just as we find it hard to keep up with children's growing and to address them in a way appropriate to the age they have actually reached, so we find it hard to keep up with the curve of transformation in almost every aspect of human life, including our own. Keeping up with what is occurring rather than lagging and getting caught in things that no longer exist, is one of the great disciplines of life. We can also become attached to ideas and concepts, like my finding the woman and rescuing her even though she was, in the end, better left alone. Which does not mean to say we stay at home and do not look for the lost; we must do what we think is right but detach from the specific outcome. Sometimes the outcome of our search-and-rescue effort is a deep exhaustion out of which we are provided with the revelation we were looking for. Perhaps I myself, sitting in peaceful clarity in the dark and the rain, was involved in a kind of vigil with her, we can never know. We can be imprisoned by even our best hopes, just as we can be imprisoned by believing these Four Noble Truths.

ITEM THREE. *Of great comfort to those who like contradictions.*

It is possible to attain a state where we are free from suffering. We free ourselves from suffering by *being* fully in the conversation rather than something static *having* a conversation and trying to defend that something at every turn. Again, we can stop complaining about the weather, the guide and the lack of overnight accommodation in central Bhutan. As an individual, I must learn to identify my self with the bigger picture, a picture that includes the weather, the history of Himalayan Buddhist culture and its lack of emphasis on roadside accommodation. I must learn to live at a kind of frontier between what I think is me and what I think is not me, so that my identity is more of a meeting place; an edge between past and present rather than an island around which the events of life swirl and move on. Even the pouring rain is part of my identity, though if I have the choice, I may move out of it. Even grief and loss, if felt in a timeless way, can be free from disconnection or suffering. In summary: It is possible to be happy while cold, wet and exhausted.

ITEM FOUR. *Of great comfort to those who want to improve themselves and make the world a better place.*

There is a disciplined way to sustain this experience of being free from suffering. It is possible to live without a constant sense of anxiety that something is not right and something is not complete. There is a way of living in which we can feel instinctual joy while letting time work its way toward our eventual disappearance; there is a way of being utterly in the present while holding responsibilities, finding people who are lost and getting things done. There is a way of not choosing, of being a crossroads where all the many qualities we try to hold together so willfully meet naturally. There *is* a peace that passes all understanding and it is attainable, though it will not give us any special privileges.

There is an interesting parallel between the Buddhist understanding of personal unhappiness and the suffering individuals may go through in divorce. Pema Chödrön's initial glimpse into the self came through her outer experience of divorce and separation. What is difficult and painful in a divorce is not so much losing the other person (by the time of the actual divorce, our feelings at being apart may be of relief) but losing the dreams we shared and built together as a couple. There is an intuition that no matter who we find ourselves with in the future, no matter how much happiness we find with an other, those shared intuitions of a possible future will not occur again, including the way we parent our children. Our approach will be different, and our children will be different because of it. When I let go of another, I let go of a different future, a future I did not credit with informing my present so fully. When I change my relationship with reality, I also have a different future, but if I cannot let go of the old dreams, I will be full of nostalgia and grief for my old future. Even if this previous relationship was not good for me and brought me deep unhappiness, it was one that I knew and had helped to build myself.

Many of us live in a constant state of separation, as if in a permanent process of divorce with the reality that confronts us. As in a real divorce, we draw battle lines, make endless self-justifications and retell all the stories to put us in the right. We may even excise certain people from our memories as we might erase them technically from photographs. Vulnerability can be the hardest place to go, to understand that there is no person who is all right and no person who is all wrong. My exasperated and easy judgments of the guide could be brought to bear on my own life. How much of my own inherited foundations are muddled and unresolved and create a certain amount of ongoing chaos around me? My Irish and Yorkshire sides work well together for the most part, but there is a definite, painful confusion when an Irish rugby team plays England. I don't know whom to cheer on. I solve this by not watching such an intimate, painful encounter between the two sides of myself. Which is exactly the dynamic that occurred when I refused to confront the guide. Living with such different streams of history inside my psyche has always made me give a person the benefit of the doubt and asked me to see both sides, to look, and too often for too long, for understanding. The guide's confusion was but a magnified, less subtle version of my own.

So, having compassion for the guide does not mean that I do not confront him when he endangers my group of mountain walkers. It does mean, however, that if I can inhabit the bigger context that the noble truths have invited me into, I am able to confront him with some understanding and compassion for the inner struggles that led to him making such bad decisions. There is a possibility, only a possibility, around the evening campfire, for an opening. Pushed to the limit, of course, and asked to choose between his personal safety and that of my group, I would push him compassionately off the side of the mountain, but almost always we are not given these stark choices. No real conversation can occur without some vulnerability. We often close the conversation by forcing ourselves to make a premature and sometimes absurd choice between our self-preservation and having a proper conversation, even when there is no real threat to our person. We exaggerate and even create a sense of threat so that we are saved the necessity of a real dialogue. Calling someone a "little Hitler" may feel satisfying at the time, but it is a very efficient way of closing down any possibilities of redemption, either for the little Hitler I am judging or the little Hitler inside me that called him a little Hitler in the first place.

My greatest enemy is my greatest teacher has a very long history in Buddhism and in almost every other spiritual tradition. The statement is not an excuse to pardon bad behavior, or to roll over and die when persecuted. We use the sense of threat and competition as a way of looking at the parts of us that feel attacked whether there is a real enemy present or not. Especially in the marriage with the self, we are more likely to find there is indeed no other enemy than the false self we continually present to the world as the real one.

Why should it be so difficult for the Bhutanese guide to feel at home with himself? Why should it be so difficult to live with that very thing that shares our own skin and with which we are most familiar: our own self? How can it at times be so uncontrollable and so destructive, when we have grown with it, walked around with it and suffered along with it? We know its biography and its complaints, what it needs to feel happier about the world and what it doesn't need: those things that anger it and make it feel hard-done by. We can tell exactly what it is going to say in most situations. We have listened to its endless and repeated requests for versions of the same thing all our life, and yet, we seem just as powerless to make this self truly happy as we do with any other self outside us. What is really strange is that this self constantly seems to be doing things that we later regret or want to hide or forget.

We seem to spend half the time coercing it to do things that we want it to do and half the time being coerced by it into things we don't want or like. It is indeed like a stranger and like a partner all at the same time.

A strange and seemingly eternal dynamic that seems to keep us both apart and firmly cemented together in any marriage is our refusal to give our partners the very thing they most want in the relationship. There seems to be something almost instinctual about our targeted withholding of specific forms of requested love. We withhold these intimacies not only because we sometimes cannot find the wherewithal to offer them, but many times because some interior whispered voice tells us that what is being requested is the very thing partners must grant themselves. That we, in effect, cannot supply what is being demanded, even if we tried. Some wiser part of us refuses to buckle under the coercion and though it may not be able to articulate why, withholds the desperately needed commodity in an unconscious effort to educate the other person into their own inherited sense of lack.

In the same way, if I spend any time in silence, any time at all watching the way my mind works, I will find, as Pema Chödrön did in the years of discipline that lay ahead of her, that there is a parallel way in which we withhold the very thing from ourselves that might provide us with the possibility of happiness. As Pema Chödrön says, "The first noble truth . . . is that people experience *Dukka*, a feeling of dissatisfaction or suffering, a feeling that something is wrong . . . only in the West is this articulated as '*something is wrong with me*.' "

What we withhold from ourselves is the willingness to understand our own imperfection. The strategic, intellectual self, looking in from the outside, cannot have the experience of sheer physical vulnerability that the deeper internal self must gain to walk through the door of self-compassion. Just as we must leave our partner with certain struggles that are entirely their own, so we must leave our deeper self alone to suffer through the confrontation with its own flaws and imperfections. By letting ourselves alone in this radical way, we actually demonstrate a freeing form of love for that emerging inner person.

MY OWN FLAWS AND MY OWN FEARS
ARE MY GREATEST TEACHER

If I am afraid of something and especially if there is no logical reason I should emphasize that particular fear beyond all the other fears that human beings feel, then I have the possibility of coming to terms with and questioning the premises on which my sense of self pivots. My flaws are my doorway to self-understanding and my way of understanding the flaws and fears of others.

The strange irony is that we take these very personal problems too personally. We think that if we investigate the self we will find out that there is something wrong at the core, and we want to defend against that revelation at all costs. The surface personality feels as if it is going to die and becomes deathly afraid of the conversation. The task is to shift the identity more toward the movable conversation that stands behind us, a deep undercurrent we can tap into that carries on unconcerned with the surface tribulations. In this depth we try to create a real silence in which to keep our long-standing, well-established, self-protective stories away, to let ourselves alone so we can experience the physical vulnerability of the question and be transformed by it. We give these smaller protective stories away so that we can see how they come back to us once we have established a larger way of being in the world.

We call this unremitting wish to create a silence in which to see to the truth meditation. The outer form looks like silence as we see a practitioner sitting quietly, but meditation can take many forms, beginning usually with simply following the breath, getting to the very foundations of the way we physically give and take. It can be quite revealing to find out how much willpower we put into that autonomous bodily function; we find that we are controlling a process that can be left well alone and doesn't need so much outside intervention. Meditation can also take conceptual forms in which we dig down deep in one area, asking a question about why we are so afraid of a certain thing, or by which we attempt to come close to a physical sense of hurt we carry.

We could see meditation as the equivalent of the kitchen or a bedroom in a marriage. It's the place where most of the significant transformative conversations happen; significant conversations that may be silent but that can shift the relationship with the self to a new level. The act of physical transformation can at times be an almost ecstatic, sexual experience. It can also be a fierce, unrelenting and prolonged daily confrontation. One of the disciplined forms of conversation with the self that Pema Chödrön learned from her Tibetan Buddhist tradition was a practice called Tonglen. It was a practice I was unwittingly performing with my difficult friend and enemy the Bhutanese guide.

Tonglen is the willingness to get not only to the center of particular forms of suffering that affect us deeply but also to the vulnerability and physical heartache that come with the experience. I might choose the suffering I witness in Darfur, or the unhappiness of an abused child I am powerless to help, or in my own experience, an unresolved hurt I felt from my father. In Tonglen, I will attempt to breathe that hurt in and give it back with each out-breath as something more spacious and generous. The object is not to solve my unresolved hurt or the endless griefs of the world, but to feel the heartache and vulnerability itself and to try to deepen that sense of hurt. The sense of vulnerability itself becomes a doorway into a bigger understanding of it and a way to hold it at the same time. It's not a way of abstracting the suffering of the world and then doing nothing about it, but a practice for making ourselves able to bear it and work with it despite the many reflected fears it brings up inside us.

This is the marriage with the self that Pema Chödrön has publicly committed to and to which she has actually made vows. In the consummation of this marriage we find this personal self cannot be separated from all the other selves in the world. "To study the self is to forget the self," said Dogen Zenji. The out-loud vow that Pema Chödrön made in her marriage is called in the Tibetan tradition the Bodhisattva vow: "Human beings are numberless, I vow to save them." Our own vows to self-understanding; to taking this invisible, very personal marriage seriously may not have a name, and we may not get an official ceremony. It may be a moment on a mountaintop or at a table in a small café, or a second alone by a window in a high building in Manhattan. The essential thing is that we see its necessity and make that often unconscious relationship with the self as conscious and as generous to others in this world as a happy marriage can be.

Conclusion: On Letting One's Self Alone

What is needed in a marriage with the self is what is needed in the marriage to another: a radical letting alone of our partner, the deeper self, to let it live its own life without our necessity for a constant, overarching control. We must stop trying to protect that deeper, more vulnerable self from the way it feels things keenly and at their essence. This self that we are attempting to "marry" can look after itself as much as our partner can. Its vulnerability is not a weakness but actually a faculty for understanding what is about to happen. It does not wish to survive its encounters with its previous reality intact and untouched; it actually wants to be transformed by what it meets. In a sense it wants to be the conversation itself.

Conclusion: On Letting the Self Meet Another

There is no self we can construct that will survive a real conversation. A real conversation always involves our moving the small context we inhabit to the next-larger context that will transform and enlighten us and that seems to have been waiting for us all along.

What we withhold from ourselves is the very thing we need to complete ourselves. This act of completion is often seen as a form of death and something to be fought against. We quite often do not want to know what we need. We will try to offer false gifts to the self in order to keep the real gift at bay.

Conclusion: On the Difficulties of Vulnerability

The real gift and the crux of our difficulty is our constant and entirely natural experience of vulnerability. Trying to live without feeling vulnerable means we do not understand the fierce nature of the reality we inhabit. In closing off our vulnerability, we close off the authentic exchanges that tell us we are actually having a real conversation. Vulnerability is the door through which we walk into self-understanding and compassion for others. Being enlightened does not mean we assume supernatural powers or find a perfection that exalts us above the daily losses other human beings are subject to; enlightenment means we have accepted thoroughly our transience, our vulnerability and our imperfections and live just as robustly with them as without them.

The relationship between the ego and the deeper enlightened self is much like the relationship between the rescuer on the muddy path and the person who does not "wish" to be rescued, who must gestate through the lonely night in the woodcutter's hut. The ego is meant to look after us, to care for us and protect us, and perhaps come looking for us when we seem to be lost. But when we identify completely with that protective figure, we lose the more important story and halt the possible transformation occurring in the depth of the night. Sometimes the best thing to do is to hold a kind of silent vigil beside

the part of us that is going through the depths of a difficult transformation. When the outer story that the ego
tells, merges with the one the inner self has come to, this
becomes "the marriage of true minds." The ego seems to
disappear, but actually it has simply assumed its rightful
place in the hierarchy of priorities; it has become a good
servant to the soul's desires.

Conclusion: On the Nature of the Path

I wrote the following piece, recalling all those paths I had
walked in various parts of the Himalaya and the invisible, personal transformations I experienced along the
way. The poem includes in an unspoken way my friend
and helper the Bhutanese guide. It begins with a quotation from Han Shan, a Chinese Taoist who spent a long
time gestating on a mountainside and who established a
faithful marriage with the elusive and ever-changing
center we call a self.

NO PATH

There is no path that goes all the way.

Han Shan

Not that it stops us looking
for the full continuation.

The one line in the poem
we can start and follow

straight to the end. The fixed belief
we can hold, facing a stranger
that saves us the trouble
of a real conversation.

But one day you are not
just imagining an empty chair

where your loved one sat.
You are not just telling a story

where the bridge is down
and there's nowhere to cross.

You are not just trying to pray
to a God you imagined
would keep you safe.

No, you've come to the place
where nothing you've done

will impress and nothing you
can promise will avert

the silent confrontation,
the place where

your body already seems to know
the way having kept

to the last its own secret
reconnaissance.

But still, there is no path
that goes all the way

one conversation leads
to another

one breath to the next
until

there's no breath at all

just
the inevitable
final release
of the burden.

And then
your life will
have to start
all over again
for you to know
even a little
of who you had been.

from D.W., *River Flow: New & Selected Poems 1984–2007*

CHAPTER 14

Not a Question of Balance:
A Marriage of Marriages

Each of the three marriages is nonnegotiable. They cannot be "balanced" against one another—a little taken from this and little given to that—except at their very peripheries. To "balance" work with relationship and with the self means we only work harder in each marriage, while actually weakening each of them by separating them from one another. Each of the marriages represents a core conversation with life that seems necessary for almost all human beings and none of the marriages can be weakened or given up without a severe sense of internal damage.

The three marriages are eternal and internal human conversations; they can occur whether we are officially married or not, whether we have a real vocation or a terrible job, whether we have astonishing revelations about our identity or have never given a second thought to our place in creation. These three conversations occur in the human psyche, consciously or unconsciously, whether we decide to speak them out loud or hide them away. They are part of the way we pay attention to the world and part of the way we attempt to make a home in it. To ignore them is to be caught constantly in invisible, internal battles, which become a source of puzzlement and unhappiness to the personality struggling on the surface.

The three marriages are especially nonnegotiable in their early stages. Only later do we learn to put them into conversation with one another. In youth we abandon our parents to go out in the world, in love we often abandon our friends for a good while, and in work we abandon "other interests" when we start to concentrate on our vocation.

But each of the marriages must be lived out physically or imaginatively, whether we attempt to choose among them or not. I may never, literally, marry a person, and I may even hold myself at a physical distance, but like Queen Elizabeth I, keeping at bay the kings and princes of Europe, I will refuse the outer match only because I am already married to some other "kingdom." Equally, in the second marriage, I may not choose an actual career, but I must have some internal definition of my work even if it is the undefined, uncelebrated invisibility of parenting. In the third marriage, I may not shave my head and enter the cloister as a monk, but to have any real possibility of contentment I must cultivate a relationship with silence and with the ever new self that can emerge out of that silence. To ignore any of the marriages causes a glacial buildup in large parts of the human psyche that may easily avalanche across the other two marriages, flattening them and smothering them in the process.

Our refusal to have these conversations out loud, to take these marriages seriously, makes no difference; they will occur with our conscious participation or without it: they are foundational to human belonging. My refusal to follow my vocation to please my spouse will only result in my demanding of her, at emotional gunpoint, all the qualities I cannot garner myself through my work. She will only be imprisoned by my frustrations and the very sacrifices she may have asked me to make. The refusal to participate fully in any of the marriages, to make them overt and speakable, causes endless friction in a relationship. Not speaking about them, a couple can often become afraid of each other's desires and eventually see each other as unspoken enemies. To speak of these marriages out loud at the very least creates a crossable frontier between the couple. Each couple stands at the turbulent edge between the surface attempt to control these other powerful marriages and the Dionysian underground energies that carry them along, trying to flow around all outer obstacles. When we attempt to stop the conversation our partner might be having in the two other marriages because of natural jealousies, we become an obstacle to the one we are supposed to "love," and then wonder why it is so difficult to make this first marriage work in isolation.

To "love" another in the first marriage, we must love the desires that the other person holds for the other two marriages. These desires are indicators of who our partner is at the moment and who the partner is becoming. They are essential to the person's identity, and to dismiss them or become frightened of them is to lose sight of the person to whom we committed in the first place.

We might ask ourselves, How is it possible to talk to a partner about these other marriages when I am confused and unsure about them myself? It might be difficult to track and keep up with the first marriage, but the act of creating a conversation with our partner on the subject of the other two marriages of work and self helps us both to understand the other's struggles and, importantly, to overhear ourselves say things we didn't realize we knew about our own lives. We become co-conversationalists in the marriage of marriages. Once each of the marriages is in conversation with the others, there can be a mutual support among them: each enlightening and emboldening the other. For instance, in the third marriage, my understanding of how I am changing at any of the big thresholds of life—moving into my thirties, becoming a parent or reaching midlife—can have a radical effect on what I want from my work or my relationship. My partner's bold moves in life can also affect and encourage me to do the same. I start to see the relationship with my partner as not only a place of shelter and retreat from the world, but also a crucible for navigating change, a more movable center than I could have imagined myself, around which the relationship and the future can pivot.

It is instructive to note that when we talk about work-life balance we are almost always talking about the effect work has on a marriage, rather than the way a marriage can also affect work or a sense of the inner self. Perhaps because the person to whom we have committed is flesh and blood, and the other marriages can seem, to begin with, like abstracts; perhaps because there are often children involved and before their priorities we are rightly helpless. But keeping a relationship or marriage alive with a flesh-and-blood partner or even with our children almost always involves the ability to keep an out-loud conversation alive with those other two marriages of work and self, which, in the heart and mind of the individual, are not abstracts at all.

The other two marriages most often become a threat when we have found no way to consciously hold them between us in the daily conversations of our relationship. We suffer especially when we have found no way to put that first marriage into a robust dialogue with the other two.

It might be useful to sit down and widen the scope of our marital conversations by asking our partners how they feel they are doing in each of the three marriages. In bringing these other marriages in as necessary friends, we change the context of our struggles, open a window of fresh air and probably surprise our partner at the same time. We begin to see these other two marriages, not as the usual rivals, or as competing lovers, but as necessary allies or even extended family, who must be invited in to help with the greater happiness of the first marriage.

The difficulty may come when I find that I have overburdened this first marriage with my partner and asked it to carry not only my own expectations of connubial bliss but my happiness in the other two marriages as well. I may find I have freighted my relationship with very heavy weights, asking it to deliver me more happiness than is humanly possible in the area of relationship and as a substitute for the other two invisible vows I have as yet refused to make. I may have put all of my eggs in this basket of relationship because I am actually afraid of asking about the greater dimensions of my work or afraid of getting to know myself in a more honest and intimate way. It can be much easier to ask someone else to give these commodities to me and then punish the person in large and small ways when I see that they have not been delivered to my door.

The conversation between the marriages—the marriage of marriages—can be as difficult to hold together as any of the individual marriages, and like each of the individual marriages this marriage of marriages is best entered, like any other conversation, through the doorway of vulnerability. If I have to learn a certain kind of vulnerability in each of the marriages individually, then there is also vulnerability in trying to make a marriage of marriages work. I may be very fearful in one of the marriages and not want to open up the conversation to look at my possible weaknesses. If I am afraid of the particular picture I see in one of the marriages, I may be especially afraid of the big picture with regard to the other marriages and may feel that I will be swamped in all three marriages rather than just the particular marriage, say, of work, that seems to be overwhelming me now. I also often don't know how the big picture is going to fit together. I can feel powerless and I can find myself becoming protective and defensive about one of the particular marriages to the detriment of the others.

I may find, for instance, that though I am a master of the universe in my work, my wish for control in the workplace is most likely to run up against a brick wall in the kitchen at home. I may find that I want the conversation that holds these marriages together to be held in a very certain way—if I want to be the boss at home in the way I am the boss at work, I may find that I want to control not only the outcome but also the way I get there. I may find that really, underneath it all, there is a more stubborn difficulty, that I don't want to learn anything new anymore. I want to coast on the momentum of my previously hard-won experience. I may spend so much time assuming the mask of invulnerability and righteousness that I find it difficult to admit that I don't know where this conversation will lead or whether my partner, if I let down this mask of control, will be still there at the end of it; if she will really love the one underneath all the protections.

We often find it hard to find faith in the conversation itself, a faith that in following the vulnerable exchange it will actually give me the spaciousness that I so desperately want in the end. It is tempting to see it as something else to do, to throw on the jogging clothes and disappear around the block, to find the time we need for the elusive self and to reassert a sense of control by stealing it from the foundational conversation. We may find that if we take time for this foundational and sometimes vulnerable conversation that we find we can have a lot of gladly agreed to jogging in the future. But one of the central vulnerabilities is that it can be hard to admit we do not know, after all, where this marriage of marriages will take us.

It is a difficult discipline in all three marriages to let a person go, continually, to see if that person comes back, to let a work go so that it can be reimagined or to let a fixed idea about ourselves evaporate and be replaced by something more flexible.

Establishing a marriage of marriages means not only that I start to learn from each of the marriages by letting them speak back to me in their own voices rather than make them say things I want them to say. It means also that I am willing to let each of the marriages speak to one another and, indeed, learn from one another.

After a recent talk I gave at a large global chemical company, I had a private conversation with one of the executives in an adjacent room. His present grief in life was that his wife's work aboard a hospital ship off the coast of Africa took her away from him for months at a time. The voice of her second marriage with her work had become so insistent after she raised her children that she had to follow it back into nursing and out to the coasts of West Africa. Her husband confided in me that her wholehearted commitment made him question the underpinnings of his own successful career; demanding that he ask questions about what he wanted at this point in his life and bringing him perilously close to seeing his primary work as supporting his wife's newfound career just as she had supported his career in the early days of their marriage.

The vulnerability and indeed the tears in this man's eyes as he talked were both surprising and emboldening. The robust way he held these qualities spoke to his ability to see their marriage of marriages as both a continual surprise and an invitation to new territory, as if the larger dimensions of all their original promises were becoming clearer with each step in their lives. His vision was enlarging beyond the perspective of the company that had been his world, beyond the country club that was to host his retirement and beyond the images he had held of his wife as a good servant to his career desires. He seemed vulnerable and yet strangely equal to what was being demanded of him. Out of his marriage he was learning about his self; out of this new self he was looking again at his work and in that buoyant, mutually reinforcing conversation, he was reordering his place in the world. We had a good exchange, in which he seemed to be saying certain things to himself he had not said out loud before. When I left him, he looked as if he was about to do something innocent, dangerous and wonderful all at the same time.

Doing something innocent, dangerous and wonderful all at the same time may be the perfect metaphor for understanding one of the demands made by a marriage of marriages: the need to live in multiple contexts, multiple layers and with multiple people all at the same time without choosing between them. A kind of spiritual and imaginative multitasking, but in which we attempt to be present to everything that is occurring, to have a foundation that will hold them all and not be distracted by passing details. In a marriage we must relate to the person we have before us while keeping in mind the ideal to whom we made the vows, who may at the time, bear no resemblance at all to what we are seeing and hearing. In a successful marriage we do not get to choose between them.

It is instructive to see how J. K. Rowling refused to make the mistake of choosing between her vocation as a writer and the obligations of motherhood. Despite the fact that she almost always put her daughter first and took her with her everywhere, she also refused to lose her relationship with the internal characters who had also recently been born inside her and were now growing just as quickly in her mind. On the outside a passerby would see her at a café table, alternately spooning food into her daughter's mouth and looking at her notepad; on the inside she was a mother who was laying the ground plan for Hogwarts and its many future imagined inhabitants, and at the same time she was looking after a very real and particular child. There is a fascinating faith displayed in that image, where faith is not the belief in a received set of facts but the ability to keep one's star in sight, to pay attention to the horizon to which we belong while not betraying our present responsibilities.

The language that describes the attempt to integrate all of these layers into one needs a Dante to do it full justice: as he did in the last lines of the *Commedia*.

> *So struck was I by this strange new sight.*
> *I wanted to see how everything could live together . . .*
>
> *Though here my mighty vision lost its power,*
> *My will and my desire, like wheels beginning to move*
> *With an even motion, were turning with*
> *The Love that moves the sun and all the other stars.*
>
> (Translation by D.W.)

But we all have a little of Dante in us, fainting in the face of what we desire; all of us have a little Robert Louis Stevenson in us, crossing whole oceans in pursuit of our desires; all of us have a little of Fanny Osbourne, testing and trying the waters to see if what she wants is true and good. All of us may have a touch of Jane Austen, looking on from a distance, examining the larger metaphorical patterns of a very physical experience, and all of us have something of the lost, fearful Deirdre Blomfield-Brown about to change into a very dedicated, very courageous, very clear Pema Chödrön.

Thinking of work, self and other as three marriages offers the possibility of living them out in a way in which they are not put into competition with one another, where each of the marriages can protect, embolden and enliven the others and help keep us mutually honest, relevant, authentic and alive.

I stop trying to work harder in each of the marriages and start to concentrate on the conversation that holds them together. Instead of asking myself what more I need to do, and killing myself and my creative powers in the process of attempting to carry it out, I ask myself: What is the courageous conversation I am not having? Out of the conversation will come as much action as I want, but the action will be simpler, clearer, more central to what I want than a stressed reaction that exhausts me for the real encounters I desire.

What we desire in the three marriages is a sense of profound physical participation with creation, the reconfirmation that we are not alone in the world and the reminder that there is a larger context to existence than the one we have established ourselves.

In the three marriages and in their possible resolution into a marriage of marriages, we look to recognize the outer external representations of all the internal elements that already live inside us. We want to give this meeting of inner and outer a voice in the world. We bring what is inside us into conversation with what seems to be outside us. We do this because it is only in this form of created joy and satisfaction that human beings lose their fear of death and disappearance. This is the eternal to which we commit in each of the marriages: the self-forgetful self, intimately joined to a world other than the one it has created for itself. At that frontier we can look around and find, without too much stress or willful action, without feeling inadequate to the many challenges that each of the marriages holds, that we are already living the courageous conversation that holds everything together.

ACKNOWLEDGMENTS

To the patience, companionship and daily wisdom of my wife, who sat with me each day through a very close, creative and conversational summer that quickly became a memorable parallel to the writing. Her equally close reading, comments, encouragement and perspectives were an integral part of the happy urgency and endeavor from which the book emerged.

To the memory of my literary and philosophical brother, John O'Donohue, who always inhabited another parallel elsewhere to my specific somewhere, whom I greatly prized as a laughing companion in arms, a confidant on the hills of Connemara, and without whom my remaining days are irredeemably and immeasurably impoverished.

To Edward Wates, my close and well-tried friend on the mountain or at the dinner table, who over the years has been a natural conversational companion for me on the subject of the Three Marriages, and whose beautiful flat in Oxford provided a spacious and prized enclosure for writing the Himalayan chapters.

To Jake Morrissey, my editor, first for his generous understanding when the prolonged illness and eventual passing of my father prevented me from writing, then, and impressively, for his leaving me alone to produce the piece in its entirety, and finally, for his finely calibrated, critical encouragement, which improved and enhanced the finished book beyond anything I could have achieved under my own devices. A great thank you to him and all the good editors who have invisibly benefited writers through the centuries.

To Sarah Bowlin, editorial assistant, who clears a delightful way for authors with regard to the numerous and endless details necessary for publication: most especially, an enormous, heartfelt thank you to her for tracking down and securing permissions.

To my agent, Ned Leavitt, constantly alert to the possibilities and openings for new thought and new writing to go out into the world and to make the necessary arrangements for that to happen, keeping the interests of his author in mind. It is a pleasure to have developed over the years such a firm and easy friendship out of a very good working relationship.

To my assistant, Julie Quiring, who, as ever, managed to be my eyes and ears to the world while my head was actually buried deeply, month after month, in the manuscript. A fine writer in her own right: her reading of the book and her comments, especially on the marriage with the self, were a great help to the formation of the final chapters.

I would like to thank also Karen and Pete Backwell and Sharon Jansen, of Johannesburg, South Africa, whose generous hospitality and arrangements for me to speak in that remarkable country first gave birth to these thoughts and their elaboration. Their hard work and many introductions opened me up to new themes, a new circle of friends and a new country, with which I and my family have fallen deeply in love.

Last, to my son, Brendan, and my daughter, Charlotte, who are truly *le choix du roi*, whose presence in the world makes sense of any amount of endeavor and application, literary or otherwise. In their future lives may they find the elusive but obtainable happiness beckoning from inside each of the Three Marriages.

JOAN OF ARC

Barrett, W. P., ed. *The Trial of Jeanne d'Arc.* New York: Gotham House, 1932.

Brooks, Polly Schoyer. *Beyond the Myth: The Story of Joan of Arc.* New York: Houghton Mifflin, 1999.

Pernoud, Régine, and Marie-Véronique Clin. *Joan of Arc: Her Story.* Trans. Jeremy Duquesnay Adams. New York: St. Martin's Griffin, 1999.

Spoto, Donald. *Joan: The Mysterious Life of a Heretic Who Became a Saint.* San Francisco: HarperSanFrancisco, 2007.

JANE AUSTEN

Austen, Jane. *Emma.* Ed. Richard Cronin and Dorothy McMillan. Cambridge, England: Cambridge University Press, 2005.

————. *Mansfield Park.* Ed. John Wiltshire. Cambridge, England: Cambridge University Press, 2005.

————. *Northanger Abbey.* Ed. Barbara M. Benedict and Deirdre Le Faye. Cambridge, England: Cambridge University Press, 2006.

————. *Persuasion.* Ed. Janet Todd and Antje Blank. Cambridge, England: Cambridge University Press, 2006.

————. *Pride and Prejudice.* Ed. Pat Rogers. Cambridge, England: Cambridge University Press, 2006.

————. *Sense and Sensibility.* Ed. Edward Copeland. Cambridge, England: Cambridge University Press, 2006.

Honan, Park. *Jane Austen: Her Life.* London: Weidenfeld & Nicolson, 1987.

Jane Austen's Letters. Philadelphia: Pavilion, 2003.

Lane, Maggie. *Jane Austen and Food.* Continuum International, 2003.

Nokes, David. *Jane Austen: A Life.* Berkeley: University of California Press, 1998.

Shields, Carol. *Jane Austen.* New York: Viking, 2001.

Tomalin, Claire. *Jane Austen: A Biography.* New York: Alfred A. Knopf, 1997.

PEMA CHÖDRÖN

Chödrön, Pema. *The Places That Scare You: A Guide to Fearlessness in Difficult Times.* Boston: Shambhala, 2007.

————. *When Things Fall Apart: Heart Advice for Difficult Times.* Boston: Shambhala, 2000.

————. *The Wisdom of No Escape and the Path of Loving-Kindness.* Boston: Shambhala, 2001.

Kullander, James. "Turning Toward Pain" (interview), *The Sun,* January 2005.

DANTE ALIGHIERI

Dante. *The Comedy of Dante Alighieri, the Florentine.* Trans. Dorothy Sayers and Barbara Reynolds. Harmondsworth, England: Penguin, 1949.

Dante. *La Divina Commedia.* Ed. Giorgio Petrocchi. Milan: Arnoldo Mondadori, 1966–1967, for the national edition of the works of Dante sponsored by the Società Dantesca Italiana.

————. *The Divine Comedy.* Trans. John Ciardi. New York: W. W. Norton, 1977.

————. *The Divine Comedy: Inferno; Purgatorio; Paradiso.* Ed. Peter Armour. Trans. Allen Mandelbaum. New York: Everyman's Library, 1995.

Luke, Helen. *Dark Wood to White Rose: Journey and Transformation in Dante's Divine Comedy.* New York: Parabola, 1989.

CHARLES DICKENS

Jordan, John O., ed. *The Cambridge Companion to Charles Dickens.* Cambridge, England: Cambridge University Press, 2001.

Kaplan, Fred. *Dickens: A Biography.* Baltimore: The Johns Hopkins University Press, 1998.

Sanders, Andrew. *Authors in Context: Charles Dickens.* Oxford, England: Oxford University Press, 2003.

Smiley, Jane. *Charles Dickens.* New York: Viking, 2002.

RAINER MARIA RILKE

Gass, William H. *Reading Rilke.* New York: Alfred A. Knopf, 2000.

The Letters of Rainer Maria Rilke. Trans. Jane Bannard Greene and M. D. Herter Norton. New York: W. W. Norton, 1945.

Rilke, Rainer Maria. *Diaries of a Young Poet.* Trans. Edward Snow and Michael Winkler. New York: W. W. Norton, 1997.

―――. *Selected Poems.* Trans. Robert Bly. New York: Harper & Row, 1981.

Rilke's Book of Hours. Trans. Anita Barrows and Joanna Macy. New York: Riverhead, 1996.

The Selected Poetry of Rainer Maria Rilke. Ed. and trans. Stephen Mitchell. New York: Random House, 1982.

ROBERT LOUIS STEVENSON

For a more extensive bibliography, see pages 291–295.

Carpenter, Angelica Shirley, and Jean Shirley. *Robert Louis Stevenson: Finding Treasure Island.* Minneapolis: Twenty-first Century, 1997.

Colvin, Sidney, ed. *The Letters of Robert Louis Stevenson to His Family and Friends.* London: Methuen, 1899.

Holmes, Richard. *Footsteps: Adventures of a Romantic Biographer* New York: HarperCollins, 1996.

R. L. Stevenson Memories. London and Edinburgh: T. N. Foulis, 1912.

Stevenson, Robert Louis. *Across the Plains, with Other Memories and Essays.* London: Chatto & Windus, 1892; New York: Charles Scribner's Sons, 1892.

―――. *The Amateur Emigrant from the Clyde to Sandy Hook.* Chicago: Stone & Kimball, 1895; New York: Charles Scribner's Sons, 1899.

―――. *In the South Seas.* New York: Charles Scribner's Sons, 1896; London: Chatto & Windus, 1900.

―――. *Kidnapped.* London: Cassell, 1886; New York: Charles Scribner's Sons, 1886.

―――. *The Silverado Squatters.* London: Chatto & Windus, 1883; New York: Munro, 1884.

―――. *Strange Case of Dr. Jekyll and Mr. Hyde.* London: Longmans, Green, 1886; New York: Charles Scribner's Sons, 1886.

―――. *Travels with a Donkey in the Cévennes.* London: Kegan Paul, 1879; Boston: Roberts Brothers, 1879.

―――. *Treasure Island.* London: Cassell, 1883; Boston: Roberts Brothers, 1884.

―――. *Virginibus Puerisque and Other Papers.* London: Kegan Paul, 1881; New York: Collier, 1881.

Stevenson, Fanny and Robert Louis. *Our Samoan Adventure.* London: Weidenfeld & Nicolson, 1956.

WILLIAM WORDSWORTH

Barker, Juliet. *Wordsworth: A Life.* Abridged ed. New York: Harper Perennial, 2006.

Gill, Stephen. *William Wordsworth: A Life.* New York: Oxford University Press, 1990.

William Wordsworth: Selected Poems. London: Penguin, 1994.

Wordsworth, William. *The Prelude: The 1805 Text.* Oxford, England: Oxford University Press, 1970.

Wordsworth: Poetical Works. Ed. Thomas Hutchinson. Oxford, England: Oxford University Press, 1904.

Wordsworth William: A Life in Letters. Ed. Juliet Barker. London: Penguin, 2007.

MISCELLANEOUS

William Blake (The Oxford Authors). Ed. Michael Mason. Oxford, England: Oxford University Press, 1988.

Bloom, Harold, ed. *Sylvia Plath.* Comprehensive Research and Study Guide (Bloom's Major Poets). New York: Chelsea House, 2001.

de Botton, Alain. *The Art of Travel:* New York: Vintage, 2004.

Perkins. *A History of Modern Poetry.* Cambridge, MA: Belknap Press of Harvard University Press, 1989.

Paglia, Camille. *Sexual Personae.* New York: Vintage, 1991.

Plath, Sylvia. *Rough Magic.* New York: Viking, 1991.

Schmidt, Michael. *Lives of the Poets.* Weidenfeld & Nicolson, 1998.

Stevens, Wallace. *Collected Poems.* New York: Alfred A. Knopf, 1955.

Vendler, Helen. *The Art of Shakespeare's Sonnets.* Cambridge, MA: Belknap Press of Harvard University Press, 1997.

Whyte, David. *Everything Is Waiting for You.* Langley, WA: Many Rivers Press, 2003.

———. *Fire in the Earth.* Langley, WA: Many Rivers Press, 1992.

———. *The House of Belonging.* Langley, WA: Many Rivers Press, 1997.

———. *River Flow: New & Selected Poems 1984–2007.* Langley, WA: Many Rivers Press, 2007.

———. *Songs for Coming Home.* Langley, WA: Many Rivers Press, 1984: rev. 1986.

———. *Where Many Rivers Meet.* Langley, WA: Many Rivers Press, 1990.